KYOTO AREA STUDIES ON ASIA
CENTER FOR SOUTHEAST ASIAN STUDIES, KYOTO UNIVERSITY
VOLUME 13

People on the Move

KYOTO AREA STUDIES ON ASIA

CENTER FOR SOUTHEAST ASIAN STUDIES, KYOTO UNIVERSITY

The Nation and Economic Growth: Korea and Thailand
YOSHIHARA Kunio

One Malay Village: A Thirty-Year Community Study
TSUBOUCHI Yoshihiro

Commodifying Marxism:
The Formation of Modern Thai Radical Culture, 1927–1958
Kasian TEJAPIRA

Gender and Modernity: Perspectives from Asia and the Pacific
HAYAMI Yoko, TANABE Akio, TOKITA-TANABE Yumiko

Practical Buddhism among the Thai-Lao:
Religion in the Making of a Region
HAYASHI Yukio

The Political Ecology of Tropical Forests in Southeast Asia:
Historical Perspectives
LYE Tuck-Po, Wil DE JONG, ABE Ken-ichi

Between Hills and Plains:
Power and Practice in Socio-Religious Dynamics among Karen
HAYAMI Yoko

Ecological Destruction, Health and Development:
Advancing Asian Paradigms
FURUKAWA Hisao, NISHIBUCHI Mitsuaki, KONO Yasuyuki, KAIDA Yoshihiro

Searching for Vietnam:
Selected Writings on Vietnamese Culture and Society
A. Terry RAMBO

Laying the Tracks: The Thai Economy and its Railways 1885–1935
KAKIZAKI Ichiro

After the Crisis:
Hegemony, Technocracy and Governance in Southeast Asia
SHIRAISHI Takashi, Patricio N. ABINALES

Dislocating Nation-States: Globalization in Asia and Africa
Patricio N. ABINALES, ISHIKAWA Noboru and TANABE Akio

People on the Move: Rural–Urban Interactions in Sarawak
SODA Ryoji

KYOTO AREA STUDIES ON ASIA

CENTER FOR SOUTHEAST ASIAN STUDIES, KYOTO UNIVERSITY

VOLUME 13

People on the Move

Rural–Urban Interactions in Sarawak

SODA Ryoji

Kyoto University Press

TRANS PACIFIC PRESS

First published in 2007 jointly by:

Kyoto University Press
Kyodai Kaikan
15-9 Yoshida Kawara-cho
Sakyo-ku, Kyoto 606-8305, Japan
Telephone: +81-75-761-6182
Fax: +81-75-761-6190
Email: sales@kyoto-up.gr.jp
Web: http://www.kyoto-up.gr.jp

Trans Pacific Press
PO Box 120, Rosanna, Melbourne
Victoria 3084, Australia
Telephone: +61 3 9459 3021
Fax: +61 3 9457 5923
Email: info@transpacificpress.com
Web: http://www.transpacificpress.com

Set by digital environs, Melbourne

Printed in Melbourne by BPA Print Group

Distributors

Australia
Bushbooks
PO Box 1958, Gosford, NSW 2250
Telephone: (02) 4323-3274
Fax: (02) 4323-3223
Email: bushbook@ozemail.com.au

USA and Canada
International Specialized Book
Services (ISBS)
920 NE 58th Avenue, Suite 300
Portland, Oregon 97213-3786
USA
Telephone: (800) 944-6190
Fax: (503) 280-8832
Email: orders@isbs.com
Web: http://www.isbs.com

UK and Europe
Asian Studies Book Services
Franseweg 55B, 3921 DE Elst, Utrecht
The Netherlands
Telephone: +31 318 470 030
Fax: +31 318 470 073
Email: info@asianstudiesbooks.com
Web: http://www.asianstudiesbooks.com

Japan
Kyoto University Press
Kyodai Kaikan
15-9 Yoshida Kawara-cho
Sakyo-ku, Kyoto 606-8305
Telephone: (075) 761-6182
Fax: (075) 761-6190
Email: sales@kyoto-up.gr.jp
Web: http://www.kyoto-up.gr.jp

Japan, Asia and the Pacific
Kinokuniya Company Ltd.
Head office:
38-1 Sakuragaoka 5-chome
Setagaya-ku, Tokyo 156-8691
Japan
Phone: +81 (0)3 3439 0161
Fax: +81 (0)3 3439 0839
Email: bkimp@kinokuniya.co.jp
Web: www.kinokuniya.co.jp
Asia-Pacific office:
Kinokuniya Book Stores of Singapore Pte., Ltd.
391B Orchard Road #13-06/07/08
Ngee Ann City Tower B
Singapore 238874
Tel: +65 6276 5558
Fax: +65 6276 5570
Email: SSO@kinokuniya.co.jp

ISSN 1445–9663 (Kyoto Area Studies on Asia)
ISBN 978-1-920901-96-7 (hardback)
ISBN 978-1-920850-67-8 (paperback)

Contents

List of Figures

List of Tables

List of Plates

Preface

It was 1995 that I visited Sarawak for the first time to undertake pilot research in the mid-Rajang Basin, and I began intensive research in a village in the Kanowit District in 1996. At the beginning I was interested in how the villagers' rural lives had been changed by the modernization process, and made a survey of family composition, social structure and agricultural activities—including swidden agriculture, wet paddy planting, rubber tapping and other cash crop cultivation. I also tried to make clear the villagers' evolving concept of land ownership, by recording traditional land tenure and modern land holding practices authorized by the Land and Survey Department.

As my research was mainly based on participant observation and interviews with local inhabitants of the village, I repeatedly visited each 'household' in the case village, and found that their perception about 'household' and 'family member' was substantially different from mine. Although it is quite natural to think that each society has a different concept of family and household, what was strange to me was that they often counted adult children, who seemed to have set up a home in town, into the parents' household members. Thus, I became interested in out-migration from the village and its effects on structural change in the rural household and village community.

Before knowing the Iban urban lives, I thought that the absent adult children were going out of the village for *bejalai*—wage-working away from home. But when I was talking to Iban people who lived in town and when I sometimes visited their home, I found that many of them lived with their spouses and children and worked in the formal sector; some even possessed their own house in town. This triggered a range of research questions such as: Why do they recognize themselves as a village member? Why do their parents count them in with the other household members? What does rural–urban migration mean within Iban society in the modern context?

In 1996, an election for the Sarawak State Assembly was held and a person who usually lived in town returned to the study village to stand as an independent candidate in the constituency of Kanowit. Even before the campaign period started, many urban dwellers came back home to support the candidate and were busily canvassing for the election. I was surprised that many villlages (longhouses) in the constituency were crowded with urban dwellers who had temporarily returned home. As the point at issue of the election in the area was a plantation development proposed by the Sarawak government, longhouse people and urban dwellers spent much time discussing land and its development.

After the election, villages in the area were restored to quietness. In 1998, however, villages thronged with people again. When questionnaires regarding the disposition of land were distributed by the government to individual villagers, and when villagers were considering whether to sign contracts accepting the development of land for the oil-palm plantation, most of them called their relatives or adult children in the city to discuss these issues together. Some longhouses that did not have a telephone called the persons concerned using message-exchanging programs provided by the local radio stations.

Large-scale 'village meetings' concerning rural development that I observed during my research always included a number of urban dwellers, and 'public opinion' within the longhouse community often seemed to be led by these people. Observing how urban dwellers participated in the discussion and led collective opinion within the rural household and community, one may safely say that they are included in the rural household and as village members. However, the question remained: Why and how do they maintain or establish these family relations? To me it seemed that these questions were difficult to explain by using previous theories on rural-to-urban migration and labor-allocation systems within the household. The least I could illuminate in my research on rural communities was to show how rural activities had changed as a result of increasing out-migration and how rural residents recognized the long absence of the younger generation.

In 1998, I decided to 'migrate,' following young Iban people, to the town of Sibu—at that time the second largest town in Sarawak and the most important urban center for the Iban in the Rajang area—to undertake intensive research on the urban lives of Iban migrants. I thought this necessary in order to attain a holistic comprehension of Iban life in the modern context; to only focus the research on rural areas would be insufficient. I lived in an Iban settlement in Sibu and conducted interviews with more than 130 people in the settlement. By recording their living strategies, I tried to make clear how they approached macro-societies to improve their urban life and why they intended to maintain the membership of their rural household and village community. Observing many people penetrating urban society or power structures, and going back and forth between the two areas, I found that although they recognized their marginal status, they struggled to improve their urban life and also to prepare for their future return to the original village. They were shrewd in their approaches, sometimes withdrawing benefits through various political negotiations, and developing channels to move these benefits from one place to another. Moreover, their way of restructuring relations with the rural family and community was closely correlated to their perception of development policy in Sarawak, and in many cases their practices made rural people acutely aware of the state and national context of rural development. In other words, their living strategies connected—whether consciously or unconsciously—both macro and micro-societies.

The Iban are widely recognized as highly migratory people. At the beginning, I also focused on their patterns of migration. In effect, the rate of the Iban working in formal and informal sectors in urban areas is much higher than other indigenous groups in Sarawak, and the frequency and length of their absence from rural villages are also considerable. However, can their movement, between the rural and the urban, be explained by the concept of migration? Can their lives in rural and urban areas be described separately? Does the rural/urban dichotomy have any significance in their living strategy? These questions arose during my research in Kanowit and Sibu, and forced me to consider various factors that had been neglected in some of the studies on the topic. For instance: Does the process of economic and political marginalization of the Iban have any effect on their migration patterns? How is their household strategy and development policy correlated? What does the so-called rural–urban interaction mean in Sarawak and how is it reflected in their migration strategy?

This study started from my ingenuous question about the changing life of indigenous people in rural areas. In pursuing their activities within and outside the village, I realized that their movement provides us with the key to understand their life in the modern context, and also provides an awareness of the nature of rural–urban interactions in a development state. Thus, my interest shifted from studies on rural activities and migration patterns, to urban studies and rural–urban interactions. Following this change of research focus, the composition of this book generally coincides with the sequential process of my research in Kanowit and Sibu. The major themes include: human mobility, rural–urban interactions, development policy and family relations.

The book is composed of three parts. Part I briefly reviews previous studies of the Iban, outlines the geographical features and historical background of the study area, and also provides preparatory examination of this study's significance.

Part II describes the details of the Iban in the study area based on the data obtained from my intensive fieldwork. Chapters in this section examine out-migration from the village, the Iban's living strategy in urban areas, the frequent movement between rural and urban locations, and kinship relations between those still living in rural communities and those now living in the cities. Through discussion from both the rural and urban perspectives, it is pointed out that understanding Iban movement as migration practices is insufficient. We should comprehend the movement as a part of their endeavors to expand their living space. This section is an attempt to provide an updated ethnography of the Iban within the modern context.

Based on the exploration of Part I and II, Part III tries to place the Iban case study within a discussion of contemporary academic literature. I believe that the Iban case in Sarawak adds a new dimension to the theoretical framework for understanding the dynamics of rural–urban interactions.

Acknowledgements

My research in Malaysia actually began with a misunderstanding. In the spring of 1995, when I was in graduate school, I had a general interest in Southeast Asia and I had met a number of scholars who were engaged in Southeast Asian studies. Yoshimi Komoguchi, who was a professor at Komazawa University at the time, assumed that I was very interested in Malaysia, and decided to take me to that country. He was so determined in fact, that I was unable to refuse.

After spending about one week in a farming village in the State of Johor, which was the location of Professor Komoguchi's research, I flew to Borneo. I did not have any specific location in mind, but I wandered into an Iban village, where I was welcomed and treated with great kindness. That village, which I still visit frequently, is the central stage for this book. I am indebted to many people from this village, including Datin Francisca Sadai, Barnabas Panggau, TR. Angki, TR. Henry, Apai Sabai, and the late TR. Klukok. Datin Francisca Sadai, in particular, 'adopted' me, and taught me a great deal about Iban language, customs and ways of thinking.

As I mentioned in the Preface, however, I did not think it would be possible to gain a full understanding of the Iban's lifestyle by only spending time in the village. I therefore shifted the focus of my research activities to the town of Sibu, where I mainly lived while also occasionally returning to the village. In other words, I aimed for a lifestyle similar to an Iban person who was living in the city. In Sibu, I lived in the home of Fabian Ajah Saging, and received invaluable assistance from him and others, including Indai Raymond, Ujang Ak Ajah, Sanggau Kuling, Apai Apoi, Apai Umil, Apai Unai, and Juntaro Arakawa. Mr. Fabian Ajah operates a small local NGO, and was also involved in the planning of study tours for Japanese tourists, focusing on Iban longhouses. I participated in these tours on a number of occasions, which gave me even more opportunities to interact with the residents of those longhouses. While I was in Sibu, I gathered materials from various companies and public agencies and during this time, I received extremely valuable advice and suggestions from Sii Gie Chew. Mr Sii, a local civil engineering contractor, showed me effective methods of gathering maps, land ledgers and other materials from the Land and Survey Department. He also explained the relationship between politics and development in Sibu, and offered many other thoughts and opinions from the perspective of a Chinese developer.

Regretfully, I am unable to include the names of all the many good friends in Malaysia who helped with my research, but I remember everyone very clearly. In my mind there are still many scenes of the enjoyable gatherings that took place almost every evening with all of my dear friends.

Professor Komoguchi came to see me several times while I was in the midst of my research in Sarawak. I was also visited by Junji Nagata, an associate professor of the University of Tokyo and Toyokazu Kawamoto of Komazawa University, both of whom taught me the basics of conducting field surveys. Professor Nagata, in particular, taught me a great deal about the specific activities involved in this research, as I had not previously had any formal training in this area. In addition, I received invaluable suggestions from the many friends who sometimes visited me unannounced in Malaysia.

Daniel Chew, Peter Kedit, Sim Ah Hua, Ipoi Datan, Voon Ping Keong, Terry McGee, Shamsul Amri Baharuddin, and Masbah Hj. Arrifin all provided immeasurable assistance while I was undertaking research in Sarawak. I am particularly indebted to Dr Chew (the former senior researcher of the Sarawak Development Institute), Dr Kedit (the former Director of Sarawak Museum), Dr Voon (the former Professor of the University of Malaya), and Dr Shamsul (Professor of Universiti Kebangsaan Malaysia) for their help in acquiring authorization for my research in Sarawak. This field research would never have been possible without their support. When I undertook additional research at a later point in time, I made several new friends, including Joseph Jawa Kendawang, Logie Seman, Sota Tanaka, and Kyosei Arakawa, who all helped me to expand the scope of my research. I would like to express my deep appreciation to all of these individuals.

I began this study when I was a student at Kyoto University, as part of my Doctoral research. The professors in my geography classes, Hiroshi Ishihara, Kozo Narita, Akihiro Kinda, Yoshitaka Ishikawa, and Toshiaki Ohji always offered their unreserved opinions and criticisms during seminars and other presentations, and although I occasionally became dejected, or even argued with them, I was always assured of receiving many valuable suggestions. Professor Ishihara was particularly patient, constantly offering words of encouragement when I encountered difficulties in my surveys and research. It was thanks to Professor Ishihara that I was able to continue my research, despite being on the verge of dropping out, and to secure a job as a researcher.

In 2000, when I obtained a position as a Research Associate at the Research Center for Regional Geography, Hiroshima University, I was concerned that it might be difficult to travel overseas, but the Director of the Center, Takashi Nakata along with the rest of the staff, provided me with an extremely flexible research environment, so that I was able to conduct my research and still fulfill my employment duties. The broad-minded approach of the professors at Hiroshima University gave me the courage to continue my research overseas. From 2002 onward, I worked in the Graduate School of Letters, Hokkaido University. The academic staff at the University also did everything they could to accommodate my overseas travels.

When I submitted the manuscript for this book to the Center for Southeast Asian Studies at Kyoto University, the professors who acted as anonymous referees at the request of the Center's Editorial Office offered many harsh but valuable comments, leading me to make revisions that changed the original draft beyond all recognition. During this revision stage, I sometimes felt discouraged, but Noboru Ishikawa, an Associate Professor at the Center for Southeast Asian Studies offered words of encouragement on countless occasions, and this gave me the strength to see this book through to publication. Even so, I may not have been able to fully incorporate all of the comments I received from so many people. As the author, I take full responsibility for the content of the book in its current form.

Tetsuya Suzuki and Shigekazu Takagaki of Kyoto University Press and Mariko Yonezawa of the Editorial Office of the Center for Southeast Asian Studies both helped a great deal in the publication of this book. I also received immeasurable assistance from Cathy Henenberg of Trans Pacific Press, who worked to correct my poor writing in English. To all those who helped me, I offer my heartfelt thanks.

Several of the chapters in this book are based upon papers that have already been published in academic journals. The original publications are listed below. I would like to thank the academic societies and other organizations that gave their approval for the re-publication of those papers in this book.

- Chapter 4: (2001) 'Rural–urban migration of the Iban of Sarawak and changes in long-house communities,' *Geographical Review of Japan (Series B)* 74 (1), pp. 92–112.
- Chapter 5: (2000) 'Living strategies of the urban poor in a local town in Sarawak, Malaysia: population mobility of the Iban between urban and rural areas,' *Geographical Review of Japan (Series B)* 73 (2), pp. 139–164.
- Chapter 6: (2003) 'Development policy and human mobility in a developing country: the voting strategy of the Iban in Sarawak, Malaysia,' *Southeast Asian Studies* 40 (4), pp. 459–483.
- Chapter 9: (2006) 'Agents on the move,' *The Annual Report on Cultural Science (Hokkaido University)* 119, pp. 79–101

The Japan Society for the Promotion of Science (JSPS) provided funding for this research. Assistance in the publication of this book was also received from the JSPS as part of the funding for the publication of research results. Several valued teachers and friends, however, passed away before this research could be presented in its current form. The sudden passing of Professor Komoguchi, and of Mr. Sii and his son, came as a great shock to me. TR. Klukok, the head of the village where I conducted my research, died a natural death from old age. I mourn the loss of these great friends and teachers, and deeply regret that the tardiness of my work has prevented me from repaying my debt to them for their guidance in my studies, and for their support during my time in Malaysia.

Part I

1
Introduction

Key themes in the study of Iban migration

The Iban of Sarawak have been defined as one of the 'major ethnic groups' that practice slash and burn agriculture in Southeast Asia. This depiction is partly the result of the work of Freeman (1955), who identified key features of Iban agricultural practice in his social anthropological research, undertaken in the Upper Rajang Basin (Balleh River) during the 1940s and the 1950s (Pringle 1970). While Iban society and culture encompass a range of significant features such as shifting cultivation, longhouse living, headhunting, the custom of *bejalai* (going on a journey) and great mobility, it is their movement, in particular, that has been emphasized as significant (Sandin 1967; Padoch 1982a; Kedit 1980, 1993; Sutlive 1992; Morrison 1993).

Sandin (1967) and Sather (1994) made clear that the Iban originated in the Upper Kapuas River in West Kalimantan, Indonesia, and began to migrate into the Sarawak side in the sixteenth century (Pringle 1970). At present, they are distributed throughout the state of Sarawak and several Iban villages also exist in the state of Sabah. As Pringle (1970) noted, the term 'Iban' is said to be a corruption of a Kayan word *hivan,* which means 'wanderer,' and was used by the Kayan of the Rajang headwaters as a term of contempt for the Iban people, whose restless disposition made them unpleasant neighbors. These characterizations have influenced us to see the Iban as a migratory, nomadic and wandering people; however, we need to be cautious of this image. While in broad terms there is variety in human movement, for example human migration, seasonal or circulatory movement, and job rotation and resettlement, the mobility of the Iban in different contexts and dimensions has been conflated and is often discussed in quite a confused manner. Their movement varies in type as well as in level—from individual to family migration, village (longhouse) resettlement and in expansion of their living space. It is difficult to deny that all of these types of movement are interconnected; however, the confused and conflated descriptions give rise to a one dimensional and stereotypical definition about the nature of Iban mobility.

The foci of Iban movement and migration studies can be roughly classified into three key areas: ecological aspects—including subjects pertaining to forest use and land-population ratio (Padoch 1982a, b; Cramb 1986; Sather 1990); historical aspects—including cultural and political factors (Richards 1949; Sandin 1956, 1967; Pringle 1970; Sather 1994); and attention to the custom of *bejalai* in the modern context or themes relating to rural-to-urban migration (Sutlive 1985, 1986, 1992; Kedit 1980, 1993; Morrison 1993).

This book commences its discussion by focusing on the out-migration from rural areas of the younger generation of Iban. In this sense, the main theme of this study is closely related to the topic of rural-to-urban migration, mentioned previously. Not surprisingly, the migration patterns practiced by the Iban have changed notably in the twentieth century. While Iban longhouses have been equipped with sedentary features, individual and family migrations have become similar to the circulatory movement in nature. In other words, for the Iban, the longhouse has become a more important foundation as a 'home village'—a starting base and a place to which to return.

Iban migration in the modern context

Kedit (1993) categorized the various types of mobility among Iban males and focused on changes in the custom of *bejalai*. According to Kedit, *bejalai* means to go on journeys with the view of acquitting wealth, material goods and social prestige. Traditionally, these journeys had a leader and were conducted in small groups. The men who went for *bejalai* left the village after the completion of the main work associated with slash and burn agriculture and then returned during the following year. Thus, the period of *bejalai* was usually three to six months. During this journey, the men often collected and traded in products from the jungle or engaged in work associated with the jungle. This practice occurred not only in Sarawak but also in Malaya (Peninsular), British North Borneo (Sabah), Papua and Kalimantan. For example, Kedit pointed out that in the modern era, the major destinations of contemporary *bejalai* were to logging sites, oil fields and construction sites. The main purpose of *bejalai*, had therefore, shifted from wealth acquittal and social prestige to one of earning cash for the purchase of material goods and other modern necessities. Kedit also examined the various cultural activities related to *bejalai* and the social impact of the absence of men on the village community.

During the 1960s and 1970s a considerable proportion of Iban males who worked on *bejalai* were engaged in oil and timber-related industries. In the last few decades, however, wage-earning jobs in urban centers have become diversified, and cities and towns in Sarawak are now major destinations of *bejalai* journeys. On this point, Sutlive (1985, 1986, 1992) mentioned *bejalai* in his examination of Iban rural–urban mobility and their in-migration to the town of Sibu. Thus in the modern context, an important part of the study of Iban mobility is rural-to-urban migration.

For Iban males, the contemporary form of *bejalai* has become a means to earn cash away from the village. In spite of its transformation, Kedit insisted that the spirit, ritual methods and institution of the custom still remain. In other words, he analyzed from a cultural point of view, the meaning of the relationship between the journey and the work away from home, for cash earnings. Although similar views on the continuity between traditional ways of thinking and modernized economic activities have been depicted in other cases (Burawoy 1976; Curry and Koczberski 1998), most studies have emphasized the vital role of migration from an economic point of view. In this sense, Kedit's standpoint, that pays attention to the cultural aspects, is significant for the exploration of rural-to-urban migration. However, whilst acknowledging his contribution, the migration patterns of the Iban have changed even further since the 1970s when both Kedit and Sutlive undertook most of their research. As will be discussed at a later point, various factors such as the diversification of wage earning opportunities in urban areas, degradation of agricultural activities in rural areas, and the advancement in rural development, have all affected the socio-economic significance of migration for the rural household. Thus for instance, in the 1980s, we saw the increase in migration of the family unit. However, within a framework, which focuses on *bejalai* of Iban males, the unit of the family is difficult to take account of and to understand. Moreover, considering that many urban Iban who migrated in a family have established their formal living base in the city, their movement and living strategy also appears to surpass the themes previously discussed in the labor migration literature.

As Kedit (1993) concluded, over time *bejalai* has become less integrated with the local economy than in the past, and the cumulative effects of frequent and long absence of Iban males has had a destabilizing impact on the rural communities. Furthermore, in recent years, the diversification of both migration patterns and the migration unit has accelerated discord and fissure in the rural household and in the longhouse community. However, according to my research in the lower Rajang Basin, urban Ibans have endeavored to maintain various types of ties with their original household and their longhouse community in the village. They do not cut themselves off from their rural community, but instead, the relations between the rural household and urban migrants are becoming more complicated and multifaceted. In short, what we need to do is to reexamine Iban movement between the rural and the urban from a range of perspectives, and explore family relations and other human relationships between those Iban who are now split between the two locations.

Geographically extended households and dispersed village members

Migration studies have a long history of examining the factors of individual decision-making pertaining to migration. For instance, the 'push and pull' factors are well known concepts, which can be replaced by rural factors for out-migration and urban factors for in-migration in the discussion of rural-to-urban migration. In the Todaro model, 'expected earnings' from urban employment was seen to encourage migrants to move to urban areas in spite of the initial period of unemployment, explaining over-population in urban areas in the Third World. These models are in principle, based on the so-called neoclassical idea, and have an underlying premise that migration is driven by the desire and effort of individuals to maximize their profit. The models overlook the fact that the behavior of individuals is usually bound to family relations or a household strategy. In examining rural-to-urban migration, it is necessary to consider labor allocation strategies within a household. On this point, since the late 1980s, family relations and household strategies have been emphasized. The discussions by Stark and Lucas (1988) and Katz and Stark (1986), for example, are modifications of the former unsophisticated point of view. This more recent model, which is often referred to as the 'new economics of migration,' sees the household, rather than the individual, as the unit of analysis.

In the case of Iban migration, since the main focus has been on *bejalai* activities, the household has been rarely considered as the unit of analysis. It is therefore necessary to reexamine the significance of Iban migration practices within the household, given the substantial change in their migration patterns observed in recent years. The difficulty of using the household as an analytical unit is how to distinguish household members from non-household members or others. In general, a household is defined as a group of persons who reside in the same home or compound and share a livelihood. However, when analyzing migration by the family unit, a person who temporarily works away from home is usually regarded as an original household member. This means that he or she is included in the category of a village member. Thus the definition of a household member is closely related to the definition of a village member.

Not surprisingly in this study, the conceptual clarity of these categories was also a problem; that is, how to define village members and household members. Those Iban who move from their village to another village upon marriage, adoption or for other reasons, are clearly defined according to which community they are affiliated with, in keeping with traditional custom. But those who sojourn to the city have an ambiguous sense of belonging. In principle, I defined the village population according to the perception of the rural household heads, and those who sojourn to the city, but are regarded as a member of a rural household by the head, are counted as part of the village population. In Chapter 4, these sojourners are categorized as 'stay-out' village members. Among them, however, some people have settled in the city for many years and have a stable job in the formal sector. Those who get married in the city, in particular, seem to set up an independent household and secure their own livelihood separate from their parents' household in the village. Why do these parents in the village recognize their adult children in the city, as rural household members? How do adult children in the city, have a sense of belonging in terms of both a household member and a village member? These questions are central to the subject of Iban migration in the contemporary context, and are examined in detail in Chapter 7.

As a consequence of Iban patterns of migration, and their relationship to their village households and method of categorization, we are inevitably drawn to deal with those people who are out of both the geographical domain of the village and a conventional concept of the household. This is because with the Iban population, a socially and spatially extended family unit has become the unexceptional type of household. Actually, since the 1980s, this type of household or family component has been a point of discussion in migration studies; 'shadow household,' for instance, is a well-known model that was drawn from the case in the Philippines (Caces et al. 1985). Caces et al. suggested:

> When one or more members of a household migrate but there continues to be a significant degree of participation by the migrant(s) in the activities of the household of origin, it becomes possible to regard the household as having a bi-local or multi-local structure' (Caces et al. 1985: 7).

In recent years, new concepts have emerged such as 'straddled household' (Curtain 1981; Curry and Koczberski 1998), 'multi-active households'

(Krokfors 1995), and 'one family, two households' (Agesa and Kim 2001; Agesa 2004), all of which examine spatially extensive relationships between wage-workers in the city and their rural families.

In the past, many researchers and policy makers have viewed the rural economy of developing countries as being synonymous with agriculture (Adams 2002). However, the change in migration patterns and extended relations among household and family members prompts us to reconsider our concept of village economies, and to think about integrated economies that spread over hundreds of kilometers, occasionally across political borders, and straddling different agro-ecological and socio-economic zones (de Haan et al. 2002). This viewpoint is closely related to the problem of defining the geographical range of a village and the unit of the rural economy (Takada 1991; Hart 1992, 1995; Rigg 1998; de Haan et al. 2002).

In Southeast Asia, as Rigg (1998) has pointed out, it is almost impossible to assign discrete spatial addresses to people moving between rural and urban areas. This means that where a person is assigned to is largely attributed to his or her sense of belonging. Thus, the extended concept of the household forces us to broaden our research further a field, and also if we place migration as the main subject of analysis, the research site itself should not be geographically confined to a village only.

Development policy and rural–urban relations

This study aims to carry out a multi-faceted investigation of Iban mobility between rural and urban areas. One of the most important factors influencing their movement is economic development. As will be explained in detail in Chapter 6, most countries in Southeast Asia have been promoting development policies since their independence, and the state of Sarawak is no exception, even though it lagged behind other states in Peninsular Malaysia and neighboring countries in the commencement and pace of economic development.

In terms of rural–urban relations in developing countries, themes pertaining to development have often been discussed on the basis of Lipton's well-known model of 'urban bias' that depicted the disparity of rural and urban regions and pointed out that the urban biased development would increase the vulnerability of the rural economy (Lipton 1977). Lipton's model invoked the discussion about balanced development between urban and rural regions, and also affected the views on rural-to-urban migration. The idea was widely accepted that the increase in rural-to-urban migration and overpopulation of cities was brought about by an urban-biased development policy. However, as there was increasing dissatisfaction within the rural population as a result of the limited or negligible economic improvement, each successive government came to attach importance to the notion of rural development. It was seen as a means by which the government could alleviate the discontent of their rural population, and was also seen as a way to reduce the rate and extent of rural-to-urban labor migration (de Haan 1999; Mosse et al. 2002).

The case of Sarawak can be understood as operating within a similar context. Although the population density in urban areas in Sarawak is considerably low in comparison to the primate cities of Southeast Asia, Sarawak has experienced an over-concentration of their population in the city, causing for instance, housing problems with squatters occupying sections of the urban centers. Moreover, rural indigenous peoples began to express their discontent about lagging behind in their economic prosperity compared to people in urban districts. In the 1980s, the state government of Sarawak began investing in rural development on the pretext of upgrading rural welfare and reducing in-migration to the city. However, these rural development projects were, in most cases, attributed to agricultural development—especially large-scale oil-palm plantations. Furthermore, most of the 'Rural Growth Centers,' designed by the government to establish regional bases to promote rural development, were located in areas, which overlapped with planned commercial plantation sites. As a result, while the number of Indonesian workers increased in these development areas, there was no perceptible effect on the reduction of out-migration among the rural indigenous population. As many scholars have indicated, policies to immobilize the population have been based on a false assumption that rural agricultural communities are sedentary (Mosse et al. 2002; de Haan and Rogaly 2002).

What is characteristic in the case of Sarawak, and more importantly in relation to this study, is that the issue of rural development in Sarawak arose in parallel with political friction within the parties in the coalition government. As will be discussed in Chapter 6, when a new Iban-led political party, *Parti Bansa Dayak Sarawak* (PBDS), was established in 1983, separate from the coalition, the party adopted the slogan 'ruralism,' which aimed at improving economic development and alleviating poverty among indigenous peoples in the rural sector. Since then rural development has become the main theme of the party and in order to alleviate the sense of disparity of access amongst some of the ethnic groups, the government has focused on the importance of rural development. In other words, there is recognition, to some degree, that ethnic inequality and the gap between the rural and urban economy are two sides of the same coin.

It is also noteworthy, that those who move between rural and urban locations are often involved in introducing development projects to the rural areas. During the election period, in particular, a considerable population movement occurs between different constituencies, to cast a ballot. This means that to win these movers over to their own side has been vital for candidates. For urban sojourners, on the other hand, it is important to ascertain who will bring development projects into their village of origin, because many of them intend to return home after retirement in the city and are eager to prepare for a comfortable rural life. Moreover, urban dwellers are influential in leading opinion among the rural population, in that they are usually regarded as having a wider perspective and greater access to knowledge and information. In this sense, negotiations between the urban dwellers and the local political leaders have had the potential to influence the promotion of rural development.

In the so-called Third World, the vulnerability of indigenous or minority groups is often linked to government led development projects. The relationship of structural disadvantage is a topic that the government is reticent to discuss. Furthermore the position of these groups has often been reinforced by various development projects and subsequent environmental degradation (Chambers 1983; Bryant and Bailey 1997). Although the Iban is the largest ethnic group in Sarawak, consisting of approximately twenty-nine per cent of the population, they feel that they have been socially and politically marginalized under the Muslim-preferred policy. In other words, the Iban tend to consider Sarawak's political system and development schedules as being controlled by the Muslim power structure and they feel like minor actors in this political and economic scheme. Within such a system, the Iban struggle to maximize their own interests, albeit within a limited range of choices. Some people engage in negotiations with local politicians to gain subsidies—sometimes in cash—for rural development, and transfer the profit from the village to their current residence in the city. The Iban know that it is easier for them to withdraw profits from the rural development funds by negotiating with local political leaders, than to directly apply to a public office in the city for the improvement of urban infrastructure. In other words, the Iban not only endeavor to introduce development into rural regions, but also play a role in facilitating the flow of profits backwards from rural to urban areas.

In this study, I regard these activities as the living strategies of people who have moved in order to improve their lives in both locations (Chapter 5 and 6).

Both the use of low-profile tactics and proactive efforts by the Iban to secure economic profits, have the potential to influence political leaders and government policies. If we emphasize this possibility, we can examine their activities as an expression of 'human agency' that may go some way to transform the structure. This topic will be examined in some detail in Part III.

As has been suggested, it is important to take into consideration the way in which development is a critical factor, which influences the movement of the Iban. Conversely, rural development policy and rural–urban relations in Sarawak cannot be understood without an examination of the role of Iban mobility.

Scope of this book and research setting

A new ethnography of the Iban in the modern context

In Sarawak, there have been few attempts to conduct intensive research in both the rural and the urban setting. This study, focusing on Iban mobility, aims to locate the research in both locations—the rural village and the migrants' community in the city. A holistic explanation of Iban life that includes *bejalai* and urban life is required. As stated above, Kedit (1993) proposed that there is a continuation between the traditional journey and wage earning away from home; however, his research was based only on a rural perspective. In addition, most other studies concerning rural-to-urban migration of the Iban have been mainly interested in its effects on rural change (Morrison 1993; Wadley 1997).

On the other hand, Sutlive (1991, 1992) conducted research in the town of Sibu and identified some of the negative aspects of urban life for Iban migrants, such as squatter settlements and prostitution. The work of Sutlive grasped some of the important implications of rural–urban migration experienced by the Iban that are comparable to 'urban problems' in other Third World cities. Although he paid only minor attention to the relationship between research in rural and urban locations, his brief description of the Usaha Jaya squatter settlement in Sibu suggests that the 'true Iban' can no longer be understood only from a rural perspective. In examining the present Iban life holistically, his suggestion forces us to not only grasp Iban activities on *bejalai,* but also take into consideration the growing number of 'urbanite Iban' who may bring about further changes in migration patterns and the social structure, of both the rural and the urban landscape.

According to Sutlive (1992), the Iban began to squat on the riverbank of the Lanang on the southern tip of the Sibu urban center in 1980. He insisted that the changes during the 1970s and 1980s were critical and they can be summarized in four categories: settlement patterns, occupations, roles and relations. He also suggested by implication, that these changes have affected and will affect the identity and values of the Iban. As for the settlement pattern, however, the late 1990s saw a further significant change. In negotiation with local political leaders, the squatters in Usaha Jaya area were each provided with a legally guaranteed allotment in a nearby resettlement scheme. In other words, the sedentary nature of urban Iban has become prominent in their settlement pattern. Therefore, we cannot continue to naively regard such urban sojourners as labor migrants on *bejalai;* they set up a household, hold relatively stable jobs, secure a legal base in which to live, and also to some degree, exert political influence.

This study reexamines the effects of migration by the Iban on the rural community and also focuses on the family and female out-migrations. It positively evaluates the role of those urban dwellers who gained a legally allocated allotment, and demonstrates how because they never terminated their ties with the rural community, they developed and re-created family relations, maintained a rural living base, and were influential in leading the rural population. Thus one purpose of this study is to illustrate the ways in which the Iban have established multiple living bases in both urban and rural locations, and to investigate the significance of these living strategies in the regional, state and national contexts.

Given many Iban secure multiple living bases in geographically separate places, as a result of rural-to-urban migration, we must inevitably broaden our horizons and conduct research in both settings in order to grasp their life holistically. In addition, their recent mobility has become difficult to explain within the framework of current migration theories. As will be illustrated in Chapter 8 and 9, by frequently moving between the two areas, the essentials of the 'rural' and the 'urban' are intermingled and embodied in their everyday life. By undertaking intensive research in both places and by focusing on the activities and perspectives of the Iban who move, this research has the possibility of describing Iban life beyond the static rural/urban dichotomy. In this sense, this study is an attempt to present a new ethnography of the Iban in the contemporary context.

Theoretical framework

In addition to providing an ethnography of contemporary life of the Iban, this study also aims to locate this work within a theoretical framework. Although there is an extensive literature on Iban culture, previous studies have been concentrated primarily in the field of anthropology, and are collectively known as Iban studies. It is true that Iban studies made valuable theoretical contributions to several sub-fields, such as the study of shifting agriculture, ritual methods, land tenure, ethnic relations, and relations between the state and the indigenous population (Freeman 1955; Pringle 1970; Fidler 1973, 1978; King 1976, 1979; Uchibori 1978, 1984; Uchibori and Yamashita 1986; Cramb 1989, 1992; Cramb and Wills 1990; Jayum 1991; Appell 1997). On the topic of rural–urban migration, however, theoretical considerations and comparisons with other cases have been rarely attempted. In other words, there has been a separation of Iban research from some key theoretical themes.

Although Iban migration has a peculiarity in its history and cultural meaning, examining their rural-to-urban migration in relation to state and national policy, regional development and family composition, provides the possibility of expanding theoretical contributions to the research fields of migration and rural–urban relations, both of which have been discussed primarily in the discipline of human geography. For instance, Potter and Unwin (1995: 65) suggested that rural and urban studies remain poorly articulated and little understood. This is despite the fact that research on rural–urban interactions, linkages and interdependency is rapidly becoming an important subfield within development geography and rural studies in general (Watts 1996; Rigg 1998). It is anticipated that the Iban case in this study will present a key to the articulation of rural and urban studies.

In order to locate this case within the body of literature on migration and rural–urban relations, a review of previous work from several fields in the social and human sciences will be undertaken in Part III of this book. Human geography, in particular, has a long history of exploring these themes; therefore, this study mainly refers to and draws upon this body of literature. However, the methods of this discipline have been criticized, as geographers have been extremely dependent on census and quantitative data. McHugh (2000: 72) suggested the limitations of census and survey-based measures of migration that center on change in a single usual place of residence between two points in time. Another area of weakness is that they have given short shrift to the 'human' in human migration. The fact that migrations are cultural events rich in meaning for individuals, families, social groups, communities and nations has been largely overlooked (Fielding 1992; McHugh 2000).

In order to avoid these shortcomings, this study largely draws upon ethnographic methods (McHugh 2000) and partly adopts a biographical or narrative approach (Halfacree and Boyle 1993, 1995); the use of which will lead to an interdisciplinary research of the subjects. On this point, recent studies in various fields have adopted the notion of 'agency' or 'human agency,' to incorporate both individual motives and the structural factors in which the migrants operate (de Haan 1999). In the field of migration studies, this concept is used to reevaluate individual actions that have a possibility of transforming structure; this is a useful concept, which questions the linear and individualistic ideas about the impact of migration. In this study, I describe these aspects of Iban activities as a 'living strategy' that might affect change in their current social systems. In this sense, the nature of Iban rural-to-urban migration may be explained by using the concept of 'agency.' It is also noteworthy that their living strategies are not limited to being only a migration strategy, but concern all aspects of their life. Therefore, reviewing migration studies on their own is insufficient theoretically in explaining the Iban case; we must also involve some studies pertaining to rural–urban relations, family relations and regional development.

I suggest in advance, as part of my concluding remarks that, although this study commences its discussion by focusing on the out-migration of the younger rural generation, it will pose the question of whether Iban activities straddling both the rural and the urban, should really be grasped as a pattern of migration. As described in Chapter 4, it is indeed considered as out-migration from a rural perspective, and similarly in-migration from an urban perspective (Chapter 5). Thus, based on the viewpoint from either rural or urban, we can regard the Iban as experiencing continuous migration between the two areas. However, within the literature, this perception cannot be understood or explained within the rural/urban dichotomy.

What becomes visible by focusing on the perspective of the movers themselves is that the ambiguity of migration needs to be considered in relation to concepts such as straddled household, multiple residences, bi-local family structure and spatially extended family relations. Examination of this ambiguity leads to a possibility of explaining the embodiment of the rural–urban continuum of the Iban movers at the individual level, and also adds another way of seeing in order to rethink the rural/urban dichotomy, prevalent in much of the earlier academic literature.

Research setting

This study is set in Sarawak, Malaysia. The colonization process in Southeast Asia brought about the development of a multi-ethnic society to independent Malaysia, adding complexity to the changing rural–urban relations in the face of rapid modernization. In particular, East Malaysia—the states of Sabah and Sarawak—comprise an extremely complex ethnic composition compared to Peninsular Malaysia. This complexity and difference necessitates undertaking detailed empirical field research at the micro-level on rural–urban relations.

The research for this study focused on the middle and lower ranges of the Rajang River, the longest river in Sarawak, as well as in Malaysia, and participant observation was carried out in the town of Sibu and a hinterland village in the Kanowit District. While the case village in the Kanowit District, Rantau Kemiding, is an Iban community that was historically largely dependent on slash-and-burn rice farming, Sibu is the nearest and most important urban center for the Iban in Kanowit and neighboring districts.

We selected this area as the research site for the following reasons: (1) rural villages in the area experienced various interactions with the colonial government through agricultural improvement projects; (2) the area is now in the front line of rural development in Sarawak, enabling us to observe contemporary interactions between rural residents and the present government concerning land; (3) the area has a high level of rural-to-urban migration; (4) the pattern of migration is worthy of consideration in terms of the cultural traditions of the Iban; (5) people who have migrated to Sibu often return temporarily to their village of origin, and many people return for their retirement years; (6) numerous squatter settlements in Sibu have been built by rural-to-urban migrants; (7) squatters in Sibu established effective cooperation between different ethnic groups to acquire legal residential lots from the government; (8) the opinions of urban dwellers strongly influence opinions among the village community; (9) land issues in the area draw the interest from both rural peasants and various actors such as urban dwellers, developers, and the government; and (10) Sibu and its hinterland are thought to provide new and wider living spaces for those who frequently move between the rural and the urban.

Locating the research in a regional urban center, Sibu, and a hinterland village, Rantau Kemiding in Kanowit, enables us to comprehensively explore and examine the range of themes, previously outlined, that have changed the traditional patterns of Iban village life.

Research for this study was conducted in August and September 1995, from June to September 1996, from July to October 1997, from September and October 1998, from December 1998 to February 1999, from June to September 1999, and in January 2000. In 2002 and 2003, additional supplementary research was carried out for short periods. During these times, I mainly undertook participant observation and door-to-door interviews in the town of Sibu and the village of Rantau Kemiding in Kanowit. In addition, questionnaires were used to complement the in depth personal interviews. To gather official data, published and unpublished documents were collected from various government agencies in Kanowit, Sibu, Kuching and Kuala Lumpur.

2
Geographical and Historical Features of Sarawak and the Study Area

Sarawak: its geography and population distribution

The State of Sarawak is located on the northwest coast of Borneo and is 124 449 square kilometers in size—is almost as large as West Malaysia (Peninsular Malaysia)—and in Malaysia, it forms the largest constituent state. Much of the state has a cover of residual soils derived principally from the tertiary sands and shale in the rugged hill country. These are characteristically thin with high acidity and low fertility. Used mainly for shifting cultivation, these soils are suitable over large areas, for the growth of rubber. On the steeper slopes of these hillsides thinner, poorer soils develop and these are known as *lithosols*; often planted with hill paddy, these areas have been recognized as having little agricultural value (Jackson 1968). In some parts of the inner region, however, the recent development of a road system has improved large-scale land use such as oil-palm plantation and commercial forestation.

The State of Sarawak is sparsely populated with a total population of 2 071 506 (Department of Statistics Malaysia 2001). This means that while the state occupies around thirty-eight per cent of the country's land, less than ten per cent of the population lives in the state. The major ethnic groups in Sarawak are the Iban, Chinese, Malay, Bidayuh, Melanau and the Orang Ulu (a collection of smaller groups such as the Kayan, Kenyah, Kelabit and other indigenous peoples) (Jayum 1994: 23). The most recent data on ethnic composition in Sarawak is shown in Table 2.1.

The population distribution in Sarawak is often explained in relation to its topographical features; the Malay and Melanau live in coastal lowland areas, the Iban and Bidayuh in the middle reaches of large rivers, including lowland and hilly land, and the Orang Ulu in the upriver and mountainous interior areas (Figure 2.1).

As indicated in Figures 2.2 and 2.3, this stereotype seems close to the truth. In effect, the Iban call the Malay/Melanau 'Orang Laut' which means coastal and maritime peoples, and the term 'Orang Ulu' meaning upriver people is

Table 2.1 Population distribution by ethnic group in Sarawak (1991, 2000)

	1991		2000	
	Number of persons	Percentage	Number of persons	Percentage
Iban	506,528	29.5%	603,735	29.1%
Chinese	475,752	27.7%	537,230	25.9%
Malay	360,415	21.0%	462,270	22.3%
Bidayuh	140,662	8.2%	166,756	8.0%
Melanau	97,122	5.7%	112,984	5.5%
Other *bumiputera*	104,391	6.1%	117,690	5.7%
Others	33,510	2.0%	70,841	3.4%
Total	1,718,380	100.0%	2,071,506	100.0%

Source: Department of Statistics Malaysia (1995b, 2001)

Figure 2.1 Stereotypical perception of ethnic distribution in Sarawak

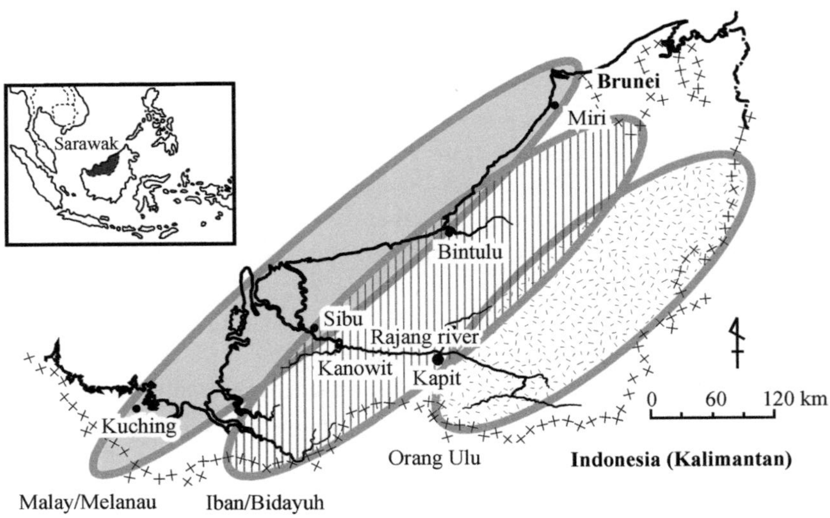

originally an Iban word, which suggests that the Iban have mainly lived in-between Malay/Melanau and Orang Ulu groups.

As a matter of course, however, the actual situation is not so simple, and the Iban have an uneven geographical distribution in the state. They are mainly concentrated in the lowland areas of Saribas and in the Rajang River basins (see Figures 2.2 and 2.6). According to Jayum (1994), about twenty-five percent

Figure 2.2 Distribution of major ethnic groups in Sarawak

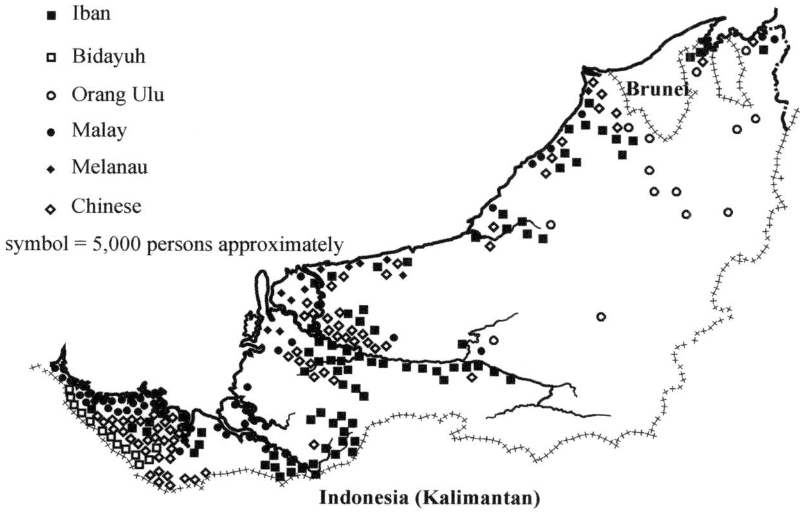

Source: Jayum (1994) modified by the author

of Iban are found in Saribas, or what is now known as the Sri Aman Division, and about forty-three percent are in the Rajang Basin, covering the present day Administrative Divisions of Sibu, Sarikei and Kapit (Jayum 1994: 22–23). Besides, in the process of historical migration and resettlement projects, the Iban have spread widely throughout the state and we can find a number of settlements along the Kemana River in the Bintulu Division and the Baram River in the Miri Division as well. In addition, considering the rapid increase in the number of rural-to-urban migrants in the last few decades, a new explanation for changes in population distribution is now required; this theme is one of the main subjects of this study.

Peripherality of Sarawak

The historical process of Sarawak's peripheralization

The history of modern Sarawak began in 1839 with the arrival to Kuching, of James Brooke. At that time the area lay under the control of the Brunei Sultanate. Inland from Kuching, antimony mining had begun more than a decade earlier, and in the late 1830s the miners were in revolt against their Brunei overlords. Brooke returned to Kuching in 1840. In return for his successful assistance in

Figure 2.3 Distribution of major ethnic groups by state constituency in Sarawak

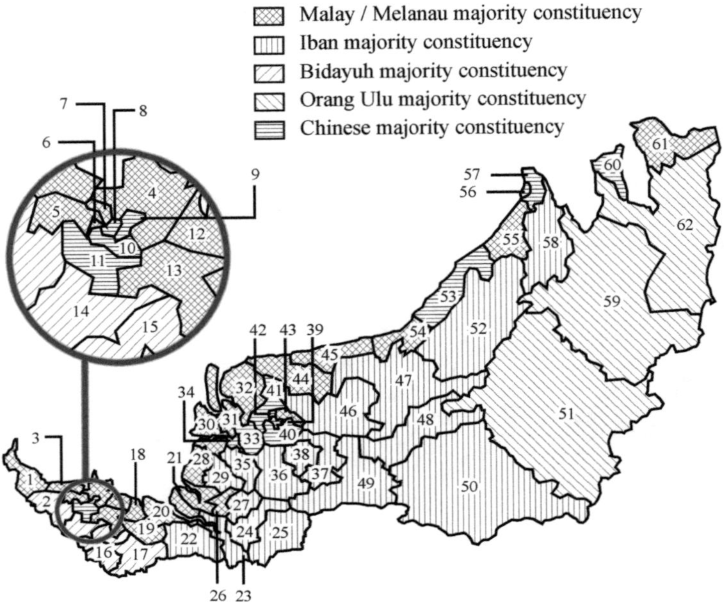

Source: New Strait Times (August 28, 1996) and Borneo Post (August 16, 1996)

suppressing the revolt, he was offered, as his personal domain, an area roughly equivalent to the present Kuching Division and in 1841 he was installed as the first 'White Rajah.' In 1853 and then again in 1861, further territory was acquired from Brunei, and in 1864 Britain recognized Sarawak as an independent state. Charles Brooke, a nephew of James Brooke, succeeded as Rajah in 1868 and continued to extend the territory. The present boundaries were settled in 1905 when Lawas area was transferred to the domain of Sarawak (Jackson 1968) (Figure 2.4).

In 1917 Charles Brooke was succeeded as Rajah by Sir Charles Vyner Brooke and the state remained as the personal domain of the Brookes until 1941, just before the Japanese invaded Sarawak. After the Second World War the third Rajah, Vyner Brooke returned to Sarawak in 1946, but upon pressure from the British Government he ceded sovereignty of Sarawak to the British Crown. On July 1, 1946 Sarawak became a crown colony and remained so until 1963 when it achieved independence and joined the new Federation of Malaysia.

King (1990) perceived the modern history of Sarawak as a process of 'peripheralization.' The Brookes had paid little attention to the economic

Figure 2.4 Expansion of the Brookes' territory

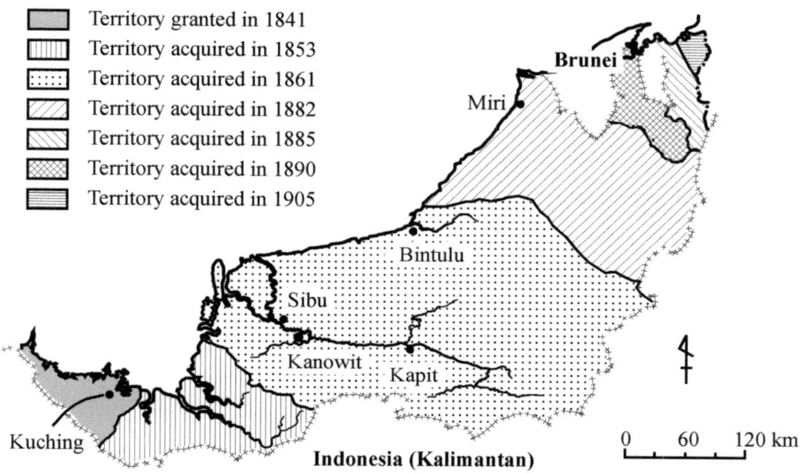

development of the indigenous population and operated a policy of native protection; unlike British Malaya, they did not establish a large-scale, foreign-owned plantation industry in Sarawak (King 1990; Ishikawa 1998). The British colonial period from 1946 to 1963 did little to alter Sarawak's economic backwardness, and therefore, it was relatively undeveloped before its incorporation into the wider Federation of Malaysia. King (1990) also remarked that although there has been some development in Sarawak since its incorporation, it has been highly localized and urban-centered, and has resulted in the emergence of considerable economic and political inequalities. What one now sees in Sarawak are the affluent urban rich alongside the rural poor.

Since the 1960s, economic development has been concentrated in the resource-exploitative industries such as logging, oil and natural gas. Large-scale plantation development and expansion of infrastructure in rural areas have only just commenced, lagging far behind other states in the Peninsular.

During my research in Sibu, a Chinese government official expressed his dissatisfaction and commented:

> To be sure, Malaysia has achieved rapid economic development and industrialization in the last few decades, but it is true only in the case of Kuala Lumpur. Sarawak has greatly contributed to the development of this country and Kuala Lumpur, through its resource exploitation, but it cannot be said that our state has received enough in return. We are exploited by the Peninsular and by Kuala Lumpur.

Similar complaints about economic disparity between Peninsular Malaysia and Sarawak are often heard amongst the Iban and other indigenous peoples as well. Thus, Sarawak is not only geographically separated, but also has a different historical background to that of Peninsular Malaysia—Sarawak has been economically marginalized in the national context of the Federation of Malaysia.

Political aspects of Sarawak's peripherality

The political situation in Sarawak is more complicated than in Peninsular Malaysia because of the complexity of its ethnic composition. In the Peninsular, ethnic composition is roughly described by the division of Malay/Non-Malay, that is, an absolute majority of Malay-Muslim, with around twenty-seven percent of ethnic Chinese and eight percent of people of Indian ethnicity. In Sarawak, on the other hand, the major ethnic group is the Iban, who account for only twenty-nine percent of Sarawak's total population, followed by twenty-six percent Chinese, twenty-two percent Malay, eight percent Bidayuh, six percent Melanau, and other indigenous and non-indigenous peoples (Table 2.1). In short, there is no absolute majority in Sarawak. Therefore, politics and political alignments have been relatively fluid and politicians rely on securing the support of people from outside their own ethnic group (Leigh 1974; King 1990).

Party political activity came relatively late to Sarawak commencing just before its independence. In 1963, in the premature political arena, Kalong Ningkan, an Iban, gained the position of Chief Minister of Sarawak. He remained in that position until 1966, and during this period, the Iban were effectively in the political majority. King remarked that Kalong Ningkan and his Iban dominated Sarawak National Party were considered to be confrontationist towards Kuala Lumpur, constantly asserting the rights, identity and autonomy of Sarawak within the Federation (King 1990).

In 1966, the federal government dismissed Kalong Ningkan, and appointed another Iban politician, Tawi Sli as Chief Minister—he was more compliant with federal wishes. But his government was transitional (Jayum 1994), and during his rule, communal and multi-ethnic parties were continually competing with one another and there was always a sense of political instability. Jayum (1994) inferred that the Federal Government felt that they had to appoint an Iban, considering the then power balance in Sarawak. Although the election for the state assemblymen in 1970 resulted in a precarious balance between the Malay/Melanau, Chinese and Iban, a powerful Muslim-Melanau leader, Abdul Rahman Yakub, the former Federal Minister of Education, became the Chief Minister of Sarawak. Since then, Sarawak has been progressively integrated politically and economically into Malaysia and a climate of cooperation has been established between the Sarawak State Government and the federal authorities. Abdul Rahman Yakub's government ended in 1981, and his nephew, Abdul Taib Mahmud became the Chief Minister, and still held the position up until the period of the publication of this book in 2007.

Iban marginality in Sarawak

Since 1970 the Iban have never been in the majority in Sarawak politics, although they are the majority of Sarawak's population. This is partly the result of the securement by the Muslim-Melanau of the support from the federation, referred to as 'federalism' or the 'federal factor.' From the Iban perspective, repeated cleavages within Iban dominated parties have also contributed to the reduction of their political influence. Moreover, as the intimacy of the relationship between the Sarawak Government and the Federation has been developed, the Iban gradually became excluded from the arena of decision-making and political power. In short, they have been marginalized from the politics of Sarawak since its formation, in 1970, of the Muslim-oriented cabinet.

In the last few decades, many Iban have felt increasingly frustrated by their political situation. Their dissatisfaction is often expressed as antipathy toward Muslim groups in Sarawak and toward the Federal Government, but they also feel irritated by the cleavages within Iban parties themselves and they sometimes disparage their own political failure.

It is true that since the 1970s indigenous peoples, including the Iban, have enjoyed advantages bestowed to them under the New Economic Policy; an affirmative action plan to propel poorer indigenous people into the economic mainstream. This plan is often called '*bumiputera* policy.' '*Bumiputera* (literally sons of the soil)' is an administrative term to clearly distinguish the 'indigenous' peoples from the 'non-natives,' such as the Chinese and Indians who have mostly migrated into Malaysia since the colonial period. While in Peninsular Malaysia the term *bumiputera* is normally used for the Malay and Orang Asli groups, in Sarawak it includes the Malay, Iban, Bidayuh and all other small indigenous groups. However, in terms of the beneficiaries of this policy, priority is clearly given to the Muslim *bumiputera*, while the Iban, mostly non-Muslim, are relegated to a 'second class' *bumiputera* status (Chin 1996). In this sense, too, the discontent felt by the Iban has deepened.

While the sense of political and economic marginalization is felt and expressed by the Iban who have migrated into the city, more than by those who have remained in the villages in the country, the perceived general disadvantage is seen to be directed at the Iban in general, no matter whether they are urban or rural-oriented. An Iban man who graduated from lower high school (Form 3) in 1976 and is now working for a government office as a driver of an official vehicle spoke of his experience from an urban perspective:

> I have a job in the government sector in Sibu. Although my education level is not high I was adopted as a government servant, maybe because I am a *bumiputera*. But we Iban are always allocated petty works such as garbage collectors, road maintenance, grass mowing and office boys. Even if we have the same education level and the same social background as a Malay man, we are never given a raise or a promotion over the Malay. As long as we are Christian or pagan, we cannot win against a Muslim.

Another Iban man who worked as a garage mechanic in Sibu emphasized the disparity between rural and urban areas in relation to ethnic differences:

> There are many job opportunities in Sibu and many rural people come down to this town to look for employment. But do you know why this urban area grew like this? It is because there have been many Chinese and Malays. The Chinese have a source of funds and know-how of various businesses in their community, and the Malay is given preferential treatment from the government. On the other hand, we Iban lack funds, business skills and government favors. Nonetheless, the Iban are always torn by internal strife and lose political power. So, we not only lag behind in the urban economy, but rural development also does not advance. Urban areas are developed for the Chinese and Malay, and rural areas are left behind because the Iban are the rural majority.

Thus, the Iban see themselves as marginalized in urban and rural areas, and often express discontent, sometimes in terms of the political situation of the State and the Federation. Considering the peripheral status of Sarawak within the national context, the Iban are structurally embedded in a multi-layered marginality. We must not overlook this point in order to understand the living strategy of the Iban in their contemporary context.

The study area: geographical features and historical background

This study focuses on Iban rural-to-urban migration in the middle and lower reaches of the Rajang River. The Rajang area, along with the Saribas Basin, is one of the main areas where the Iban reside. For the rural study site, an Iban community was chosen in the Kanowit District, and intensive research was also

Figure 2.5 Map of administrative districts in Sarawak

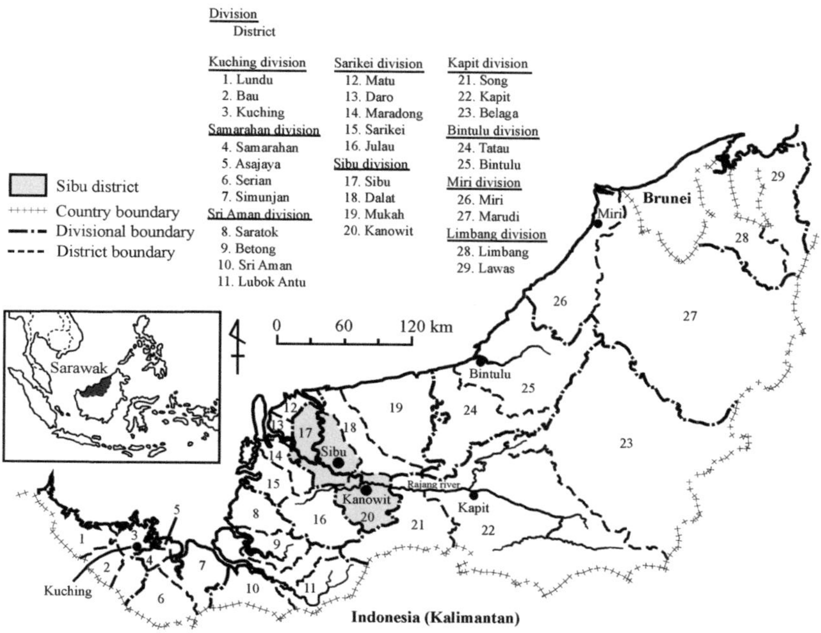

conducted in an urban area, with a focus on the Iban resettlement community in the town of Sibu. The details of these research sites in both Kanowit and Sibu will be discussed in Part II. In this section, I will provide some general information about the area of Kanowit and the town of Sibu (Figure 2.5).

Kanowit

The geography and history of Kanowit

The Kanowit District forms the area of the middle reaches of the Rajang. In 2000, the population of the district was 27 982 persons, of which the Iban accounted for eighty-three percent, the Chinese twelve percent and the Malay three percent (Table 2.2) (Department of Statistics Sarawak 2002). It takes about one and half hours, either by express boat or bus, to travel from Sibu to the town of Kanowit, the administrative center of the district. The town of Kanowit is located at the junction of the Kanowit and Rajang Rivers; it is a small market town with a population of 815 people in its Town District (Department of Statistics Sarawak 2002). People from neighboring villages visit this town by bicycle, motorcycle, car, boat, or informal bus, to purchase daily goods and to access government

Table 2.2 Population distribution by ethnic group in the Kanowit District (1991, 2000)

	1991	2000
Iban	20,732	23,168
Chinese	3,622	3,408
Malay	637	859
Melanau	248	355
Bidayuh	58	57
Others	83	135
Total	25,380	27,982

Source: Department of Statistics Malaysia (1995a) and Department of Statistics Sarawak (2002)

offices. Some villages surrounding the town are accessible by feeder roads, and there are public bus services from Kanowit to other much smaller towns, which link villages at the roadside of these feeder roads.

In the town, the Chinese control most of the commercial activities, while there are scattered villages of other ethnic groups such as Malay, Kanowit (Rajang), and Iban, surrounding the town (see Figure 3.1 in Chapter 3). Kanowit has primary and secondary government schools, a mission school, a public hospital, a post office, private banks, District Office, District Council and other social amenities. Thus, the town can meet the minimum requirements of people in the district.

As is shown in Table 2.2, the Kanowit District is one of the Iban dominated areas along the Rajang River. Historically, however, the Kanowit (Rajang) people had occupied this area until the first half of the nineteenth century when the Iban came into the vicinity from the upper Kanowit River (Kaboy 1965; Sandin 1967; Edward and Stevens 1971). In this period, groups of Iban engaged in fierce raids on the lower Rajang River and coastal sago-producing Melanau areas. These Iban people were thought to be mainly from the areas of Saribas and Skrang, arriving to the new area along the Kanowit River system (Figure 2.6). They conducted expeditions into the lower areas, and also began to migrate, becoming the first Iban settlers in Kanowit. According to Edward and Stevens (1971), within a relatively short time period, the Iban replaced the Kanowit as the major population group and political force in the area.

At that time, the Kanowit area was not a part of Sarawak, but the Rajah was eager to put an end to piracy, so as to protect the sago-producing communities in the lower Rajang. After several visits to the area, the Rajah decided to build a fort at the junction of the Kanowit and Rajang Rivers. Even after the construction of this fort, in 1851, and the incorporation of the area into Sarawak some ten years

Figure 2.6 Iban migration history

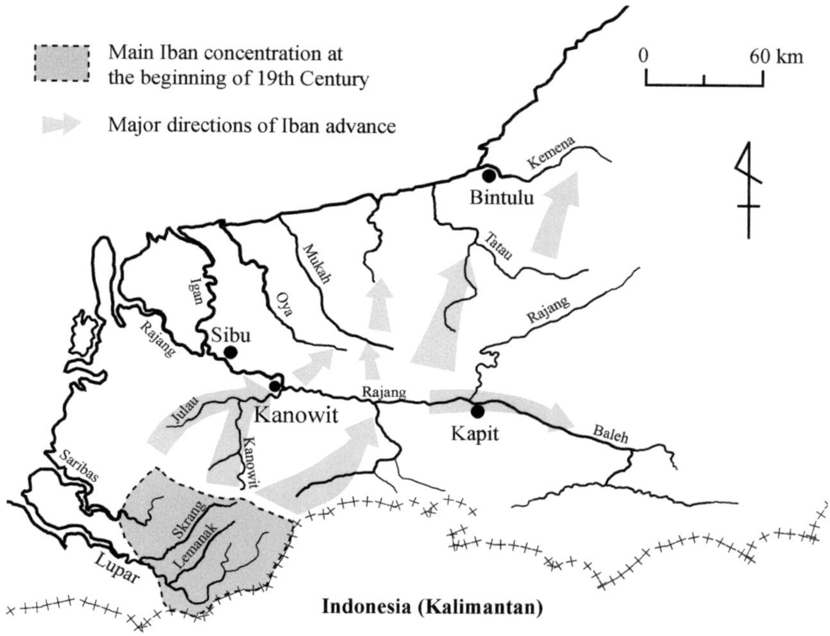

Source: Jackson (1968) modified by the author

later in 1861, there were still attacks on the fort and trouble continued in the Rajang, Kanowit, and its tributaries. What is important here in relation to this study, is the point that not all of the Iban were pirates and that in the latter half of the nineteenth century there were many Iban who came down to the area to escape from the disturbance of war in the upper area, expecting the protection of the White Rajah. People of the case village, discussed in Part II, are mostly descendants of these relatively moderate Iban people.

The Kanowit Catholic Church

In 1881, the first missionaries of the Roman Catholic Church arrived in Kuching. The Rajah had no wish to promote inter-missionary rivalries in Sarawak, so he decided to send the newly arrived Catholic priests to areas where no other missionary station (e.g. Anglican Church) had been built. The Rajah wanted the mission to be started at Kanowit, where the Iban were numerous and often troublesome (Edward and Stevens 1971). The Catholic missionary station of Kanowit was established in 1883 as the first base along the Rajang Basin, and in 1887, the first church was constructed (Edward and Stevens 1971; Rooney 1981). At that time, the Catholic Church was trying to modernize the Iban's agricultural practices with the clear intention of encouraging them to settle down in accordance with Brooke's policy (Rooney 1981: 31–33). This church not only introduced wet paddy, rubber, coffee and pepper cultivation, but also founded schools and hospitals, and the schoolboys were engaged in various agricultural activities on the church's land.[1] Although the influence of the church's demonstration farm only extended to a small area, their contribution to the expansion of rubber planting in Kanowit was seen to be successful.

Their missionary work not only contributed to changes in the area's agricultural production and practice, but also had an impact on changing the Iban's social structure. The Kanowit Catholic Church trained some local Iban men as catechists, enabling the local leaders to engage in missionary work throughout the district. They often went for *bejalai* to visit longhouses in the interior and persuaded longhouse residents to believe in Christianity. In some cases, people were encouraged to resettle on the land nearer the Kanowit town and to serve the church. According to old people in Kanowit, in the early twentieth century, some longhouses near the town were reorganized on the basis of social ties of Christianity, rather than as traditionally defined through kinship. The case longhouse in this study is from one of the villages that experienced this transformation in social structure. The head of the longhouse, at that time, had served in the church in the early twentieth century, and on the basis of their shared Christian beliefs had accepted people from other areas to join his longhouse.

Relations between the Iban and Chinese in Kanowit

The town of Kanowit, which began its history as a fort town, came to be equipped with a commercial function when the Malay from the lower Rajang and the Dutch Kalimantan began trading in the town. By the 1870s, however, Chinese merchants—mostly from the Hokkien dialect group—who migrated from Singapore, established businesses and within a short period, had almost dominated the town economy.

Although details of the relations between the Iban and Chinese, in the late nineteenth century, have not been elucidated, it is thought that the Iban mainly provided the Chinese merchants with jungle products. It was in the early twentieth century that the relations between the two groups became more significant, when the Iban in the area began to produce rubber.

In small towns in Sarawak one can see many grocery shops. These shops are very similar to each other in their business style, in that they sell almost all of the necessities of life such as soap, cleanser, kitchenware, dry foods, canned foods, salt, sugar, seasoning, coffee, carpenter's tools, agricultural chemicals and fertilizers, and also buy agricultural products such as cocoa, pepper and rubber from the indigenous peoples. Fidler (1973), who conducted anthropological research with the Chinese community in Kanowit, explained why almost the same shops could co-exist in this type of small town; there was a kind of patron-client relationship between the Chinese shopkeepers and the Iban farmers.

In former days, the income source of the Iban in rural areas was largely limited to the production of cash crops, and very few people had enough money to buy even everyday goods in town. Chinese shopkeepers allowed the Iban to buy goods on credit on the condition that they would clear away their debts by carrying rubber sheets. The Iban who had debts were not allowed to buy any necessities nor sell agricultural products at other shops, and Chinese shopkeepers had an unspoken agreement between themselves not to take clients of other shops. In other words, the Iban were usually tied to a specific shop. As this system was established in the first half of the twentieth century, what appears as an overabundance of grocery shops have been able to co-exist in small towns like Kanowit.

Present day Kanowit

The town of Kanowit is now accessible in a day trip, from most areas within the district, mainly because of the improved road system and the diffusion of outboard motors. In 1998 the town had thirteen store buildings (shophouses) in which about one hundred shops were operating. Other than permanent stores, there are two market corners for perishables that are run by the district office, one for meat and fish, and another mainly for vegetables. These market corners are opened every morning. The Chinese own most of the permanent stores in the shophouses, and a range of people, including the Chinese, Iban, Malay, Indonesian and Pakistani operate the stalls in the market corners

Access to Sibu has also been easier than in the past and people, who are relatively wealthy, come there to buy everyday goods in bulk because prices are slightly lower than in Kanowit. Although patron-client relations are to some extent still alive, these ties have been loosening. The diminution of these types of patron-client relationships has occurred as the result of the accessibility to Sibu, the decline in the agricultural activities of the Iban and the diversification of their income source.[3]

Kanowit is a regional market town, which has been integrated into the range of daily life activities of the Iban. The town has a hospital, post office, government offices, banks and branches of political parties, which, to some extent, provide local people with the opportunity for contact with the macro-society. Kanowit, however, does not have many employment opportunities except for a small

Plate 2.1 The town of Kanowit

Plate 2.2 The port of Kanowit[2]

number of positions in the government sector, and therefore, those who look for work have no choice but to go to other towns and cities, such as Sibu. One of the informants in the case village noted:

> Kanowit is a very small town and there is nothing to do there. But I go to town almost every morning to sit in a coffee shop, eat a bowl of noodles, and talk with somebody else from the other longhouses.

It seems that the Iban in the district do not regard the town as an urban center, but see it as a place to go to in their daily life to exchange information with Chinese merchants, Malays and Kanowit (Rajang) villagers, as well as with Iban from neighboring longhouses.

Sibu

The history of Sibu

As will be shown at a later point in this book, Sibu is the most important regional center for those who live in the lower Rajang Basin, especially for the Iban of Kanowit. According to Sutlive (1972), the founding of Sibu may be attributed to the second Rajah, Charles Brooke, whose policies were influential in the early development of the town. These policies were also important in establishing the demographic patterns and the smallholders' economy in the supporting hinterland.

Sibu was built where no permanent settlement had previously existed. The continuing movement of the Iban into the Rajang through the Kanowit and Sarikei Rivers, and their spread to the Igan and northern tributaries of the Rajang, prompted the Rajah to construct a fort at the junction of the Rajang and Igan Rivers. The fort was constructed in 1862, a historical point, which can be regarded as the commencement of Sibu as a town and regional center of the area (Sutlive 1972).

The construction of the fort attracted Chinese traders and the encouragement of Chinese immigration, in particular, created a radical transformation of the demography of the area. The Foochow, a Chinese dialect group originating from Hokkien (Fujian) province, southern China, began to migrate to Sibu in 1901 under the sponsorship of the Sarawak Government. In 1902, under government contract, a total of 997 farmers, including women and children, arrived at the port of Sibu (Kiu 1997). From the original 997 people, the population of the Foochow has increased rapidly, and they are now the largest Chinese dialect group in the town of Sibu.[4]

Plate 2.3 The town of Sibu

By 1947 the total population of the Sibu Urban area had reached 9983 persons, and in the 1960 Census there was a three-fold increase in population, or a total of 29 630 persons. With the expansion in 1980 of the gazetted Sibu Urban area, the population sharply increased to 126 381 (Department of Statistics Malaysia 1995a) (see Figure 5.1, Chapter 5).

Sibu was located at the junction of broad rivers that form a large delta region and a deep-water passage into the Rajang River, thus permitting the thoroughfare of larger ocean-going vessels. This has meant that historically, the town developed as an import-export center, which expanded as the economy

Plate 2.4 The port of Sibu[6]

became more bound to the hinterland areas. Since the 1960s, in particular, the exploitation of timber and its export to foreign countries has boosted its economy. According to the 1991 Census, Sibu was the second largest urban center in Sarawak.[5] Although in the last decade, with the exhaustion of timber in the Rajang area, there has been a deceleration of development, the town of Sibu still remains the most important regional center in the Rajang area.

Sibu as a macro-society

Since its inception, Sibu has continuously increased its population size (Table 2.3). If we refer only to population size, urban centers in Sarawak seem to be typical of local cities or towns in Malaysia, in contrast to the primate city of Kuala Lumpur (Table 2.4).

It is noteworthy, however, that the ethnic composition of Sibu's population is fundamentally different from many of the cities and towns in other parts of Peninsular Malaysia (Table 2.5). To the Iban, within the regional context of the Rajang Basin, the town of Sibu is a place dominated by the Chinese. At the same time, within the national context of Malaysia or Sarawak, it is a place where the Iban first feel frustrated by government policies that give preference to Muslims. As described above, many people from rural areas have come to Sibu to look for employment, and found that business in the private sector was almost dominated by the Foochow Chinese and that non-Muslim indigenous peoples were often allotted unimportant positions, even in the government sector.

Table 2.3 Population in urban and rural areas by administrative district in Sarawak

	1980			1991			2000		
	Urban	Rural	Total	Urban	Rural	Total	Urban	Rural	Total
Kuching	72,555	226,775	299,330	277,905	91,295	369,200	422,240	71,869	494,109
Lundu	-	21,576	21,576	-	24,493	24,493	-	27,345	27,345
Bau	-	31,449	31,449	-	35,958	35,958	-	41,824	41,824
Samarahan	-	-	-	-	46,583	46,583	23,064	23,902	46,966
Serian	-	64,542	64,542	-	71,874	71,874	-	79,632	79,632
Simunjan	-	34,914	34,914	-	45,971	45,971	-	37,287	37,287
Sri Aman	-	65,589	65,589	18,503	40,136	58,639	21,243	41,532	62,775
Saratok	-	33,956	33,956	-	37,939	37,939	-	42,035	42,035
Betong	-	36,821	36,821	-	43,993	43,993	-	50,392	50,392
Lubok Antu	-	19,735	19,735	-	22,234	22,234	-	23,255	23,255
Sarikei	12,618	28,540	41,158	21,156	28,475	49,631	25,053	32,043	57,096
Maradong	-	27,028	27,028	-	26,957	26,957	-	28,942	28,942
Daro	-	16,387	16,387	-	13,179	13,179	-	14,851	14,851
Matu	-	-	-	-	9,154	9,154	-	11,183	11,183
Julau	-	26,240	26,240	-	28,104	28,104	-	31,723	31,723
Sibu	85,231	45,328	130,559	133,479	36,920	170,399	167,427	42,691	210,118
Dalat	-	20,160	20,160	-	22,022	22,022	-	23,462	23,462
Mukah	-	33,205	33,205	-	41,831	41,831	-	44,837	44,837
Kanowit	-	26,690	26,690	-	25,380	25,380	-	27,143	27,143
Bintulu	-	54,800	54,800	51,862	34,270	86,132	103,733	35,279	139,012

Tatau	-	-	-	-	21,124	21,124	-	23,241	23,241
Miri	52,125	43,374	95,499	102,878	58,495	161,373	169,005	52,050	221,055
Marudi	-	49,219	49,219	-	71,958	71,958	-	71,713	71,713
Kapit	-	35,847	35,847	-	55,608	55,608	13,610	43,099	56,709
Belaga	-	11,497	11,497	-	22,284	22,284	-	22,896	22,896
Song	-	15,528	15,528	-	17,576	17,576	-	19,236	19,236
Limbang	-	24,047	24,047	11,054	22,845	33,899	19,018	20,799	39,817
Lawas	-	19,777	19,777	-	29,276	29,276	-	32,726	32,726
Asajaya	-	-	-	-	-	-	-	28,513	28,513
Total	222,529	1,013,024	1,235,553	616,837	1,025,943	1,642,771	964,393	1,045,500	2,009,893

Note: Figures have not been adjusted for under-enumeration.

Source: Department of Statistics Sarawak (1998, 2005)

Table 2.4 Population and number of households in major cities and towns in Malaysia (1991)

STATE	CITY/TOWN NAME	POPULATION	RANKING	NO. OF HOUSEHOLD	RANKING
Federal Territory	Kuala Lumpura[a]	1,145,342	1	244,267	1
	Labuan	26,271	25	5,272	25
Johor	Johor Bahrua[a]	328,436	2	70,032	2
Kedah	Alor Star	124,412	10	25,385	8
Kelantan	Kota Bharu	58,335	24	11,853	24
Melaka	Melaka	75,909	20	15,282	19
Negeri Sembilan	Seremban	72,958	21	14,771	20
Pahan	Kuantan	86,360	15	17,724	14
Perak	Ipoha[a]	301,424	3	67,512	3
	Taiping	62,321	23	12,820	22
Perlis	Kangar	14,247	26	2,978	26
Pinang	Seberang Perai (Tenggah)	236,270	4	47,739	4
	Georgetown	219,603	5	43,456	5
	Pulau Pinang (Barat Daya)	122,764	11	24,892	10
	Seberang Perai (Selatan)	84,771	17	16,383	16
	Butterworth	78,640	18	15,864	18

Sabah	Sandakan	125,841	9	21,666	11
	Tawau	86,289	16	16,263	17
	Kota Kinabalu	76,120	19	14,481	21
Sarawak	Kuching (Selatan/Utara)[a]	148,059	7	26,748	7
	Sibu	126,381	8	25,275	9
	Miri	87,167	14	17,358	15
Selangor	Klang	161,773	6	30,347	6
	Shah Alam	102,019	12	20,392	12
	Bandar Petaling Jaya	88,338	13	18,464	13
Terengganu	Kuala Terengganu	67,027	22	12,464	23

Notes.
a = a place with city status
Cities and towns with municipal status are listed. The population outside urban areas (bandaraya/bandar/pekan) is not counted.
Source: Population Report for Local Authority Areas (1991), Department of Statistics Malaysia (1995b)

Table 2.5 Population distribution by ethnic group in the town of Sibu (1991)

ETHNIC GROUP	POPULATION	PERCENTAGE
Malay	13,255	10.5%
Iban	16,922	13.4%
Bidayuh	922	0.7%
Melanau	8,960	7.1%
Other *bumiputera*	585	0.5%
Chinese	84,267	66.7%
Others	1,470	1.2%
Total	126,381	100.0%

Source: Department of Statistics Malaysia (1995a)

The Iban in the Rajang area call Sibu '*negeri*.' This term has multiple meanings—country, state, city and large town. They never use this term to describe small market towns such as Kanowit. The Iban who migrated to Sibu from rural areas perceive that '*negeri*' has a different institutional structure from their home place and they are conscious of relations with other ethnic groups in the state and national contexts. An Iban man in Sibu commented:

> In this '*negeri*,' we cannot survive without cooperation with the Chinese and the Malay, because the government policy often overlooks the Iban.

In this statement, the regional situation of Sibu and the levels of state and national government overlap. Here, Sibu represents a symbolic feature of the experience of the 'macro-society' for the Iban in the area.

Notions of 'rural' and 'urban' in this study

Statistical definition of rural and urban areas

It is rather difficult to clearly distinguish between the urban and the rural, because 'urbanness' and 'ruralness,' or 'urbanity' and 'rurality,' do not necessarily correspond to administratively defined areas. However, as the focus of this study is primarily the subject of Iban mobility between rural and urban areas, we need to provide a definition of 'rural' and 'urban' before continuing with our discussion.

When we refer to population statistics in this book, we depend on the official classification of rural and urban areas. In Malaysia, urban areas are, in principle, composed of '*bandaraya*' and '*bandar*,' that is, city and town. In Sarawak, as of 2005, Kuching (Kuching Selatan and Kuching Utara) and Miri have the status of a city, and other urban centers such as Sibu, Bintulu, Sarikei and Sri Aman are classified as towns. The Sibu District is administratively divided into Sibu Rural District and Sibu Urban District, both of which have a council; Sibu Rural District Council and Sibu Municipal Council respectively. In this study, the town of Sibu refers to the area administrated by the Municipal Council, which in 1981, was extended to cover 129.5 square kilometers.

The Sibu Division is comprised of four districts: Sibu, Kanowit, Mukah and Dalat. The Kanowit, Mukah and Dalat Districts are classified entirely as rural areas (see Table 2.3), even though they include numerous market towns such as Kanowit. Small market towns in these districts are called '*pekan*,' and do not have a municipality. In this sense, the town of Sibu is the only urban center in the division.

An Iban village in the Rajang area

As mentioned previously, the whole Kanowit District is classified as a rural area. However, the district is too large to deal with as an analytical unit, and if we consider the rurality or ruralness of the indigenous people, the smaller unit, the village, has great significance. This study choose an Iban village in Kanowit as the analytical unit of the rural community, however, it is also necessary to clarify how the term 'village' is being utilized here, because this term is not defined as an administrative category in Sarawak.

As for the concept of village, in Peninsular Malaysia, Shamsul (1996) remarked that as a Malaysian administrative category, the village is important in two interrelated ways: for the organization of land revenue and for development purposes. With regard to the former, each village in Peninsular Malaysia is seen as having a definite, fixed and identifiable physical boundary. The annual land tax is assessed according to commercial or subsistence use, and part of the land tax is reallocated to villages in the form of development expenditure. With regard to the second point, the village has been officially recognized as the basic administrative unit in the overall hierarchy of 'development administration' in Peninsular Malaysia. It is also an important local component of national and state development-oriented bodies (Shamsul 1996). In Sarawak, on the other hand, there is no administrative and physical boundary of the village. The smallest administrative unit that has clear geographical demarcation in Sarawak is the district, although some districts have sub-districts within the territory. However, when minor rural development projects are implemented, the smaller unit is usually taken into consideration, that is, the longhouse community. In other words, the longhouse is an important local component of state development-oriented bodies. As will be discussed in Chapter 6, when an Iban dominated political party launched their campaign in 1983 and asserted 'rural development,' the backwardness of rural areas was narrated in relation to the rurality of the Iban in the longhouse community.

The longhouse has often been used as a symbol of rurality and is considered as synonymous with the indigenous community, not only in the political arena but also in various fields, including the mass media. While this study makes clear that the activities of the Iban are not limited to those within the longhouse community, we do concede that the longhouse can be regarded as the 'home village' for the Iban; that is, the starting base and place to which to return. Besides, the longhouse reflects rurality in terms of the context of development policy in Sarawak.

Urbanness for the Iban

Although, in a statistical sense, it is clear that Sibu is an urban area, which has a definite administrative and geographical boundary, we would like to think of 'urbanness' as the essence of the city. Yoneyama (1987) and Wazaki (1988), who further developed Glick's (1973) argument on urbanness, asserted that what is important for the study of migrants' urban lives is not to classify a city on the basis of its administrative form and geographical scale, but to investigate the emergence of new urban communities with respect to the nature of the city. Yoneyama defined the term 'urbanness' as the nature or the essence of the city, regardless of its population size. He enumerated variables for analysis such as developed social stratification, connections with the higher reaches of society, the role of mediators in negotiating with the macro-society, and so on. Yoneyama and Wazaki called these elements,[7] which are important for the survival of rural-to-urban migrants in the cities, 'urban essentials.' Sibu has almost all of the urban essentials that are listed by Yoneyama.

As will be described in this book, the Iban in Sibu are obliged to interact—sometimes competing and sometimes cooperating—with other ethnic groups, and are conscious of their marginal situation in the city. However, those who work for government agencies have the chance to obtain inside knowledge and try to make the best use of such information to improve their lives. Some of them know how to impose their will and appeal to influential persons or political leaders. To the Iban, Sibu is a place to feel anguish as a minority and, at the same time, to investigate the possibility to make inroads into the existing power structure.

Kuching: the capital city of the state of Sarawak

The most important urban center in Sarawak is the state capital city, Kuching, which has absorbed a large number of people from rural areas including those

Plate 2.5 Kuching: Sarawak's capital city

from the Rajang region. Although we will focus on the Iban in Sibu and its hinterland, we should mention how we locate the city of Kuching in this book, from the perspective of migration patterns of rural people in the Rajang area.

According to the 1991 Census, in Sibu Division (Sibu, Mukah, Dalat and Kanowit Districts) the number of people who changed residence from 1986 to 1991 amounted to 101 971 persons, and the number of non-movers were 164 888, which means almost forty percent of the population in the division experienced migration in the five-year period. Of the 101 971 movers, those who moved to the Sibu District (including the move within the Sibu District) comprised 44 770 persons, or almost half. On the other hand, 3516 persons migrated to the Kuching District, that is, less than four percent of all of the movers from the Sibu Division moved to Kuching. As for the number of out-migrations from the Kanowit District during 1986 and 1991, while 2335 persons (almost ten percent of the total population of the district) migrated to Sibu, only 214 persons moved to Kuching.

Thus, the population movement in the area is mainly oriented toward Sibu, not Kuching. The same tendency can be seen in the flow of migrants from the neighboring districts along the upper Rajang River system, such as the Song, Kapit and Julau Districts. These data show only the flow between districts, and therefore, not all of the people move to urban areas. Besides, we cannot see the ethnic breakdown of the movers, but we can easily guess that the majority of the area, the Iban, have Sibu-oriented migration patterns, and their mobility is reflected in the data shown above. In this sense, it is reasonable to deal with the mobility between Sibu and its hinterland when we consider the rural-to-urban migration of the Iban in the Rajang area.

Analysis in the middle-scale

As discussed previously, people in the Rajang Basin tend to move toward Sibu, and therefore, it is rational to analyze Iban mobility within the scale of the Rajang Basin. Here, we would like to assert the validity of such an analysis from the viewpoint of a 'middle-scale society.'

To probe diversified rural–urban interactions from the migrant perspective, it is necessary to observe in detail the living strategies of movers in both rural and urban locations. However, it is almost impossible to trace those who move from 'peripheral' villages to primate cities and foreign countries. To overcome the difficulties caused by geographical distance between the origin and destination of migrants, we need an analytical unit with a smaller scale. In other words, it may be more realistic to deal with intermediate cities or small towns as migrant destinations. As discussed in the previous sections, Sibu has a centripetal force in the Rajang area, where we can explore the nature of urbanness for the Iban migrants from rural areas. Thus, even a local city/town[8] such as Sibu and its hinterland, provide the key factors that are useful in examining and explaining rural–urban interactions.

This perspective can be reinforced by the concept of a 'middle-scale society' proposed by Yamashita (1986) in his focus on 'local towns.' The concept falls between the two pillars of anthropological studies and macrocosmic social sciences. According to Yamashita, while we already have a 'micro' (conventional anthropological) model based on data from rural communities, and a 'macro' model derived from sociological studies of metropolitan areas, we do not have an efficient model for dealing with societies of an intermediate scale and complexity. In this sense, research on the 'local town' and its hinterland has the potential for establishing a new social model.[9]

There have been previous studies on intermediate cities and towns from geographic and economic perspectives. Rondinelli (1983), Hinderick and Titus (1988), Galie (1988, 1992), Choguill (1989), Leinbach (1992), Siddiqi (1993) and Bajracharya (1995) are all good examples. However, most of these studies regard secondary cities, small towns, and intermediate cities as distribution centers for the hinterland villages. They deal with them to complement urban system theory, which has neglected smaller cities and towns, or at best, they have focused on the spatial disposition of such cities and towns to alleviate overpopulation in primate cities. These studies generally described the characteristics of cities on the basis of population size and spatial distribution, and emphasized their economic functions and administration policies. This perspective is substantially different from our study that focuses on the interactions between rural and urban areas in a middle-scale.

On this point, the discussion presented by Endo (1996) is suggestive. He comprehensively reviewed studies of local (provincial) economic zones in Thailand, and classified these studies into three categories: (1) a trickle-down perspective that views regional economic centers from the top; (2) quantitative analysis of regional economic disparity based on statistics; and (3) 'core-periphery' theory or dependency theory, which explains the mechanism of the subordination of regional centers to the over-concentrated primate city. Endo commented that all of these research frameworks neglect the local actors who perform important roles in regional economic development. He also recognized the importance of investigating relationships between various political actors and economic leaders at the local level because they are intertwined in the restructuring of the regional economy and intermediate society. This perspective is relevant to the study of intermediate cities not only in Thailand but also in Southeast Asia in general.

Rondinelli (1983, 1985), who studied intermediate cities from the perspective of their economic function and policy making, also asserted that there are a number of important factors in the type of interactions at the level of the regional economy and the demographical situation, as well as those between local leaders and groups.[10] Thus, when we deal with so-called 'middle-scale societies' (Yamashita 1986), it is essential to analyze the interactions between various actors and performers at the local level.

In this study, we choose Sibu as an intermediate town and Kanowit as the hinterland village. The perspectives that we have outlined reinforce our attempt to set Sibu and Kanowit as the analytical unit of a 'middle-scale society.' In this geographical range, we would like to analyze rural–urban interactions focusing on the actors and performers who move between the two areas.

Part II

In this section of the book, the new ethnography of the Iban in the contemporary context will be described.

Chapter 3 provides some basic information on the longhouse community, and subsequently outlines the brief history of the Rantau Kemiding Village. These facets of Iban life are important to clarify and are indispensable to our understanding of the relations between out-migration and the resultant changes in the longhouse community.

Chapter 4 specifically examines out-migration from Rantau Kemiding Village and its impact on agricultural activities and the village community. Taking into account Iban traditions and culture, the significance of structural changes in the village, in terms of the process of modernization, are examined. In recent years, the younger generation, especially adult women, have increasingly left the village. Since they play a vital role in agricultural activities, family succession, and in the inheritance of tradition, their absence has had a considerable effect on the decline of community structures. Nevertheless, the village community is still an important basis for those who earn a subsistence living in unstable situations in the cities, and also provides affirmation for Iban people living an urban life.

Chapter 5 describes the living strategies of rural-to-urban migrants. The first issue is the process by which squatter residents—the so-called 'urban poor'—acquired legal residential lots in a resettlement area through interaction with other ethnic groups and the urban administration. In the squatter area of Sibu, different ethnic groups such as the Iban, Malay, Melanau, and Chinese, reside in a pattern of loose and spontaneous segregation. However, effective cooperation among these different groups was observed in the process of negotiating with the administration. This chapter also looks at the interactions between rural-to-urban migrants and their community of origin. Urban dwellers, that have apparently obtained stable residence in town, keep moving between the two areas to maintain their ties with their native village and also to try to secure rural residence and land, with a view to their long-term life plan. The meaning of such strategies is examined mainly from a socio-economic point of view.

Chapter 6 focuses on the political aspects of rural–urban interaction. An investigation of the development policies of the Sarawak Government and the reaction of the Iban illustrates how the macro-political situation is reflected in the Iban community. This chapter also points out that urban dwellers play a vital role in influencing opinions in rural communities and in involving rural residents in the processes of political negotiation. Our observation of these factors supports our belief that those who move between rural and urban areas are extremely important actors in bringing micro and macro-societies closer together.

In an attempt to explain the contemporary living space of the Iban, Chapter 7 includes a comprehensive reexamination of the themes raised in the preceding chapters. To develop an understanding of their lives holistically, changes in kinship relations are described. While rural-to-urban migrants make use of a broad interpretation of traditional customs and concepts in elaborating their long-term life plan and furthering the expansion of their living space, they also face the problem that relationships between loosely linked members of the extended family are becoming strained in the process of rural development. This chapter points out that the balance between looseness and rigidity may be untenable for the Iban in the near future.

Thus in summary, Part II provides a multi-faceted investigation into the human mobility and living strategies of the Iban in Sarawak. The analysis, in these chapters, emphasizes the cultural, social, economic, and political aspects of the phenomena, all of which are closely interrelated. The synthesis of all of these factors provides an explanation of the living space of the Iban and of contemporary rural–urban interactions.

3
The Formation of the Rantau Kemiding Village

The Rantau Kemiding Village in the Kanowit District is the case village chosen to examine out-migration of the Iban. The patterns and effects of out-migration will be discussed in relation to structural change occurring in the longhouse community. Before commencing this discussion, and in order to understand the changes that will be described in the following chapters, it is important to outline the general features of the Iban longhouse and the historical background of the case community.

Principles of the longhouse community and the case village

The longhouse of the Iban

The longhouse is designed to house multiple families within it, and in this sense, it is a kind of communal house. According to Waterson (1990), in earlier times, longhouses were widely distributed in Southeast Asia. Loeb and Broek (1947), Sugimoto (1971) and Waterson (1990) provide an historical overview of the types of longhouses and communal houses and their distribution in Southeast Asia. Concerning the social structure of the longhouse community in particular, Sekine (1979) presented some suggestive information. He explained Iban society in relation to the features of spatial composition in a longhouse and village land use, emphasizing their dichotomous pattern of living space, discussed below. Waterson remarked that historically, longhouses and other types of communal houses shared in common some similar purposes and functions, such as defense against the enemies and unification of families within a community. Currently, however, many of these communal houses in South East Asia have dissolved and disappeared. But in Sarawak, many of the different ethnic groups' longhouses remain, and moreover, they are still constructing new types of longhouses. For example, along the major roadsides in Sarawak, we can see a large number of longhouses made from bricks, some of which have two-stories. Longhouses that are relatively wealthy have been equipped with electrical appliances such as refrigerators, washing machines and air-conditioners. While the indigenous peoples in Sarawak seem to adhere to the traditional style of residence, they are also keen to improve their lives by incorporating modern technological appliances into the longhouse, where they can.

Most of the indigenous shifting cultivators in Sarawak have different kinds of longhouses, and this residential unit is sometimes called a longhouse community. The Iban are typical of those ethnic groups in Sarawak who live in longhouses. An Iban longhouse usually contains a village community within which a number of families live together. The interior of the longhouse is mainly composed of *bileks* (separate family rooms) and a *ruai* (common corridor).[1] The *bilek* is the smallest spatial unit in which a stem family is supposed to live. This family unit, usually called a *bilek*-family,[2] forms a management unit for swidden agriculture and is rather autonomous both socially and economically. On the other hand, the common corridor, the *ruai*, runs in front of the *bileks* from one end of the longhouse to the other. This corridor is a highly public space used for meetings, rites, or group work. It also provides people with an opportunity to exchange information in their daily life (Sekine 1979: 68–70). In short, the *bilek* is a closed and domestic space for the family, and the *ruai* is a public space for all members of the longhouse community that is also open to the outside world. The social life of the Iban is mainly spent in these two sections of a longhouse. The head of the longhouse is called *tuai rumah* in Iban language.

The Iban longhouse usually contains more than 10 *bileks*,[3] and some have more than sixty. The length of a longhouse ranges from twenty to three hundred meters. Although the composition of the Iban longhouse community is mostly consanguineous, a *bilek*-family is free in principal to break away from their longhouse community and join another. Therefore, it is no wonder that some longhouse communities include *bilek*-families that have no consanguine relationship. In principle, the longhouse community has the flexibility to accept a new *bilek* whenever it needs to.

The longhouse community itself has autonomous principles and can be regarded as a small-scale village. Construction of a longhouse as the residence for a village community is considered for the purpose of defense, but in addition, the longhouse is easy to build, pull down and remove, enabling the Iban to frequently move a village from one place to another. The scale and high mobility of the Iban village has been closely related to their patterns of subsistence. The Iban have been largely dependent on shifting cultivation, which needs a relatively large tract of land. This point will be discussed in more detail later.

In addition to the general features of defense and the ease of construction of a longhouse, Uchibori (1996) pointed out that to live together in a longhouse is important for community members to maintain social relationships and secure emotional stability. For example historically, when they gathered together in the *ruai* to discuss the manner of labor-exchange in the farming season, distributed meat of hunted wild animals, performed rituals, and held meetings on important issues, they reconfirmed the cooperativeness of the community. The Iban themselves often say that the longhouse makes it easier for all village members to join the various social activities in the community, and it is also a very easy way for the head to control the whole village.

The Rantau Kemiding Village

The Rantau Kemiding Village is located along the Kanowit River, a tributary of the Rajang, and is about four kilometers south of the town of Kanowit. The village is accessible from the town by an unpaved road,[4] and an unlicensed van transportation service operated by the local Chinese is also available.[5] It takes around fifteen minutes by van, car or motorcycle to get from the town to the village, and some people commute daily to the town of Kanowit. While most of primary school children who live in the village attend the village government school, some children go by van everyday to the mission school[6] in the town. Secondary school students also go to the government school in the town. Nowadays there are very few people in the village who go to town by boat, but most *bilek*-families still possess a boat to access the paddy fields and rubber gardens on the east side of the Kanowit River.

The name of this village, *rantau* means the reach of the river that is opposite to the *tanjong* (bend), and *kemiding* refers to a kind of edible fern. Therefore, the village's name, Rantau Kemiding, means the riverside where it is abundant in edible ferns. Village people say: 'In the area we could see a lot of *kemiding* in former times, but now it is relatively difficult to find such edible ferns because of the use of agricultural chemicals and land development.'

While this area does not have officially recorded village boundaries, there has been a loose consensus on the boundaries among the Iban in the local area. The village boundary of Rantau Kemiding shown in Figure 3.1 is simply a rough sketch[7] based on interviews with older people in the village.

Although the village community of the Iban is usually made up of one longhouse, Rantau Kemiding has two longhouses in its territory. In this study we have called them 'Longhouse A' and 'Longhouse B,' because the name of a longhouse changes frequently. A longhouse is usually named after the head of the longhouse. For example, if Mr Duit heads one longhouse community,

Figure 3.1 Rantau Kemiding Village

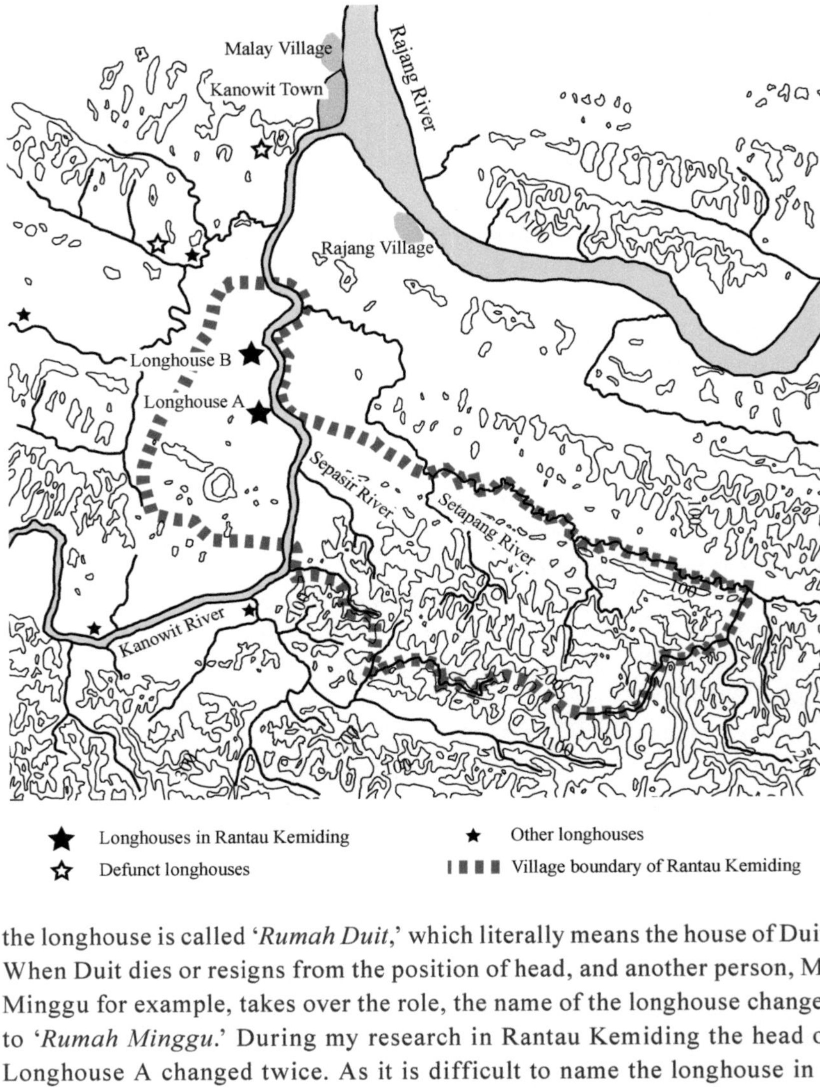

the longhouse is called '*Rumah Duit*,' which literally means the house of Duit. When Duit dies or resigns from the position of head, and another person, Ms Minggu for example, takes over the role, the name of the longhouse changes to '*Rumah Minggu*.' During my research in Rantau Kemiding the head of Longhouse A changed twice. As it is difficult to name the longhouse in a consistent way, I decided to use the nomenclature of A and B to indicate the two longhouses in the study village.

Longhouse A comprises fifty-two *bileks* and Longhouse B, located 500 meters north of Longhouse A, contains eleven *bileks*. There are five individual houses near Longhouse A and one in front of Longhouse B. In this village,

Plate 3.1 Longhouse A of Rantau Kemiding

Plate 3.2 Longhouse B of Rantau Kemiding

an individual house is regarded as a *bilek* even though it is detached from the longhouse, so in total, this village has sixty-nine *bileks* altogether. Longhouse B was constructed in 1985 when it split off from Longhouse A, and Longhouse B has its own head independent of the management of the other longhouse. As for the unity of the village community, Rantau Kemiding seems divided against itself, however, there is no geographical boundary between the two longhouses and they share the same territory. As members of the two longhouses belonged to the same longhouse community until 1985, they are still closely related in a complicated way in terms of landholding and consanguinity. In case they need to hold a meeting, for example, about land in the village, members of the two longhouses gather together. Besides, the Kanowit District Office does not recognize Longhouse B as an independent village community.[8] Therefore, this study regards the two longhouses as components of the village community of Rantau Kemiding.

Construction of a sedentary longhouse

In this section we would like to explore the process by which the Iban in Rantau Kemiding came to settle in the area. As there is limited documented evidence about how they settled and formed a longhouse community in that specific location, we are obliged to depend mainly on the memory of the old people of Rantau Kemiding.

Changes in patterns of Iban mobility

It was in the late nineteenth century that the Iban of Rantau Kemiding first came down from Mujok to the Kanowit district. According to the villagers, Salleh and his son Sawing were the leaders of the Iban community when they arrived in Kanowit. The oldest leader that they remember was called Junggol, he led his group from the upper Kapuas, Indonesia, to the Sarawak side near Simmangang (presently called Sri Aman). Salleh was one of Junggol's lineal descendants. The group led by Salleh migrated to the upper Lemanak, although it is not clear when and along which route they moved. Thereafter, they moved again to the Mujok River basin, but nobody remembers the reason why Salleh and his group migrated to this area (Figures 3.2 and 3.3).

People in Rantau Kemiding often emphasized that their ancestors came down to Kanowit to escape from the disturbances of war in the Mujok area. They also remarked that Salleh's group was looking for a place that was already controlled by the Brookes. Immediately before the fort was built at

Figure 3.2 Migration route of Salleh and his group

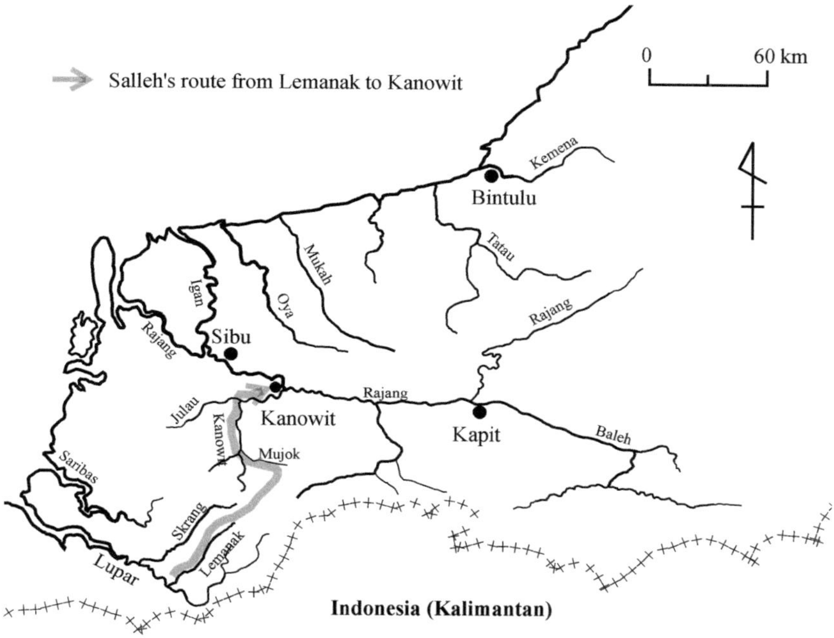

the junction of the Rajang and Kanowit Rivers, a nephew of James Brooke, Tuan Besar visited Kanowit in 1851, and gathered the Iban leaders in the area together to make them promise to restore tranquility. It is not clear whether Salleh's group knew about this or not, people in Rantau Kemiding asserted that Salleh thought that the Brookes' rule maintained public peace in Kanowit.

From the late nineteenth century to the early twentieth, there were a large number of Iban who migrated, an action that was affected by the Brookes' policy. In other words, Iban mobility accelerated and became more dynamic as a result of Brookes' intervention. At that time, Iban attitudes towards this policy can be roughly categorized as follows: (1) to be offended by the newly legislated regulations and employ guerrilla tactics against the Brookes; (2) to migrate to escape from the interference of the Brookes; (3) to join the Brookes' troops as soldiers to fight against other oppressive Iban groups; (4) to obediently follow the compulsory migration policy of the Brookes; and (5) to escape from warfare in the interior and migrate towards a place under the Brookes' rule.

Figure 3.3 Succession of *tuai rumah*

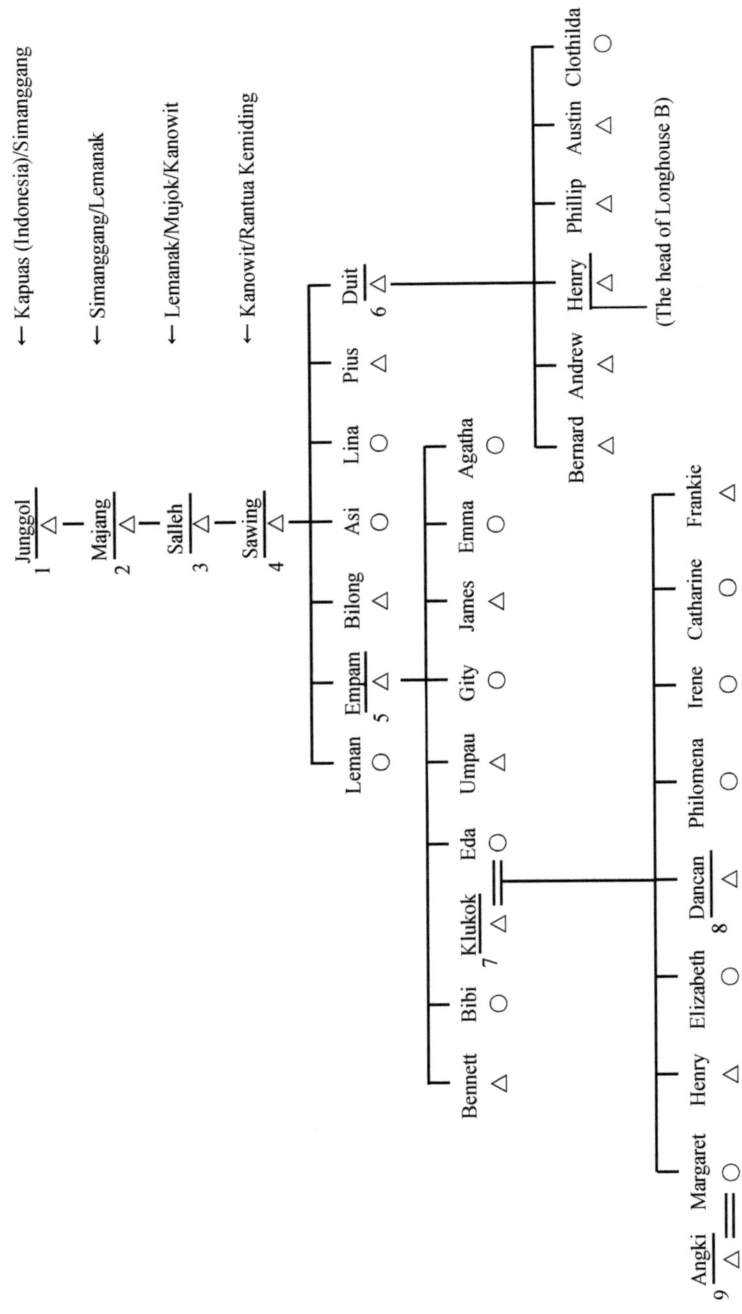

These different attitudes and responses by the Iban were reflected in their variable migration patterns. The move of the Iban of Rantau Kemiding is considered to be the result of the fifth response, one of escaping warfare and seeking protection. It is often pointed out that the great influx of the Iban from the Skrang and Lupar River systems to the Rajang Basin in the early nineteenth century gave rise to frequent bloody battles, but since the end of the nineteenth century it can be said that many Iban came to Kanowit to settle down in order to seek close relations with the Brookes' government.

The formation of a sedentary longhouse in Rantau Kemiding

Salleh's group came to Kanowit in the late nineteenth century, but even after arriving there they resettled several times near the town. The marks ☆ in Figure 3.1 show the obsolete longhouses of Salleh's group before settling in Rantau Kemiding where in the late 1920s they finally resettled. Immediately before moving to Rantau Kemiding, Salleh passed away and Sawing, one of his sons, succeeded as head of the group. In Rantau Kemiding they first constructed a temporary longhouse, called *dampa* in Iban language, and thereafter in 1936, built a sturdier longhouse just beside the temporary one. This is Longhouse A in its present form. When this longhouse was built, Sawing's son, Empam, became head of the community. He was a powerful leader and also religiously influential in the district.

Longhouse A was constructed in 1936 with twenty-one *bileks*. It is worth noticing that the longhouse community contained *bilek*-families that had recently migrated from other places to join Empam's group. According to the old people in Rantau Kemiding, before coming to Kanowit, the community led by Junggol, Majang, Salleh or Sawing was a small group, members of which had close kinship relations with each other. However, when they migrated to Rantau Kemiding, they began to include new *bilek*-families that had no ties of consanguinity with the original *bilek*-families. Most of these other families joined this group under the guidance of Empam.

In the 1920s Empam began to serve the Kanowit Catholic Church as a catechist.[9] His main work was to travel in and around the district and to visit the Iban longhouses to promulgate the Christian faith. He sometimes persuaded longhouse people to come down to the town of Kanowit to learn the Catholic doctrines and attend the divine service at the Church. In effect, at that time, many Iban from various areas in the Rajang district lived in the mission dormitory to learn Christianity, and some of them chose not to return to their original longhouse but to settle near the town to keep close to the Church. Empam accepted these people to join his longhouse community in Rantau Kemiding. Until the early 1950s, when he passed away, Empam continued to persuade the Iban in the interior to believe in Christianity. Thus, the Rantau Kemiding Village was a mixed community from the beginning, and even after the construction in 1936 of Longhouse A, some *bilek*-families were incorporated into the community through the bonds of Christianity.

Several longhouse communities in the Kanowit District were reorganized as a result of the Catholic Church's missionary work. In the early twentieth century this was a new phenomenon. How can we account for the emergence of these newly formed longhouse communities in terms of the social environment of the time?

In the process of forming the 'private' state of Sarawak, the Brookes tried to establish order by utilizing excessive power against Iban warfare in the interior (Uchibori 1987: 64). On the other hand, Christianity was used to peacefully enlighten the Iban and other indigenous peoples by establishing mission schools and hospitals, and by introducing agricultural innovation. To the Iban at that time, the Brookes' rule was a symbol of terrible violence, while Christianity was a symbol of peace, even though both the Brookes and the Church were symbols of the ruling 'Whites (*orang putih*).' In other words, these symbols were two sides of the same coin—like a carrot-and-stick approach. The Iban of Rantau Kemiding first came to Kanowit to be under the Brookes' rule and established a new longhouse community strongly influenced by the Catholic Church. In this sense, they embodied the wishes and expectations of the 'Whites' in their longhouse community; it was a mixture of Iban tradition and European modernity.

Introduction of cash crops

Traditional subsistence and introduction of rubber

The major form of subsistence for the Iban was dry paddy planting by slash and burn agriculture. The traditional agricultural cycle was as follows: from June to July they opened primary or secondary forests, in August burned the area while waiting for felled and slashed trees to be dry enough, from the end of August to early October planted seeds of paddy with other vegetables on the same field,[10] in November and December they weeded the paddy field two or three times, and in February and March of the next year, they harvested the paddy. After they used a parcel of land for dry paddy cultivation for one or two agricultural seasons, they fallowed the land for less than ten years, and in the following farming season opened new forest. Although they were largely dependent on dry paddy cultivation, if there was a small swamp or a wet sunken place near the dry paddy field, they usually also planted wet paddies (Figure 3.4). [11]

The Iban in Rantau Kemiding said: 'When our grandfathers began to settle here, this area was still plentiful of primary forest, and they could open the forest as they liked.' There is no evidence that primary forest covered the area at that time, but it is probably true that the forest had not been occupied by anybody else for a considerably long period of time, prior to their settlement in the area. Since the 1920s they began to open the forest on the east side of the Kanowit River. Although all of the members of the community had a living base (*bilek*) in the longhouse on the west side of the river, they preferred planting paddies on the opposite side, because the land nearest the longhouse was mostly flat and wet land not suitable for dry paddy and rubber planting. Those who planted paddies on the opposite side made an agricultural hut out on the paddy field and lived there during the farming season. Some people spent almost all of their time during the year living in the hut, to tap rubber trees during the off-season of paddy farming.

Before coming down to Kanowit, the Iban made their living by planting paddies and vegetables, and by hunting, fishing and gathering. In Kanowit, however, they adopted new crops such as rubber that were primarily introduced by the Kanowit Catholic Church.[12] The first rubber planting in Sarawak was recorded in 1905 (Jackson 1968), and a few years later it was introduced into the Kanowit area. The District Officer reported that in around 1910, Father Adrian Klerk of the Kanowit Catholic Church educated the local Iban in how to plant rubber trees, and tap and produce rubber sheets for sale. Immediately after rubber was introduced in Kanowit, there was a rubber boom as a result of the First World War and many Iban in the district adopted rubber planting. Thus, rubber became one of the major agricultural crops in Kanowit as well as in the whole of Sarawak. When the Iban of Rantau Kemiding built their new longhouse in 1936, dry paddy and rubber were their most important crops.

Rubber planting as a condition of settling down

The Iban not only learnt about rubber planting from the Kanowit Catholic Church, but some people were also working for *Tuan* Kedd, an Englishman who had a rubber plantation located on the opposite side of the town of Kanowit across the Rajang River. In 1926 he employed local Ibans to plant rubber trees on his plantation site, and some people from Rantau Kemiding joined the wage-work in the plantation. It can be assumed that the Iban began to plant rubber on their own land in the 1920s, and learnt the skills of rubber

Figure 3.4 Agricultural cycle of paddy planting in the early 20th century

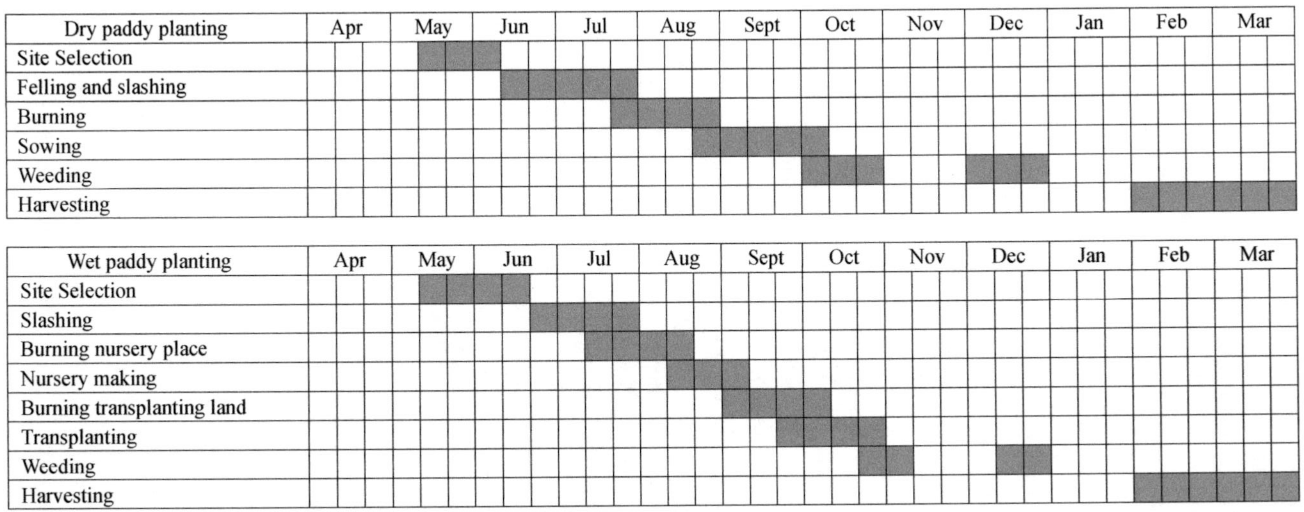

planting and tapping both through their interaction with the Church and from their experience as wage laborers in the plantation.

As rubber trees are difficult to grow on wetland, the Iban chose to make rubber gardens on the east side of the Kanowit River. However, they did not take the trouble to clear away the forest specifically for planting rubber trees. To clear the land of forest is one of the heaviest agricultural tasks, and the Iban principally felled forest trees only for preparing to plant dry paddies. So what they did was to usually use the cleared land for one or two seasons and after they harvested the paddy, they would convert this land into a rubber garden.

According to the old people, they used to make around five acres of dry paddy field per *bilek* every year. Therefore, it is estimated that they planted a maximum of five acres of rubber trees once every few years. In the 1910s and the 1920s, they were given rubber seeds, free of charge by the Catholic Church. In addition, in the 1930s they were allowed to pull out and bring back rubber seedlings that had spontaneously germinated from the dropped seeds in older rubber gardens of local Chinese smallholders and *Tuan* Kedd's plantation. In the old rubber gardens, seeds often fell from matured rubber trees and spontaneously sprouted. The extraction of rubber seedlings was necessary to maintain the stable productivity of the rubber garden. Therefore, plantation and garden owners welcomed the gathering of the seedlings by the Iban and as a result, few Iban needed to buy rubber seeds or seedlings themselves.

For the Iban, the merits of rubber planting at that time were as follows: (1) they could utilize the land that had been planted with the paddy in the previous year; (2) they did not need to invest in buying rubber seeds or seedlings; (3) it was relatively easy to manage the rubber garden after planting; and (4) they could tap rubber trees whenever they liked and utilize the time during the off-season of paddy farming. Thus, rubber was the most efficient cash crop for the Iban at that period of time. As many Iban told me 'rubber gardens used to follow paddy fields;' it is thought that rubber gardens became gradually diffused in patches as dry paddy fields were shifted (Figure 3.5).

As described in this section, the Iban established a new type of longhouse community in a complex interaction with the 'Whites,' and chose to settle in Rantau Kemiding. While they continued swidden agriculture on the east side of the Kanowit River, they also introduced rubber as an important cash crop, enabling them to earn a more stable livelihood. This income supported them and they were able to live in one location; it also made it difficult for them to migrate or resettle again to another place. In this sense, the introduction of rubber had the desired effect of the Brookes' policy, restraining the Iban's frequent migration, at least in the Kanowit area.[13]

Growth of the longhouse community

Although the community leader, Empam, died in 1953, the longhouse community was stable and continued to grow until the 1980s. This section describes its growth and also gives a brief explanation about the changes that occurred in the longhouse in 1985.

The 'second generation'

During the 1930s and up until the 1950s, Empam brought the longhouse community of Rantau Kemiding together. The number of *bileks*, when established in 1936, was twenty-one (Figure 3.6). At that time, the longhouse

Figure 3.5 Distribution of rubber gardens in the research area in the 1930s

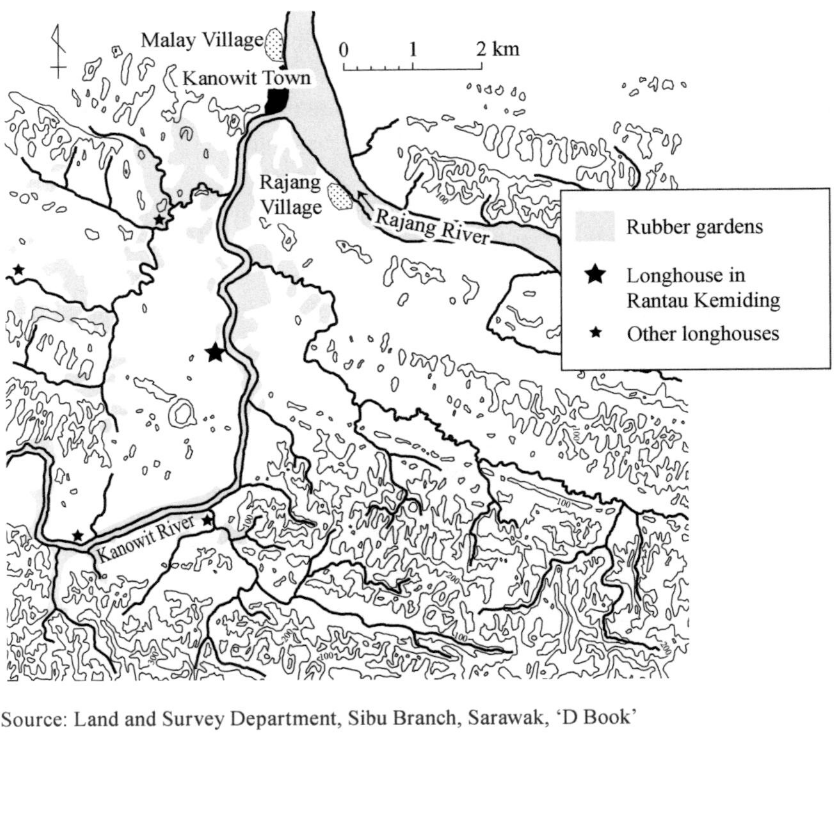

Source: Land and Survey Department, Sibu Branch, Sarawak, 'D Book'

Figure 3.6 Plan view of the two longhouses in Rantau Kemiding Village

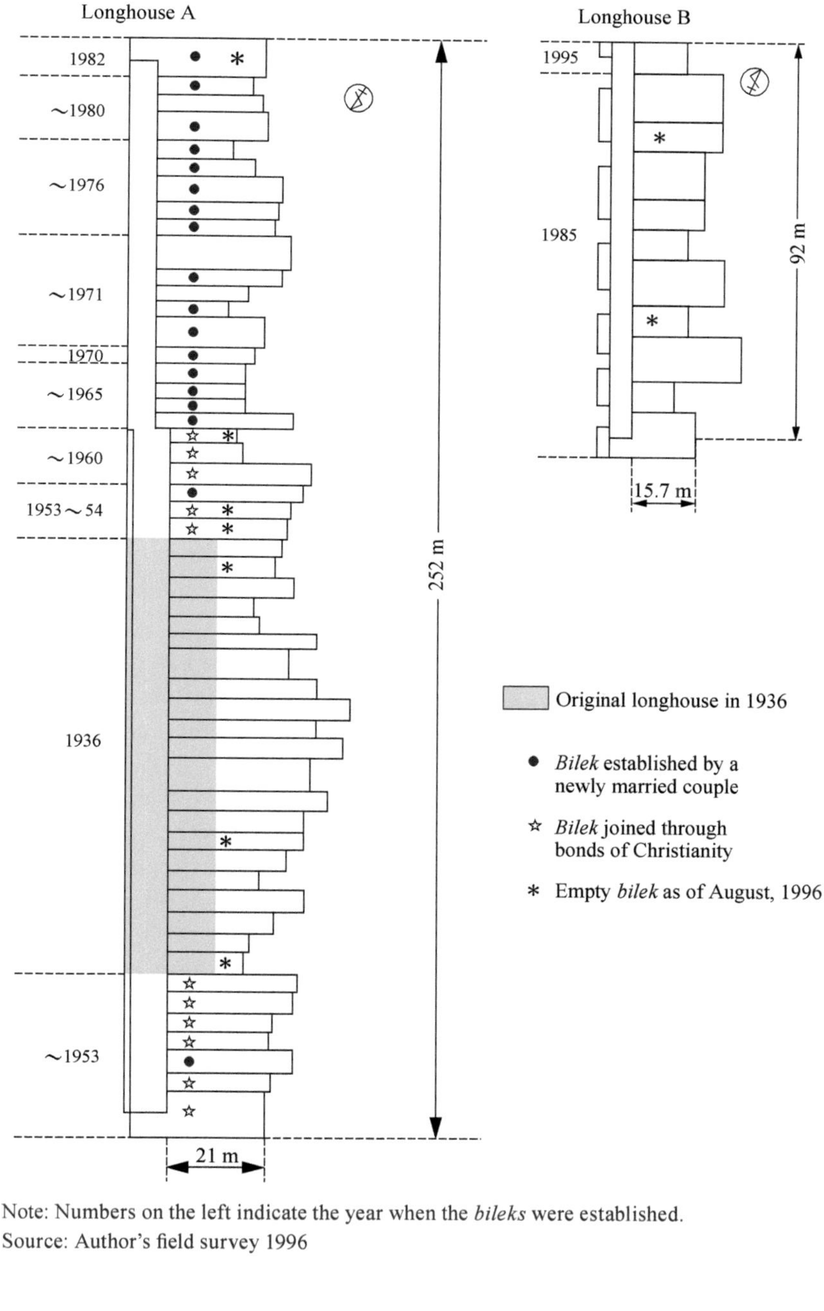

Note: Numbers on the left indicate the year when the *bileks* were established.

Source: Author's field survey 1996

community was not based solely on lineal relations. Empam, the then community leader, accepted some *bilek*-families from other areas through the bonds of Christianity. The inflow of *bilek*-families from the outside occurred until 1960 (refer to the *bileks* marked ☆ in Figure 3.6).

Even after 1960, the longhouse continued to extend itself by attaching new *bileks* on its side. These new *bileks* were mainly constructed by newly married couples that had become independent of their parents (*bileks* marked • in Figure 3.6), including the case of marriage among the same longhouse members. Considering that marriage between the same longhouse members may strengthen the ties of the *bilek*-families (Freeman 1970: 94), it can be said that since the 1960s, the slightly unstable community that had been gathered together based on the bonds of consanguinity and religion had become more solid and stable. In short, during this period, Rantau Kemiding experienced both the growth (extension) of the longhouse and the maturity of the community itself.

From the viewpoint of population change, during Empam's period, the community experienced 'social increase' of the village population, but in the 1960s saw a transition from 'social increase' to 'natural increase,' strengthening the ties among the community members.

Leaders in the stabilizing period

In relation to the maturity of this community, it should be noted that in this period the village of Rantau Kemiding produced several influential leaders. After the death of Empam, his youngest brother, Duit, became *tuai rumah* (the head of the longhouse) and remained head until 1974. He was also appointed as *penghulu* (the chief of a certain domain) of the lower Kanowit Basin. Bennett, the first son of Empam, served in the Third Division (the current Kapit and Sibu Division) as a government official, and was appointed as the District Officer of Kanowit. The most influential person in this period was Umpau, the second son of Empam. Umpau served in the Kanowit Mixed Local Authority during the British colonial period, and in 1963 when Sarawak gained independence from the Crown Colony and joined the newly formed Federation of Malaysia, Umpau stood for the Sarawak State Assembly and was successfully elected.[14] He was also a pioneer in agriculture, introducing various kinds of cash crops to Rantau Kemiding, such as pepper (1954), new species of grafted rubber (1955) and cocoa (1979).

Thus, between the 1950s and the1970s, as a result of its influential leaders, Rantau Kemiding was fairly prosperous. Many people look back on this period with nostalgia as the 'good old days' of the village. They said that leaders at that time had pleasant personalities and broad perspectives. When they came back to the longhouse for short periods, the villagers would spontaneously gather at the *ruai* to listen to their animated stories about the outside world. By discussing a range of subjects and concerns within a broader context and based on their knowledge of what was happening locally and nationally, people in the longhouse came to be equipped with viewpoints on their lives that were located within the modern context.

The prosperous days for Rantau Kemiding ended in the late 1970s; firstly, Duit, the then *tuai rumah*, died in 1975. Then as a result of illness, Umpau gave up standing as a candidate at the 1979 election and immediately after the election passed away. Bennett resigned from the position of Kanowit District Officer in 1974 and died in 1979. When these influential people, who not only demonstrated strong leadership in the village, but also played an active role in the district, passed away one after the other—the shining period of Rantau Kemiding came to an abrupt end.

Economic factors of growth

As described above, the longhouse community of Rantau Kemiding established stability, both in terms of its strengthened community ties and in the authority of its talented leaders. From an agricultural point of view, it is noteworthy that this period saw the increase in wet paddy cultivation and rubber planting. Wet paddy, in particular, allowed for population increase of the community. Here, we would like to describe the agricultural changes that occurred in the village in relation to the community's population growth.

Diffusion of wet paddy cultivation

Even before the 1940s, the Sarawak Government tried to introduce wet paddy planting in this area; for instance, the government opened a pilot farm in Kanowit in the late 1930s and gave lectures to the Iban on wet paddy farming with the use of buffalos. Although the lecture obtained cooperation from a few Dusun people from Sabah (the territory of the North Borneo Company at that time), it did not produce adequate results because the project was interrupted by the outbreak of the Second World War (Edward and Stevens 1971).

In the late 1940s a few *bilek*-families in Rantau Kemiding began to use agricultural chemicals and fertilizers, and in the 1950s these new technologies were expanded in and around the village. These technologies were introduced by the Agricultural Department for the purpose of modernizing agriculture in the area. In 1949 and 1968, we also saw the construction of small-scale

Plate 3.3 Talking in the *ruai* of Longhouse A in the 1960s

irrigation systems on the east side of the Kanowit River[15] and in the early 1950s the Kanowit Rural Improvement School was established to give local indigenous peoples agricultural education.[16] Considering these innovations, we can assume that the colonial government was keen to develop wet paddy cultivation to increase the yield of rice.

In the 1950s people were eager to plant wet paddies on the east side of the Kanowit River, especially along the Setapang and Sepasir Rivers, tributaries of the Kanowit. The reason why these areas were preferred was that they were plentiful of both hilly and swamp lands. Although they were keen to introduce new wet paddies, they were still largely dependent on dry paddy cultivation by slash and burn methods, and therefore, a large tract of hilly land was also needed.

According to the old people, wet paddy cultivation with agricultural chemicals became popular in Rantau Kemiding in the 1950s,[17] and in the late 1960s the total area of wet paddy in the village exceeded the area covered with dry paddy. The Sarawak Government encouraged indigenous peoples to adopt wet paddy for the purpose of increasing the degree of self-sufficiency in rice production in Sarawak, improving the economic level of rural life, and restraining the indigenous people from opening primary forest.[18] It is probably true that the government's intention had an influence on the expansion of wet paddy in Rantau Kemiding. However, the increase in the 1960s of wet paddy field in the village was not only affected by government policy, but was also closely related to the rubber-planting boom in this period.

Expansion of rubber gardens

The acreage covered with rubber trees rapidly increased in the 1950s and the 1960s (Figure 3.7). In 1955 budded rubber trees were introduced by Umpau, who attended a lecture on planting newly developed rubber trees and brought grafted seedlings to Kanowit. The Agricultural Department also began to distribute the new seedlings in 1957.

Although the special procurement demands of rubber, caused by the Korean War, had already abated, the production, export and planting of rubber remained at a high level in the late 1950s (Figure 3.8). As for Rantau

Figure 3.7 Distribution of rubber gardens in the research area around 1980

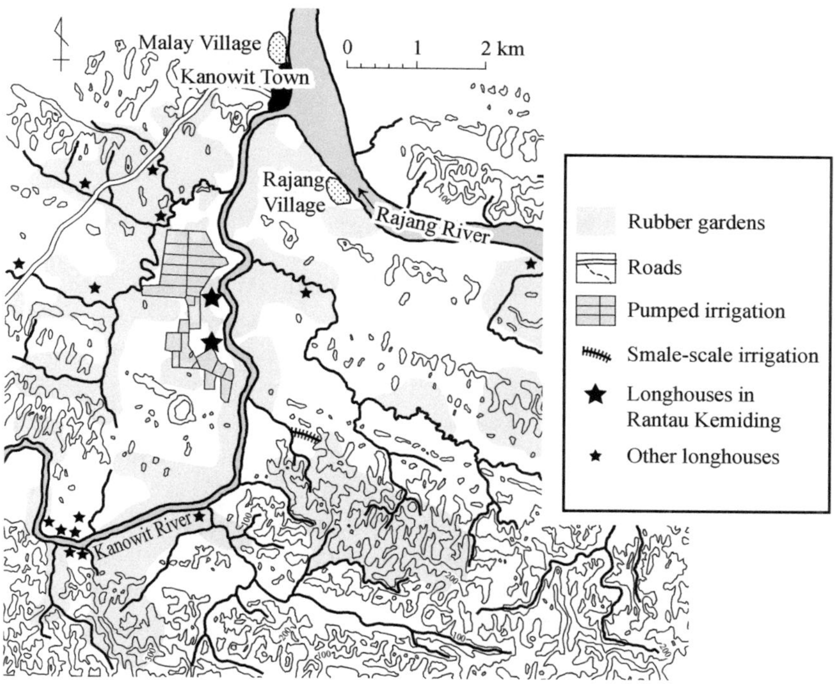

Source: Aerial photograph, Kanowit, Sortie No. 11/72, Scale 1:16,000, 1972. Aerial photograph, Kanowit, Sortie No. 2/72, Scale 1:25,000, 1976. Land and Survey Department, Sibu Branch, Sarawak, 'F Book (1st survey),' 1969–1983

Figure 3.8 Exports and market price of rubber 1946–1993

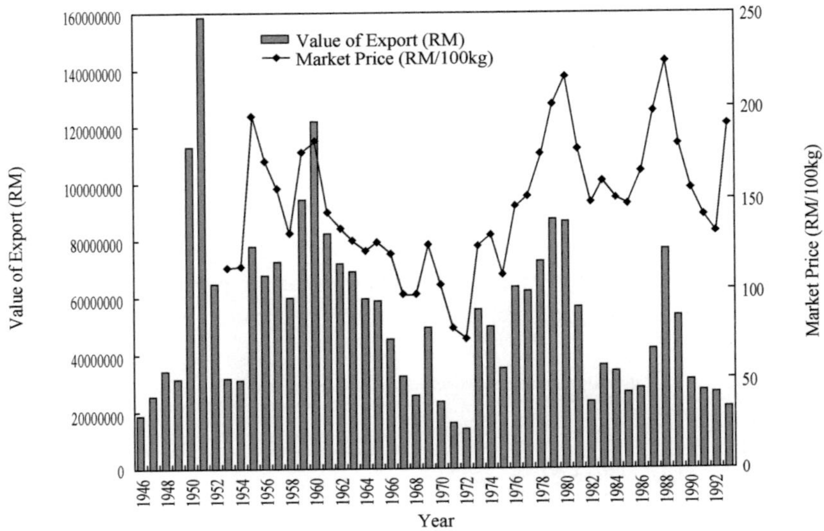

Source: Department of Agriculture, Sarawak

Kemiding village, villagers said that the increase in *bilek*-families accelerated the expansion of rubber planting.

From the viewpoint of traditional shifting cultivation, converting a dry paddy field into a rubber garden leads to a decrease in acreage of fallow land. This prevented the abandoned paddy field from returning to secondary forest, and as a result, the amount of land suitable for dry paddy cultivation had decreased. Considering the traditional cycle of the Iban's shifting cultivation, land shortage may bring about resettlement, dispersal or disunion of the longhouse community. However, Rantau Kemiding could avoid the split in the community and experienced a population growth in this period. This was partly the result of the expansion of wet paddy and rubber; that is, firstly wet paddy enabled repeated cultivation on the same land, which was impossible on the dry paddy field; secondly, intensive land use for wet paddy brought about relatively higher production of paddy per unit area; and finally, even when the yield of paddy dropped they could supplement their livelihood by cash income from rubber production.

Thus, the expansion of rubber gardens did not cause land shortage in Rantau Kemiding, but rather it complemented the Iban's livelihood as the most important cash crop. In general, in a day, an adult male can tap rubber trees in two or three acres, but most people in Rantau Kemiding continued to plant rubber once every few years. This was because they needed more than one rubber garden; that is, they wanted to try to plant new species whenever they were introduced, avoid overexploitation of rubber trees by shifting tapping sites frequently, and they had a prospect that their children would utilize their parents' rubber gardens in the future. However, it cannot be denied that they had planted an overabundance of rubber trees. In the village there were many rubber gardens that were left untapped for a long time after planting. Since the 1960s, the Iban were discouraged from producing rubber as a result of its sharp fluctuation in market price, and this also coincided with an increase in the number of younger people who were engaged in wage-earning jobs outside the village.

The split in the longhouse community

The death of Duit, Bennett and Umpau in rapid succession in the late 1970s was the moment that marked the end of the prosperous era for Rantau Kemiding. The extension of the longhouse also apparently ceased in around 1980. In 1985, however, the community established a new longhouse (Longhouse B). Although this may be regarded as part of the continuous process of expansion, it actually took on elements of political tension within the longhouse community.

After the death of Duit, Klukok, his son-in-law, succeeded as the head of the longhouse (*tuai rumah*). Klukok became the head, on the recommendation of Bennett and Umpau, but some village members were displeased with this selection because he was not a lineal descendant of the previous leaders (see Figure 3.3).[19] With this choice as a turning point, the disunity of the community began to surface.

Instability was exacerbated by the political events occurring in Sarawak. In 1983, the Sarawak National Party (SNAP), an Iban dominated party, split, and the younger members broke away to organize a new 'Dayak[20] based' party, the *Parti Bansa Dayak Sarawak* (PBDS).[21] In Rantau Kemiding most people had been supporters of another party, *Parti Pesaka Bumiputera Bersatu* (PBB), but a group in the village asserted that the Iban should join the new party, the PBDS. The difference in favorite parties paralleled the rivalry between the factions within the village, that is, the discord between the supporters of the new *tuai rumah*, Klukok, and their opponents. The PBDS supporters in the village nominated the third son of Duit, Henry, to be the leader of their faction, and subsequently built another longhouse within the village territory—this was Longhouse B.

Plate 3.4 Identity card of an owner of a rubber holding

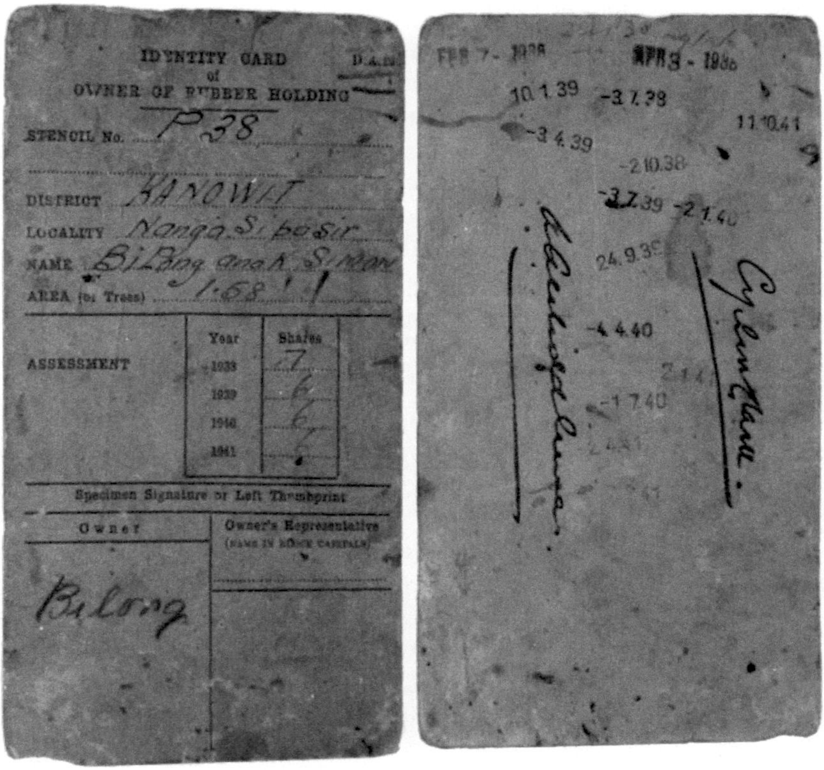

IDENTITY CARD
of
OWNER OF RUBBER HOLDING

STENCIL No. P38

DISTRICT KANOWIT

LOCALITY Nanga Sipesir

NAME Bilong anak Simon

AREA (or Trees) 1.68

ASSESSMENT	Year	Shares
	1938	7
	1939	6
	1940	6
	1941	6

Specimen Signature or Left Thumbprint

Owner	Owner's Representative (NAME IN BLOCK CAPITALS)
Bilong	

Most of the village people, however, explained that the reason for the split in the longhouse community was because of land shortages, Longhouse A could not be extended any further. This explanation is reasonable. The northern side of Longhouse A borders the government primary school, and on the south the ground is too soft to build a new *bilek*. Another explanation is that the population of the village exceeded the appropriate size for the longhouse community. However, while some village members asserted these explanations as the ostensible reasons, they emphasized that the split originated in the process of the selection of the new head of the longhouse in the late 1970s. Some other people in the village felt that the political incident in 1983 also strongly influenced the breakup of the community.[22] It is difficult to judge which explanation is correct, but we can say that the political factors within and outside the village are interconnected with land conditions and the population problem, resulting in the construction of Longhouse B.

After the breakup of the longhouse, Longhouse A and Longhouse B conducted festivals and held meetings independently. It is possible, however, to regard these two longhouses as constituents of the same community, because the construction site of Longhouse B is within the village boundaries, and did not affect the changes in land ownership in the village. Furthermore, very close relations between the longhouses remain through the bonds of consanguinity and affinity. If needed, they gather to hold meetings together, and during the farming season labor-exchange is carried out between the *bilek*-families of both longhouses. Presently, as it is not unusual that a village community is divided into a several longhouses,[23] many people outside the village also regard the two longhouses as components of the Rantau Kemiding Village. In other words, the division of the longhouse that Rantau Kemiding experienced in this period should not be regarded as a complete split. However, it is important to consider that the disunity of the community began to surface as a result of several of these symbolic incidents.

Since its establishment in the 1930s, the community has experienced fluctuations in terms of its social structure. The process, in the last 20 years

Plate 3.5 Talking in the *ruai* of Longhouse B in 1998

in particular, has been largely affected by political factors, and in this period the structural change of the community was also closely related to socio-economic factors. These changes will be explored and elaborated further in the following chapter.

4
Iban Migration and Structural Change in the Longhouse

Introduction

Objectives

Internal migration studies have highlighted some of the distinctive features of rural–urban relations in the so-called Third World countries. These countries appear to be following their own course of urbanization and change in population composition, which differs from the process once observed in developed capitalist countries. As previous studies have frequently pointed out, a consequence of urbanization and migration in the Third World has been that multifarious job opportunities absorbed the influx of labor from rural areas (Armstrong and McGee 1985; Skeldon 1990; de Haan 2002).

However, the dominant conceptualization of migration and migrant adjustment as a one-way journey is inadequate (McHugh 2000: 71). The literature highlights not only the one-way flow of labor, but also notions of circulatory migration and its effect on rural communities (Prothero and Chapman 1985). Moreover, other scholars have explored the relation between migration trends and changing household composition (Caces et al. 1985; Stark and Lucas 1988; Wolf 1992; Agesa and Kim 2001, Agesa 2004), as well as the increase of female labor migration (Fawcett et al. 1984; Chant and Radcliffe 1992; Willis and Yeoh 2000). This means that, while the previous rural–urban migration studies were mainly concerned with male labor migration and its effect on the transformation of urban societies, recent research has begun to direct attention to the vital role of females and the family, and the migrants' ties with their home village communities.

Concerning the relationship between migration and family composition, the process of migration decision-making has also attracted scholarly attention. For example, the book edited by Harbison (1981) is one of the most important works on this subject. In another notable study by Root and de Jong (1991), the authors attempted to explain family migration through an analysis of a range of variables. In addition, their focus on the family unit, in this work, is considerably different from previous emphases on individual rural-to-urban migration. The structure of rural families or village communities is also regarded as an important factor, even for female migration. This importance has been acknowledged by several authors; for example, by Thadani and Torado (1984), who presented a theoretical framework to examine female rural-to-urban migration, Smith et al. (1984), who provided an outline of the general tendencies of female migration among Asian countries, and Elmhirst (2002), who emphasized the agency of young female migrants in an Indonesian transmigration area. Willis and Yeoh (2000) collected the literature on female migrations including the cases in developing countries.

Therefore it is undeniable that the great influence of women and family on migration trends is becoming more prominent and recognized in the literature. Even in this current thinking, however, rural-to-urban migration of married women has attracted less attention because their mobility has been simply regarded as concomitant to male labor migration (Smith et al. 1984: 22). Even though some researchers such as Williams (1989) examined the postnuptial migration of married couples, his main concern was directed to the rise in social status of women within a household, paying less attention to its effect on home village communities. Out-migration of married women from rural areas is not only closely related to the substantial change in male circulatory migration, but also may have a great impact on the changes taking place in rural societies themselves, in which married women have an important role in the management of the subsistence economy and the succession of generations. The reason why this point has been disregarded in previous research may be attributed to the following conditions; even though the study of internal migration has diversified in its perspectives, rural-to-urban migration still tends to be discussed mainly from the standpoint of the urban landscape, instead of focusing on the influence it has had on the changes in social structure and subsistence activities in rural areas (Hugo 1992: 111). It is easy to anticipate that a multi-ethnic society, in particular, has varying patterns of out-migration and in rural areas has resulted in complicated forms of social transformation. These processes and outcomes can hardly be comprehended from the urban viewpoint. In this sense, micro-level empirical studies from the rural standpoint are required (Prothero and Chapman 1985: 438–439).

Thus, the purpose of this chapter is to examine how the substantial changes in male circulatory labor migration that was accompanied by the drift of females, has affected the process of social transformation in rural areas.

Methods

The Iban, who were considered typical of shifting cultivators in Southeast Asia, have gained considerable attention from a range of quarters because of their conspicuous characteristics, such as their wide-ranging mobility in order to secure land suitable for swidden agriculture, combat strength symbolized by their custom of 'headhunting,' and complicated relations with their English rulers. From an historical point of view, various types of migration by the Iban have been described in the literature (Wright et al. 1972; Freeman 1955, 1970, 1981; Pringle 1970; and Padoch 1982a). These are indeed important academic studies that enable us to imagine the Iban's traditional way of life, but contemporary themes, such as widespread rapid development and modernization, have not been thoroughly explored nor understood. Some articles have dealt with the impact of development and modernization on the rural society inhabited by the Iban (Cramb and Wills 1990; Ahmad and Noran 1991), but in-depth investigations about the topics of diverse off-farm employment opportunities, out-migration to urban areas, and their effects on Iban society, have only been provided by a few scholars, most notably Sutlive (1972, 1991) and Kedit (1980, 1993). As is pointed out in Sutlive (1992: 128) and in Chapter 3 of this book, the Iban began to adopt small-scale rubber planting at the beginning of the twentieth century to supplement their diet of 'traditional' swidden agriculture. The continuous decline of the market price of rubber and the rapid growth of the timber and oil industries in the 1960s propelled the rural-to-urban labor migration of Iban males (Cleary and Eaton 1995: 156–157). However, the works of Sutlive and Kedit, based on their prescient research activities in the late 1960s and the 1970s, already seem outdated in the contemporary context, because wider opportunities are now open to the Iban. Concerning the recent increase in off-farm employment and its relation to the economic situation and population composition in rural communities, Morrison's (1993) report is informative, but unfortunately he does not provide sufficient definitive data on the changes in social structure at the community level.

In this chapter, we will examine the contemporary socio-economic status of Iban society based on data obtained through empirical field research in Kanowit. The sections that follow will be devoted to the discussion of two main topics; firstly, the rise in socio-economic status of the Iban as it relates to the diversification and stabilization of their employment situation in urban areas; and secondly, the decline and structural change that can be observed in rural communities. In order to explain these transformations, important factors will be explored and presented, including the Iban's changing concept of occupation, the increase in female out-migration, and the modification of women's role in the subsistence economy.

As discussed above, in general, in developing countries, female and family migrations have been the key to understanding the migration process of the rural population since the 1980s. However, their migration patterns in relation to the changes occurring in the village communities themselves have not been widely examined. In this sense the disputes about themes related to gender such as the improvement of female status and the structural background of changes in female migration, have dominated the focus of exploration in more recent literature. Although this chapter mentions Iban female migration, a facet little noticed except by Sutlive (1991), the main purpose here is to emphasize the importance of female migration within the family unit. As will be described in this chapter, the pattern of female migration among the Iban, is such that it aims to ostensibly 'follow the husband,' and the 'housewife' shares a considerable portion of female status in the city. This focus may not attract the attention of gender-oriented approaches, however, here we would like to discuss female and family migration in relation to the structural changes in the rural community, because placing an overemphasis on female migration in the framework of gender may lead us to see migration as a disjuncture. From the perspective of rural–urban relations, the 'absence' of females in the village is a much more important topic that is necessary to understand in any exploration of social change of the community in the contemporary context.

As mentioned previously, the research for this study was conducted in an Iban community (Rantau Kemiding) in the Kanowit District, where the Iban is the predominant ethnic group. The research data, shown in this chapter, is largely based on information collected through participant observation, interviews with community leaders, and questionnaires distributed to all families in the community. This data was obtained during the research periods of August to September 1995 and June to September 1996.

Setting

As has already been outlined, the study village, Rantau Kemiding, was formed in the 1920s near the junction of the Kanowit River and the Rajang River. The reasons this village was selected for the study area are as follows: through the interaction with the outer world after settling down at Rantau Kemiding, widespread changes occurred in Iban society in the middle reaches of the Rajang, and the process of these changes are thought to be significant.[1] The Kanowit District, where Rantau Kemiding is located, has a high Iban population (eighty-three percent of a total of 27 982 persons), which is representative of the neighboring districts in the Rajang Basin such as the Julau District, Song District, and Kapit District (Department of Statistics Sarawak 2005). What is more, the Kanowit District provides a good research environment for observing the remarkable effects of urbanization on Iban society, most notably because the district sends the largest labor population to Sibu (State Government of Sarawak 1997).

Table 4.1 Population of Rantau Kemiding (1996)

	NUMBER OF *BILEK*-FAMILIES	NUMBER OF EMPTY *BILEKS*	CURRENT RESIDENTS
Longhouse A	52	7	182
Longhouse B	11	2	48
Individual houses	6	1	15
Total	69	10	245

Source: Author's field survey 1996

As described in Chapter 3, the research village, Rantau Kemiding, is composed of two longhouses (Longhouse A and B) and six individual houses that contain sixty-nine families and a population of 245 persons (Table 4.1). The plan view of longhouse A and B was shown in Figure 3.6 (see Chapter 3).

Each *bilek* has been lengthened backward according to its own financial capacities, which does not necessarily reflect on an increase in the *bilek*-family members. The extension of a *bilek*, though not for the satisfaction of their vanity, indicates a rise in their economic condition and also the sedentary nature of the present longhouse. Figure 4.1 shows the changes of a *bilek* in Longhouse A. In the past, a *bilek* was a space without any partition within it, but at present each *bilek* is usually partitioned into several small rooms such as a living room, bedroom (*pangking*) and kitchen (*dapur*).

A relatively wealthy family possesses the *bilek*, shown in Figure 4.1, but the number of family members who currently live in the *bilek* is only four including an old married couple. According to the *bilek* members, two bedrooms are usually unused, but during a busy farming season and annual festivals the *bilek* is full of their children who come back to stay in the village temporarily.

In other words, the longhouse is now a place to which to return for those who work in the city. Economic improvement of the longhouse community has been partly dependent on financial support from the rural-to-urban migrant workers who often come back to the longhouse bringing various kinds of consumer goods. Table 4.2 shows the possession of major household effects of each *bilek* in Rantau Kemiding in 1996.

According to interviews with the villagers, the longhouse community of Rantau Kemiding, after settling down there, did not disperse its population to other new fields, but focused on expanding their own community. However, as discussed in the previous chapter, the population increase and accompanying expansion of rubber plantations began to encroach on the land that was designated to remain fallow for dry paddy planting in the 1960s. This resulted

Figure 4.1 Plan view of a *bilek* in the 1930s and in 1996

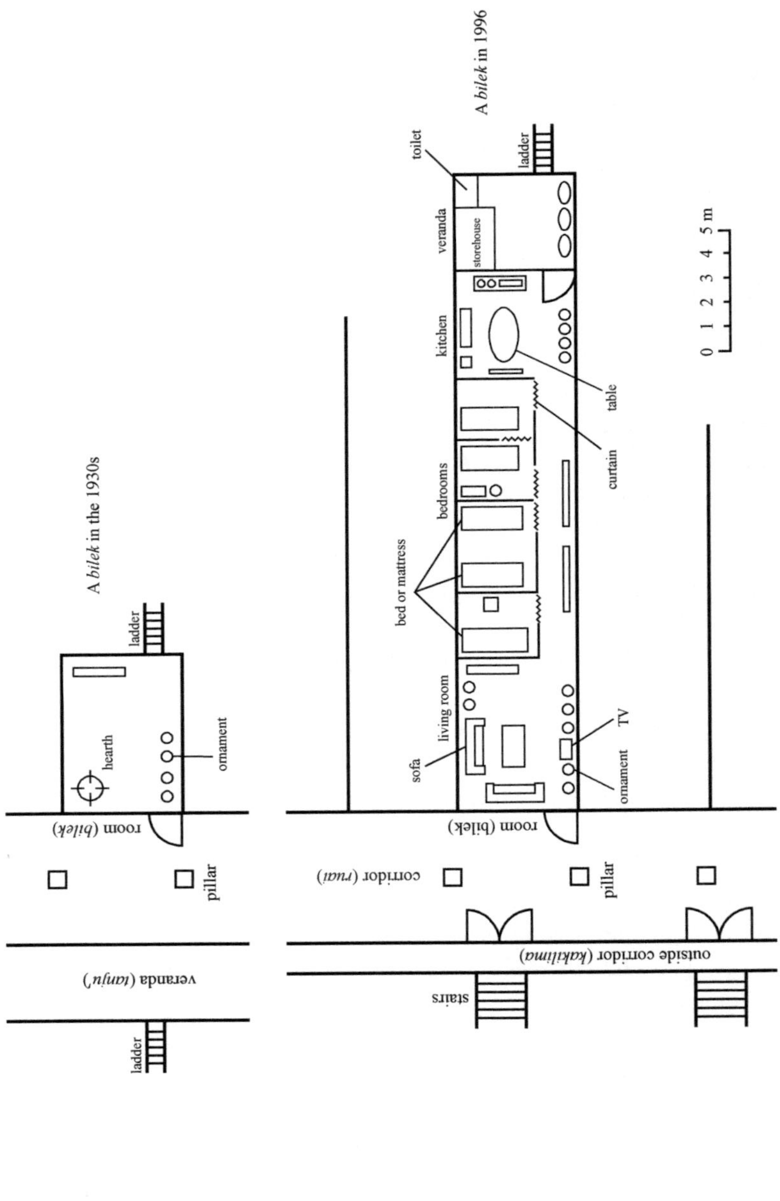

in the diffusion of wetland cultivation in combination with the government's wet paddy promotion policy of the 1950s. Since the 1950s, the increased use of agricultural chemicals and fertilizers supplied by the Agricultural Department has facilitated farming on wetlands close to the longhouse. At the same time, since the 1960s, rubber diminished in economic value because of the decline of its market price. These factors led to a gradual decline in agricultural activities on remote hill lands. Thus, the Iban began to devote less time to remote farming and spent more time in the longhouse. Furthermore, in 1982, the Drainage and Irrigation Department opened a power-driven irrigation system (127 hectors) in the swampy area northwest of the longhouse. As the irrigation area became important for wet paddy cultivation, few people carried out farming at the remote huts. This meant that the longhouse of Rantau Kemiding became a permanent residence receiving subsistence mainly from wet paddy cultivation. However, this sedentary longhouse faced a new trend of population movement, that is, out-migration of females or the whole family to the city.

A view of the occupation and employment situation

While the longhouse of Rantau Kemiding became a sedentary and permanent dwelling for the Iban, a new trend of human mobility from the longhouse to urban areas took place. Acceleration of this pattern of migration brought about substantial changes in the community. The main purpose of male migration is to seek jobs in urban areas. In this section, I will describe the changing views among Iban males about what constitutes an occupation and examine their actual conditions of migration and employment.

Changing view of an occupation among the Iban

Before examining the process of out-migration from the longhouse community, we would like to clarify how the Iban perceive an occupation. Concerning the words related to job, occupation or employment, the Iban in the Kanowit area have variations in their language such as *pengawa*, *bejalai*, *bekuli* and *kerja*.[2] The interconnection and relationship between these words, as well as the conceptual changes in meaning that has occurred over time, is indicated in Figure 4.2. *Pengawa* has a considerably wide meaning and is used for work in general. Even though *pengawa* often results in a cash income, the word is also used for daily chores and subsistence activities.

In the old days, *bejalai* meant male 'headhunting' expeditions or journeys in search of new frontiers. An Iban male was recognized as an adult after completing these journeys. Even after the Brooke government officially

Table 4.2 Household census of Rantau Kemiding (1996)

	Population			Property														Landholding (trees or acres)		
Bilek No.	Male	Female	Total	Car	Motorcycle	Bicycle	TV	Video	Compo stereo	Radio	Gas	Rice cooker	Refrigerator	Washing machine	Telephone	Boat	Outboard engine (horse)	Rubber (estimate in acreage)	Cocoa (trees)	Pepper (trees)
A-1	-	-	-																	
A-2	1	1	2						1		1					1				
A-3	3	2	5			2	1		1	3	1					7	2 (6/6)	10	1,000	
A-4	2	3	5		1	2				1	1		1			1	1 (6)	3	1,000	200
A-5	2	1	3		1	1	1		1	1	1		1			1		11		
A-6	2	1	3			2	1		1		1	1	1			1		15		
A-7	1	1	2			2	1			1	1					1		6	300	
A-8	3	2	5		1	1	2	1	1		1		1			1	1 (6)	?		
A-9	2	2	4			1	1		1									?	?	
A-10	2	2	4		2		1	?	1	?	1	?	1			1	1 (?)	?	?	?
A-11	3	3	6		1	1	2	1	2		2		1					?		
A-12	5	4	9		1	3	1	1	1		1							2		
A-13	3	3	6							1								2		
A-14	3	3	6		1		1		1	1	1					1		6	2 acres	0.1 acre
A-15	2	4	6			1	2			1	1	1	1			1	1 (6)	7		
A-16		1	1								1									
A-17	1		1			1				1	1							3	1,600	1 acre
A-18	3	5	8			1	1		1		1		1			1	1 (6)	20	2 acres	
A-19	-	-	-																	
A-20	2	4	6			2	1		1	1	1		1			1		124		
A-21	4	2	6		1	4	1		1	1	1							26		200
A-22		1	1			1	2		1		1							5		
A-23	-	-	-																	
A-24	-	-	-																	

A-25	1	2	3			1	1		1	1	1	1	1			1	1 (6)	12	1 acre	
A-26	-	-	-																	
A-27	1	2	3				1		1	1	1	1				1		6		
A-28	1	1	2				1		1	2	1							10		
A-29		1	1								1							10		
A-30	1	1	2		1		1	1	1		1	1	1					3	100	
A-31	4	2	6		2		3		1	1	1	1	2	1		6	a	170	100	500
A-32	2	3	5				1		1		1		1		1			54		
A-33	3	3	6			2	1	1	1		1	1	1		1		1 (10)	30	2 acres	
A-34	2	2	4			1	1		1		1	1	1				1 (10)	8	1 acre	
A-35	2	2	4			1	2		1	1	1	1	1		1	1	1 (2)	10	0.5 acre	
A-36	2	2	4			2	2		2	5	2	3	2	1	3	2	b	27	1,000	300
A-37	2	2	4	1		1	1	1	1	1	2	1	1	1		1	1 (5)	10		
A-38		3	3		1		1		1		1	1	1	1				10	200	
A-39	-	-	-																	
A-40	2	1	3				1		1		1	1	1				1 (10)	5	200	
A-41	2	2	4			1	1				1					1		7		
A-42	1	2	3		1		1			2	2	1	1			1	1 (6)	?	?	?
A-43		1	1				1				1		1					14		
A-44		3	3				1				1	1	1					?		
A-45	-	-	-																	
A-46	6	2	8		1	3	2		1	3	2	1	1	1		2	1 (6)	33		
A-47	1	1	2		1		1		1		1	2	1	1		2	2 (20/2)	10		
A-48	3	2	5				1			1						1		9	3 acres	
A-49	3	2	5						1	1	1	1	1			2	1 (2)	13		
A-50	1		1				1				1					2	1 (2)	35	6 acres	200
A-51	3	2	5		1	1	1	1	1	1	1	1	1			2	1 (2)	13	300	
A-52	2	4	6		1	1	1	1		1	2	1	1		1	1		2	2,000	
B-1	1	1	2		1		1		1		1	1	1		1	1	1 (4)	22	1,000	

Table 4.2 continued

	POPULATION			PROPERTY														LANDHOLDING (TREES OR ACRES)		
BILEK NO.	MALE	FEMALE	TOTAL	CAR	MOTORCYCLE	BICYCLE	TV	VIDEO	COMPO STEREO	RADIO	GAS	RICE COOKER	REFRIGERATOR	WASHING MACHINE	TELEPHONE	BOAT	OUTBOARD ENGINE (HORSE)	RUBBER (ESTIMATE IN ACREAGE)	COCOA (TREES)	PEPPER (TREES)
B-2	2	3	5		1	1	1		1		1	1			1					
B-3	3	3	6		2	1	1	1	1	1	1	1	1			1	1 (2)	250		
B-4	-	-	-																	
B-5	2	2	4		2		2	1	1	1	1	1	1	1	1	1				
B-6	2	4	6	1	1	1	1		1		1	1	1		1	2		2		
B-7	1	1	2				1			1	1	1	1			1	1 (2)	12		
B-8	4	3	7		1	1	1	1	1		1	1	1	1		1	1 (20)	6	1 acre	
B-9	-	-	-																	
B-10	7	6	13		2	3	2		1		1	1	2	1	1	1	1 (2)	25		
B-11	2	1	3				1				1							20		
I-1	2	2	4			1	3	1	1	1	2	1	1	1	2	2	1 (2)	115		500
I-2	-	-	-																	
I-3	2	2	4	1	1		1	1	1		1	1	1	1	1			15		
I-4	1	1	2				1		1		1	1	1		1	1		35	1 acre	1 acre
I-5		2	2																	
I-6	2	1	3				1			1	1	1	1		1					

Notes. a: 3(40/30/6). b: 6(30/15/8/5/2/2).

Source: Author's field survey 1996

Figure 4.2 Changing concepts of occupation: an analysis of Iban language

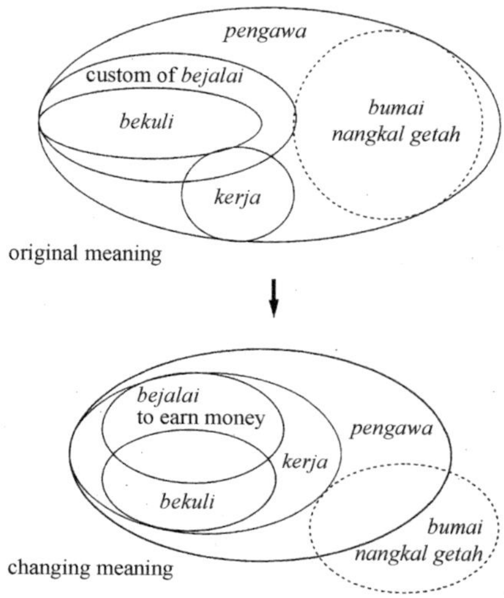

pengawa: work, business in a broader sense.
bejalai: to go on journeys with a view to acquiring wealth, material goods, and social prestige; at the present time the main purpose is to get a job.
bekuli: to carry out unskilled and hard jobs or short-term wage-labor or coolie.
kerja: to work as a salaried employee or non-manual wage-earner; at the present time, it includes wage-labor.
bumai: rice farming.
nangkal getah: rubber tapping.
——— : work with cash income.
--------- : work in village without wages.

Source: Kedit (1993) and the author's field survey

prohibited headhunting, Iban males were still expected to leave the longhouse to obtain money or material goods, and ritual preparations for this journey were conducted until recently with some changes in procedures. In this sense, *bejalai* was a very important cultural system among the Iban (Kedit 1993). The custom of going on journeys was also closely related to the division of labor between the sexes in their daily life.[3] At present, however, the word *bejalai* tends to mean only working away from home for cash income.

A connected word, often used in conjunction with *bejalai*, is *bekuli*. *Bekuli* is a derivative of 'coolie.' This word is widely used to mean unskilled physical labor such as loading work, factory work, and shop assistance. When Iban males go on *bejalai*, they often find jobs as *bekuli*. This is especially true in a small market town like Kanowit, where job opportunities are mostly *bekuli,* except in the government sector.

Kerja, on the other hand is thought to be a relatively new word among the Iban that does not have a cultural connotation.[4] This word basically means regular salaried employment such as a government employee and company clerk. But nowadays the Iban in Kanowit frequently use this word to mean not only 'occupation' but also 'work' or 'labor' in general. In other words, the concept of '*kerja,*' at present, includes short-term wage labor in the way of *bejalai* and miscellaneous work (*bekuli*) by the day.

The changing meaning of these terms seem to reflect the fact that *bejalai* is losing its social and cultural significance, while the definition of *kerja* is expanding according to the diversification of wage labor. It is noted that the word *kerja* is seldom used to describe subsistence agricultural work. Although the word is sometimes applied to commercial plantation labor, other agricultural work is described by specific words such as *bumai* for planting paddies and *nangkal getah* for tapping rubber trees. In particular, those who receive a certain amount of cash income from sources other than agriculture emphasize that their agricultural activity is just a 'pastime' (*main aja*). That is why full-time farmers, if they are questioned on their occupation, usually answer with diffidence that they have no occupation (*nadai kerja*). It seems that at present Iban males attach more importance to gaining cash income by *kerja* than subsistence agriculture. The following subsection discusses the actual working situations of the Iban in the study area.

The employment situation of the Iban

The salary and wage of those working in the city differs according to their occupation and age. It is said that in Sarawak, the education level largely affects the salary (Table 4.3).

According to the village people, as of 1996 those who graduated from Primary 6 can earn 600 to 800 *Ringgit* Malaysia[5] per month, while those from Form 3 can earn 800 to 1000 *Ringgit* and those from Form 5 earn more than 1000 *Ringgit*. If they graduated from college or university, a monthly salary would be more than 1500 *Ringgit*. There are rough estimates of the salary for regular occupations (*kerja tetap*) such as a government civil servant. Salaries in the private sector largely differ according to the ability of the workers. As for contract or temporary jobs, such as work in the construction sector (*bekuli*), people usually work by the day or the week. In such cases, they are paid between fifteen to thirty *Ringgit* a day, which means that they can earn from 400 to 800 *Ringgit* a month.

Table 4.4 shows the variety of occupations of the villagers and the out-migrants from Rantau Kemiding. While Table 4.5, indicates the place of current

Table 4.3 Education level of Rantau Kemiding villagers

	Stay-in												Stay-out											
	Less than Primary 6		Primary 6		Form 3		Form 5		College/ University		unknown		Less than Primary 6		Primary 6		Form 3		Form 5		College/ University		unknown	
Age	M	F	M	F	M	F	M	F	M	F	M	F	M	F	M	F	M	F	M	F	M	F	M	F
≥ 19			1	1	3	1	1	1					1		1	1	4	2	2					
20–29		2	5	3	3	3	6	5					2	3	6	7	14	17	17	8	2	2		1
30–39		4	2	6	2	5	5	1					1	5	10	8	9	16	15	5	3		3	1
40–49	1	7	6	5	3						2		1	1	1	1	3	4	4	1	3	1	1	2
50–59	4	13	9	1	2	2						1					2	2						
60 ≤	13	18	6		1						1	3	3	1										
unknown		1	1								1	1	2	1				1					1	1
Total	18	45	30	16	14	11	12	7			4	5	10	11	18	17	32	42	38	14	8	3	5	5

Source: Author's field survey 1996

Table 4.4 Occupation of the villagers and the out-migrants from Rantau Kemiding

	STAY-IN		STAY-OUT		
TYPE OF JOB	M	F	M	F	TOTAL
Government servant	3	1	13	3	20
Teacher	3	2	5	2	12
Clerk			3	3	6
Political secretary			1		1
Soldier	1		5	3	9
Policeman	1		7		8
Telekom employee	1		2		3
Company employee			11	1	12
Company manager			2		2
Shopkeeper	2	2	2	5	11
Cook			2		2
Waiter, Waitress			2	1	3
Nurse			2	1	3
Baby-sitter		1			1
Charwoman				3	3
Security guard	2		3		5
Welder			1		1
Driver	4		5		9
Tugboat crew	2		5		7
Construction laborer			8		8
Timber company laborer			9	2	11
Factory laborer			3		3
Other laborer	12		9		21
Farmer	32	44	3	12	91
Housewife		24		60	84
Longhouse headman	2				2
Priest			1		1
Without regular job	13	10	1	1	25
<Pensioner>	<12>	<5>		<3>	<20>
Unknown			1		1
Total	78	84	106	97	365

Notes.

As for pensioners, their former jobs are indicated above.

Population: household heads and their spouses and children over fifteen years old, except for school attendants, as of August 1996

Source: Author's field survey 1996

Table 4.5 Population by place of current residence and by five-year age-group of out-migrants from Rantau Kemiding

	Total stay-ins		Stay-out: Kanowit district		Stay-out: Sibu district		Stay-out: Other districts in Sarawak		Stay-out: Other states in Malaysia		Stay-out: Other countries		Total stay-outs	
	M	F	M	F	M	F	M	F	M	F	M	F	M	F
0–4	13	11												
5–9	13	11												
10–14	15	9	1										1	
15–19	6	12	1	3	4	3		3	2				7	9
20–24	8	11	1		5	3	8	7					14	10
25–29	7	3	2	6	13	5	7	10	1	1	1		24	22
30–34	6	8	5	5	7	11	4	4	2		2		20	20
35–39	3	8	3	4	6	8	5	4	4	3			18	19
40–44	7	5	4		5	6	1				1	1	11	7
45–49	5	7	2	1	2	2	4						8	3
50–54	6	7	1	1				1					1	2
55–59	9	10					1						1	
60–64	7	6												
65–69	5	6												
70 ≤	8	9		1										1
Unknown	2	2		3	3	6	1	2	1		1		6	11
Total	120	125	20	24	45	44	31	31	10	4	5	1	111	104

Population: Household heads and their spouses and children as of August 1996

Source: Author's field survey 1996

residence of the out-migrants from the village. The data shown in these tables were collected through my interviews with village members.[6]

The findings based on these tables are as follows: firstly, the number of farmers (who plant paddies in the village every year) is only seventy-six of the 162 total stay-in villagers (male: 32 of 78; female: 44 of 84), that is, forty-seven percent. On the other hand, the stay-in villagers who are employed in the town of Kanowit amount to thirty-one of the total males (forty percent). While only six females are employed (seven percent), twenty-four people (twenty-nine percent) are neither engaged in farming nor wage work (categorized as 'housewife'[7] in Table 4.4).

Secondly, there are still a large number of laborers, such as construction workers and timber company employees, among the out-migrants from the village (the stay-outs). Contrary to the stereotype that the Iban are unskilled laborers,[8] they also engage in occupations such as government employees, schoolteachers, company clerks, and company managers; illustrating the diversification and stabilization of their working situation. Even for unskilled work, the contract periods are getting longer. Consequently, those Iban who are engaged in contract work in urban areas are gradually shortening their stay in the original living base, the longhouse, and spending more time in the city.

Thirdly, Table 4.5 shows that 215 people of Rantau Kemiding origin currently live out of the village (stay-out), which is close to the total stay-in population of 245. Most of the out-migrants from Rantau Kemiding are urban dwellers, except for eighteen people (seven percent) who live in other longhouse communities.[9] Moreover, most of the stay-outs who live within the Kanowit District are employed in the town of Kanowit. Even taking into consideration the expense and means of transportation, they can commute between the village and the town by bicycle, motorcycle, car, or unofficial van, but they prefer to live in the town.

Among the job variations in Table 4.4, only a few types of jobs are immediately recognized as *bejalai* at present. If one is employed within commuting range, people never recognize that person to be on *bejalai*. This is the same as the case of a person who secures full-time employment in other urban areas. Even among those who are engaged in physical labor pursuant to a short-term contract in a remote area, some do not recognize themselves as being on the *bejalai* tour.

At present, a realistic value judgment for the Iban's working experience is based on whether they have a *kerja* as regular work rather than on whether they have performed the journey of *bejalai*. The expanding meaning of the word *kerja*, which is drawn in Figure 4.2, is the result of the shift in emphasis from *bejalai* to *kerja* and the diversification of the Iban's employment situation. *Bejalai* is a kind of circular labor migration mainly for the purpose of obtaining consumer goods or cash for remittance with a clearer view to returning home. However, corresponding to the changing concept of Iban words for occupation, the period of a young Iban's sojourn into urban areas is becoming considerably longer, which may make it inappropriate to define this process as a form of circulatory migration. This new tendency in labor migration is closely correlated with changes in population composition and subsistence activities in the village. This matter will be discussed in the following section.

Female migration and subsistence activities

Out-migration accompanied by a wife and children

An important phenomenon emerging in accordance with the changes in occupational opportunities for Iban males is the trend of female out-migration. At one time, there was an accepted division of labor between the sexes in which the males were expected to work outside the village to make a fortune or reputation, and the females were supposed to remain in the village and take care of their family and the paddy fields for self-sustenance (Freeman 1970: 75; Sutlive and Appell 1991: xix; Morrison 1993: 53). As Iban society is based on bilateral kinship, inheritance of a *bilek* is open to any child who intends to stay with the parents after marriage, regardless of sex or seniority (Uchibori 1996: 58). The absence of a strict rule of succession is reflected in the relaxed social restrictions on the drift of the young generation from the longhouse. Therefore, in Iban society, where long-term journeys of adult males are taken for granted, parents can ease their anxiety for the future if they have a married daughter or a daughter-in-law staying with them in the same *bilek* in the village.

However, as Table 4.5 shows, for those originating in Rantau Kemiding, the number of females who currently live outside the village is 104 out of a total of 229, which is not very different from the rate of male stay-outs (111 out of 231). The rate of female stay-outs is relatively higher compared to the past. Villagers explained that the increase in female out-migration has been a more recent trend, which accelerated as a result of the relatively stable income and improved living conditions of their husbands who have been working in urban areas. It should be noted that, as Table 4.6 illustrates, a certain number of the urban dwellers secured relatively more stable residences such as government quarters (thirty-eight percent or seventy-four out of one hundred and ninety- seven persons) and individual houses (fifteen percent or twenty-nine persons). Moreover, according to Table 4.4, while males are engaged in various occupations, a large number of females (sixty-two percent or sixty out of ninety-seven persons) are not employed, and stay at home as a 'housewife.'[10]

Table 4.6 Type of residence by marital status and sex (1996)

	SINGLE		MARRIED		
TYPE OF RESIDENCE	M	F	M	F	TOTAL
Longhouse A and B	64	67	50	52	233
Individual house (within the village)	2	2	4	4	12
Individual house (outside the village)[a]	3	3	9	14	29
Government quarters[a]	7	4	28	35	74
Rented room of a house[a]	10	3	16	10	39
Company dormitory[a]	10	2	10	10	32
Other longhouse	-	-	6	12	18
School dormitory[a]	3	7	-	-	10
Others, unknown	4	0	5	4	13
Total	103	88	128	141	460

Notes.
Population: Equal to that in Table 4.5
a: Urban residence
Source: Author's field survey 1996

The diversification and stabilization of employment among Iban males and the accompanying phenomenon of female rural-to-urban migration are thought to result from the changes in the industrial structure of Sarawak. Since the decline of the rubber market price, the Sarawak Government has been promoting industrial diversification instead of depending excessively on the export of agricultural products or raw materials, such as timber, oil, and natural gas (Danaraj 1995: 28).[11] Indeed, it is difficult to deny that the majority of Iban males in urban areas are still largely dependent on unstable job opportunities, but it is also true that their lives have been gradually improving to make it possible for the family to follow the husband into urban areas.

Some writings, based on research conducted in the 1970s and the early 1980s, described the rapid increase of male labor migration induced by the growth of the timber and oil industries. These works also outlined the social impact of these patterns of migration on the life of females who remained in the village (Kedit 1993), as well as emphasizing the rural-to-urban migration of divorced females for the purpose of prostitution activities (Sutlive 1991). But nowadays such male-female relations among the Iban are rarely observed in the Kanowit District. According to the interviews with Iban women who live with their husbands in the urban areas, the purpose of their migration was partly to release themselves from the tedious life or human relationships in the village and, more positively, to provide their children with a better education.[12] For the aged people in the village, remittances and financial aid from their children is still an important source of income, but the migration of younger people attaches more importance to investment in the next generation. In Rantau Kemiding, as of August 1996, there were three wives living apart from their husbands in town. Two of them were sojourning with their parents only temporarily in order to take care of their infants with their parents' assistance. As such, they did not participate in agricultural work and also articulated their intention to go back to their husband after a few months or so.

If a male migrates from a rural to urban area with his wife and children, he is not considered to be on the journey of *bejalai*. Nowadays, *bejalai* of Iban males, as a short-term circulatory migration has been decreasing, while family migration and long-term sojourning in urban areas are becoming more popular, underpinned by the increased opportunities of *kerja*—steadier, regular work. There are certainly many urban dwellers who are going to enjoy retired life in their home village after a long-term stay in town, but it is too naïve to consider this trend to be a change in the migration cycle.

What is worth noticing is the potential for improvement of the socio-economic status of the next generation who may remain in the city. When I interviewed a man who usually worked in Sibu and temporarily came back to the longhouse, he asserted:

> Although I am not sure if our children will remain in the city or come back to this longhouse, I will come back here with my wife in the future. I would like to continue to work in Sibu until one or two of my children obtain stable jobs in the city.

A woman who is categorized as a 'housewife' among the stay-outs in Table 4.4 stated:

> In rural areas we cannot provide our children with a good education. Schools in the city, not like the village schools, have talented teachers, are equipped with computers, and give children chances to communicate with high-achieving pupils. Good education is necessary for children to obtain a good job in the future.

Some people emphasized the high education level of the Chinese schools in town. During my research in Sibu, a man from Kanowit told me of his experience.

> When I was small, I went to a Chinese primary school. It was lucky for me to learn the Chinese language at the time. Now I work for a small company operated by a Chinese, where I understand what my boss is talking about. They used to say bad

> things about Iban workers, but they have never spoken ill of us since they noticed my language ability. Iban workers usually work just according to the order of their boss, but if we understand Chinese, we can do a better job by knowing the intention of our bosses. In this sense, my bosses acknowledge me to be a good worker. As I believe that it is vital to know the Chinese language to look for jobs in Sibu, I send my daughter to a Chinese school in Sibu.

In short, family migration has a different characteristic to previous circulatory migration that aims to transfer wealth from urban to rural areas; instead, family migration is characterized by a deliberate long-term sojourn for the purpose of accumulating wealth through the generations who dwell in urban areas.[13] This means that the important unit of the *bilek*-family composition is also changing. While long-established continuity of the generations within a *bilek* had not necessarily presupposed that a married couple would always live together in the *bilek*, the recent migration trends seem to attach more importance to the bonds of a nuclear family based on the married couple. This change may substantially transform the longhouse community, a topic discussed at a later point herein.

The aging population and decline in agricultural activities

Recently, because married women are increasingly migrating out from the longhouse to follow their husbands who are employed in urban areas, the elderly are performing a major part of the agricultural activities in the village. Table 4.7 shows the working population in Rantau Kemiding listed by age and sex, of which fifty-seven percent of full-time farmers are fifty years old and over. This aging farm population is accompanied by substantial changes in agricultural activities.

During the farming season of 1995/1996, forty-four out of a total of fifty-nine *bileks* carried out paddy cultivation including farming as a side job.[14] The status of paddy planting of each *bilek* is shown in Table 4.8. This table illustrates several important points. Firstly, the major form of farming is shifting from dry paddy planting to wet paddy planting in swamps or irrigated fields. The number of *bileks* that planted paddies on hilly areas and dry flat lands is only eight and twelve respectively, but the *bileks* that performed wet paddy planting amounted to thirty-seven. Regarding the planted acreage, the total area under wet paddy cultivation in the village was 65.6 acres while dry paddy occupied 22.8 acres.[15] Each *bilek* has 1.7 different types of dry paddy on average and 3.7 types of wet paddy on average.

Table 4.9 shows the variety of paddy planted in Rantau Kemiding in the 1995/96 farming season. According to this table, out of the total thirty-nine types

Table 4.7 Working population by age and sex in Rantau Kemiding (1996)

Age	Farmer (full time)		Nonfarm employment		Unemployed, housewife		Total		
	M	F	M	F	M	F	M	F	Subtotal
≥ 19	1		2	1	2	2	5	3	8
20–29	2	3	7	2	5	8	14	13	27
30–39	2	9	6	1	1	6	9	16	25
40–49	5	8	6	1	1	3	12	12	24
50–59	8	9	6	1	1	7	15	17	32
60 ≤	13	13	5		3	8	21	21	42
Unknown	1	2	1				2	2	4
Total	32	44	33	6	13	34	78	84	162

Population: Equal to stay-ins in Table 4.4
Source: Author's field survey 1996

of paddy found in the whole village, fifteen types had adaptability to dry land while thirty-six types were adaptable to swamp or irrigated land (Table 4.9).[16]

Secondly, there is a tendency for continuous cropping on the same land. It was taken for granted that the paddy planting in the Iban community was dependent on shifting cultivation, whether on dry or swampy land (Pringle 1970: 26), but at the time of my research (1996) there were ten *bileks* that had been planting wet paddies on the same land for more than three years, and most of the other paddy fields were also utilized with a very short period of fallow.

The third point is the shrinkage of the average planted acreage. According to the report of Freeman (1955), who conducted his research between 1949 and 1951, the average planted area of paddy was nearly five acres, while that in Rantau Kemiding in 1996, was only 2.01 acres (there were only two *bilek*-families who planted more than five acres). According to the Rantau Kemiding villagers, in the 1960s there were many *bilek*-families that cultivated more than five acres, but in the 1970s the planted acreage began to gradually decline.

It is said that the ratio of planted wet paddy began to exceed that of dry paddy in the late 1960s. The likely reasons for this change were that since the 1950s the Sarawak Government had continuously promoted wet paddy cultivation and most of the hilly land had by this time already been covered with rubber trees. By the late 1960s there were few hilly areas remaining without rubber trees planted on it, and it was also difficult to find secondary forest that had been left fallow for a long enough period. Because the soil fertility of shortly fallowed land has not recovered satisfactorily and is subject to damage caused

Table 4.8 Status of paddy cultivation in Rantau Kemiding (1996)

BILEK NO.	POPULATION M	POPULATION F	POPULATION TOTAL	AREA (ACRES) IRRIGATED FIELD, SWAMP	AREA (ACRES) DRY FIELD (FLAT LAND)	AREA (ACRES) HILL	VARIETY WET PADDY	VARIETY DRY PADDY	CONTINUOUS CROPPING (YEARS)	*PADI PUN*
Longhouse A										
A-1	-	-	-	-	-	-				-
A-2	1	1	2	1.5			4	0	1	○
A-3	3	2	5	1			2	0	1	⊙
A-4	2	3	5	-	-	-				?
A-5	2	1	3	3			4	0	1	⊙
A-6	2	1	3	-	-	-				△
A-7	1	1	2		1.5	*mit*	0	3	1	○
A-8	3	2	5	1		*mit*	4	1	4	⊙
A-9	2	2	4	n.a.	n.a.	n.a.	n.a.	n.a.	n.a.	n.a.
A-10	2	2	4	1.5	0.8		1	0	7	⊙
A-11	3	3	6	-	-	-				△
A-12	5	4	9	1			4	0	2	×
A-13	3	3	6	1		*mit*	2	2	5	⊙
A-14	3	3	6	2.5	*mit*		5	1	2	○
A-15	2	4	6	2			4	0	1	⊙
A-16		1	1	-	-	-				?
A-17	1		1	-	-	-				△
A-18	3	5	8	3	*mit*		7	0	1	○
A-19	-	-	-	-	-	-				-
A-20	2	4	6	2	*mit*		9	2	1	⊙
A-21	4	2	6	2.5		3	1	1	1	○
A-22		1	1	1		0.5	2	2	1	⊙
A-23	-	-	-	-	-	-				-
A-24	-	-	-	-	-	-				-
A-25	1	2	3	2			9	0	15	⊙
A-26	-	-	-	-	-	-				-
A-27	1	2	3	2	*mit*		3	1	1	⊙
A-28	1	1	2	-	-	-				△
A-29		1	1	-	-	-				×
A-30	1	1	2	2	*mit*		3	1	1	⊙
A-31	4	2	6	1	1		n.a.	n.a.	1	×
A-32	2	3	5			2	0	3	1	⊙
A-33	3	3	6	2			n.a.	n.a.	2	?
A-34	2	2	4	-	-	-				⊙
A-35	2	2	4	0.8			2	0	1	⊙
A-36	2	2	4	-	-	-				△
A-37	2	2	4	0.5	0.5		4	1	4	⊙
A-38		3	3		0.5		0	2	1	△
A-39	-	-	-	-	-	-				-
A-40	2	1	3	-	-	-				×
A-41	2	2	4	1		1	7	1	1	?
A-42	1	2	3	1		1	4	1	10	△
A-43		1	1	-	-	-				⊙
A-44		3	3	5			3	0	1	⊙
A-45	-	-	-	-	-	-				-

Table 4.8 Continued

BILEK NO.	POPULATION M	F	TOTAL	AREA (ACRES) IRRIGATED FIELD, SWAMP	DRY FIELD (FLAT LAND)	HILL	VARIETY WET PADDY	DRY PADDY	CONTINUOUS CROPPING (YEARS)	*PADI PUN*
A-46	6	2	8	1.3			1	0	7	○
A-47	1	1	2	1			5	0	3	×
A-48	3	2	5	3			3	0	1	×
A-49	3	2	5	2			3	0	1	×
A-50	1		1	2			4	0	1	?
A-51	3	2	5		2		2	1	1	⊙
A-52	2	4	6	2		*mit*	1	1	1	⊙
Total	89	93	182	51.6	6.3	7.5	3.7	1.5	2.5	-
Longhouse B										
B-1	1	1	2	3.5	0.5		5	1	5	⊙
B-2	2	3	5	-	-	-				△
B-3	3	3	6	2		1.5	4	1	1	⊙
B-4	-	-	-	-	-	-				-
B-5	2	2	4	0.5	0.5		1	1	1	○
B-6	2	4	6	1			2	0	1	○
B-7	1	1	2		1	1	0	4	1	?
B-8	4	3	7	-	-	-				×
B-9	-	-	-	-	-	-				-
B-10	7	6	13	0.5	0.5		2	3	1	○
B-11	2	1	3			3	2	2	1	⊙
Total	24	24	48	7.5	2.5	5.5	2.7	2	1.6	-
Individual houses										
I-1	2	2	4	2.5	0.5		9	2	5	○
I-2	-	-	-	-	-	-				-
I-3	2	2	4	2	0.5		3	2	1	?
I-4	1	1	2	2	*mit*		5	2	1	⊙
I-5		2	2	-	-	-				×
I-6	2	1	3	-	-	-				×
Total	7	8	15	6.5	1	-	5.7	2	2.3	
Grand total	120	125	245	65.6	9.8	13	3.7	1.7	2.4	-

Notes.

n.a.: Data not available. ⊙: Sacred seed rice inherited. ○: Sacred seed rice resurrected after previous renouncement. △: Sacred seed rice renounced (*punas*). ×: no possession of sacred seed rice. ?: sacred seed rice in oblivion. *mit*: *mimit aja* = a little; excluded from accumulation.

Source: Author's field survey 1996.

Table 4.9. Variety of paddy 1995/96

No.	PADDY 1995/1996	*PAYA*[a]	*EMPERAN*[b]	*BUKIT*[c]
1	Aji	○		
2	Anong	○		
3	Banjar	○		
4	Bario	○		
5	Baro	○		
6	Belancai			○
7	Berandong	○		
8	Bingka	○		
9	Entulu (Celum)	○		
10	Bubu	○		
11	Coa			○
12	Danau (Julau)	○	○	○
13	Engkabang	○	○	○
14	Gelini	○		
15	Gemala	○	○	
16	Jambi	○		
17	Jengkanan	○		
18	Kasai	○	○	○
19	Kerangan			○
20	Lalat	○		
21	Lasak	○		
22	Lemak	○		
23	Limbang	○	○	
24	Machan	○	○	
25	Melinga	○		
26	Miyai	○	○	
27	Nibong	○		
28	Nuliang	○		
29	Pandak	○		
30	Paya Laut	○		
31	Pulut	○	○	○
32	Sayap (Lalat)	○		
33	Sebulok	○	○	○
34	Seratok	○		
35	Siumidong	○	○	
36	Tarat	○	○	○
37	Tiga Bulan	○		
38	Undang	○		
39	Wangi	○	○	○

Notes. a = suitable for wet land. b = suitable for both wet and dry land. c = suitable for dry land.
Source: Author's field survey 1996

by disease and harmful insects, extra work is required such as fertilizing and chemical treatment, in order to obtain a settled harvest. Therefore, even taking into account the tiresome work of weeding, the villagers preferred cultivating wet paddies in marshy areas close to the longhouse, and when they planted dry paddies they tended to choose flatland to minimize their efforts. Furthermore, the establishment of a pumped irrigation system in 1982 facilitated the continuous cropping of wet paddy. The decrease in the agricultural labor force, the rise in the ratio of the aged population, and the increase in the opportunity for side jobs have strengthened the tendency of alleviating agricultural work and reducing the paddy cultivation area.

Custody of 'padi pun' and the extinction of the bilek-family

Iban culture is often called a paddy cult. The cultural importance of their paddy cultivation is emphasized, particularly in their ritual activities and inheritance practices (Pringle 1970: 30). This subsection both describes the status of inheritance of sacred rice, '*padi pun,*' which symbolizes the succession of the *bilek*-family, and also examines its relation to the change in patterns of subsistence.

The Iban recognize the sacred rice, *padi pun*, as their 'root;' it is inherited by children from their parents and prohibited from transfer to others. The genealogy based on the *bilek* is the only measure for the Iban to identify their origins; therefore, inheritance of the sacred rice is an important symbol of the *bilek*-family in straight succession (Uchibori 1996: 52).[17] The seed rice (usually dry rice) inherited from ancestors is supposed to be planted every year. When they cannot plant the sacred rice themselves, due to unavoidable circumstances, the Iban ask close relatives to plant it in order to prevent its extinction.

In spite of such efforts, the inherited sacred rice may become extinct accidentally, for example, there may be no harvest because of disease or harmful insects, or the seed rice may disappear due to careless safekeeping during the agricultural off-season. In Iban language, extinction of the sacred seed rice is called *punas*. This word originally meant that a married couple is not blessed with a child or a *bilek*-family is extirpated. In this sense, too, the sacred rice can be said to have a symbolic meaning in the succession of the *bilek*-family.

According to Table 4.8, out of the forty-four *bilek*-families who cultivated paddy in 1996, thirty-one planted sacred rice (marked ⊙ and ○), eight *bilek*-families had let the inherited sacred rice die out (marked △), and eight *bilek*-families had not inherited sacred rice from their parents (marked ×). Furthermore, even among the *bilek*-families who maintained their sacred rice, ten did not plant authentic rice. In reality, these families had experienced *punas* of the sacred rice in the past and resumed paddy cultivation by substituting seed rice given by other *bilek*-families for their own sacred rice (marked ○). Thus, the tradition of succeeding the authentic sacred seed rice was successfully continued by only twenty-one *bilek*-families out of forty-four (marked ⊙), which is less than half of the total families that planted paddies.

In principle, women are responsible for the management of the paddy. In paddy cultivation among the Iban, there is a division of labor between the sexes, though it is not strict. While men play central roles in dangerous and heavy labor, such as opening forests, burning the opened fields, and making holes for seeding, women are expected to take the initiative in sowing, weeding, harvesting, wet paddy nursing and transplanting. As for the variety of paddy, while females are eager to plant new species obtained from friends in other areas, males often have no interest in this activity. In addition, women are responsible for selecting which species of paddy to plant, the safekeeping of the seed rice during the agricultural off-season, and taking measures to avoid *punas*, which most males are indifferent to. Thus, the status of females regarding the succession of sacred rice is very important.

According to the villagers, the tendency toward extinction of sacred rice succession, mentioned above, is caused by several factors. These include the shift from dry paddy cultivation to wet paddy cultivation (sacred rice is usually used for dry paddy), the stagnation of subsistence activities because of the decrease in the agricultural labor force (yearly cropping has become difficult), and careless safekeeping (the absence of married women as safe-keepers of seed rice or the lack of close communication between *bileks*).[18]

The *bilek* not only maintains high autonomy as a managing unit of paddy cultivation but also functions as a place for inheriting sacred rice, land usufruct, agricultural implements, and other household property. In other words, the *bilek* is important as both a living space and a basis for identifying one's family lineage. Its continuity is symbolized by inheritance of sacred rice in which females play a central role. In this sense, the relation between the absence of females and the tendency towards extinction of *bilek* succession should be noted from the perspective of the decline in the cultural tradition of inheritance.

The structural degradation of the longhouse community

As was discussed above, the diversification and stabilization of Iban males' employment conditions and circumstances and their long-term sojourn in urban areas has given rise to an increase in out-migration by females and, subsequently, to a decline in subsistence activities in the village. In order to clarify how these phenomena affect Iban society, it is necessary to examine them from the perspective of the longhouse as a living space. There is a dichotomy commonly recognized in Iban society that contrasts male, outside and dynamic with female,

Plate 4.1 Dry paddy planting

Top: Burning the paddy field. Middle: After the men dibble the ground, the women put paddies into the holes. Bottom: Paddies put in the hole.

Plate 4.2 Wet paddy planting

Top: Rice nurseries are usually made on the ridges between the rice fields. Middle: Rice seedlings are extracted for the sake of transplanting. Bottom: Transplanting is mainly carried out by women.

Plate 4.3 Drying paddies in front of a longhouse

inside and static. This dichotomy is closely related to the spatial composition of a longhouse, that is, the *ruai,* symbolized as an open and public space for men, and the *bilek,* symbolized as a closed and private space for women (Sekine 1979: 60–73; Sutlive 1991: 493; Uchibori 1996: 46–48).[19]

The *bilek* is the basis for succession of the *bilek*-family. When an Iban refers to his origin, he usually attaches importance to the continuity of the *bilek*, not to the history of the longhouse (Uchibori 1996: 52–53). This continuity is based on the culture of rice production, and is observed in the way land and sacred rice is inherited. However, that continuity is now threatened with extinction. For example, Tables 4.2 and 4.8, show that in Rantau Kemiding there are six persons (two males and four females) who live alone in a *bilek*—they are all elderly people.[20] In addition, five *bilek*-families are composed only of one married couple whose household heads are above fifty-five years old, the other ten *bileks* are empty. These three types of *bilek* composition account for 30.4 percent of the longhouse community (twenty-one out of sixty-nine *bileks*). This not only indicates that the longhouse community is beginning to resemble an 'old people's home,' but also augurs the crisis of passing the inheritance of the *bilek* to the younger generations. Some young people, who live in the city with their wife and children, are anxious about leaving their aged parents in the longhouse. The aged people are often encouraged to live with their children in urban areas, but rarely accept their children's invitations, because they find it more comfortable to spend time in the *ruai* where they can easily find someone to talk to. However, even the function of the *ruai* has been changing.

It can be said that the public space of the *ruai* symbolizes the longhouse community itself, in that the community is composed on the basis of territorial relations with the reticulation of affinity and consanguinity. In this sense, social functions fulfilled in the *ruai* reflect the solidarity of the community (Sekine 1979: 72). However, it is obvious that the important aspect of the *ruai* as an assembly space has been gradually declining. The changes in agricultural activities, such as the decrease in the size of the planted area, the shift from dry to wet paddy cultivation, and the fixation of the paddy fields, have made it unnecessary to mutually confirm planted areas for the year and to arrange large-scale group work or labor exchanges between *bilek*-families. This is why there have been no longhouse meetings concerning agricultural activities in the community since the 1980s. In addition, assemblies for performing agricultural rituals and other daily gatherings also have been declining.

It is easily surmised that the loosened bonds in the longhouse community correspond to the decline in these agricultural activities. However, some villagers also emphasized that the excessive expansion of the community resulted in the loosening of solidarity, reflected in the deterioration of the public characteristics of the *ruai*. They also pointed out that politics at *ruai* meetings and political events of the outside world affected the split in the community (the establishment of Longhouse B) in 1985. These tendencies confirm Sutlive's (1972: 458–459) prediction of the decline in the social importance of the *ruai*—a decline that is adversely affecting the solidarity of the community.

The two major sections of a longhouse, *bilek* (the separate room to confirm a lineal relation) and *ruai* (the common corridor to reinforce territorial relations), have been organized in such a way so as to loosen their own social function. This is a fundamental problem that not only affects the integration of the community, but also threatens the existence of the longhouse community itself.

Looking back at their history, one can detect the contradictory effects of the changes in Iban patterns of migration. For instance, in the colonial period, Iban migration was restrained by the influence of the British and the Chinese. Their choice to settle in a permanent residence subsequently gave rise to the decline in agricultural activities in distant places, especially dry paddy cultivation, reducing the pattern of some members living in remote farm huts. This change stabilized the longhouse and reinforced its character as a permanent place of residence. However, in the process of its stabilization, the dispersion of the larger population to new frontiers became stagnant. This was also the result of various restrictions, such as the beginning of rubber planting and the relative decrease in uninhabited forests, culminating in the excessive expansion of

Plate 4.4 Carrying rubber sheets to Kanowit

the longhouse community itself.[21] In the 1960s and the 1970s, the addition of *bileks* to the longhouse occurred according to the natural increase in population, which in turn gave rise to various internal frictions including political conflict. In addition, after the high point of its stabilization, the longhouse community began to face various problems such as out-migration of the younger generations including females, aging of the population, decline of agricultural activities, and weakening of solidarity in the community, all of which were closely related to the diversification of male employment opportunities in urban areas. This phenomenon can be called the 'structural degradation' of the longhouse community.

In short, from the perspectives of both subsistence activities and social bonds, the positive reasons for the existence of the longhouse community are

Plate 4.5 *Gawai* festival

declining; instead, with the outflow of the leading younger generations in the community, the longhouse is becoming a place for youths who cannot find jobs and who passively engage in agriculture and, for the aged who have given up sojourning in urban areas.

Conclusion

Many studies on the subject of out-migration from rural areas and the impact on rural communities in Southeast Asia have focused on institutionalized circulatory labor migration as a supplement to the rural economy or namely, the unremitting flow of wealth from urban to rural areas and the penetration of the monetary economy into rural regions. Even though attention is beginning to be paid to female migration, scholars' main interest has remained limited to the circulatory migration of single women and its effects on the economic structure. The effect of female migration on key social structures in rural communities has not been satisfactorily explored. In order to examine its socio-cultural meaning, this chapter highlighted the change in male circulatory migration and the out-migration of married women.

It is true that since the late 1960s there has been a remarkable influx of Iban males who work away from home, stimulated by the rapid growth in the timber and oil industries in Sarawak. But as Kedit (1993) has pointed out, for Iban males to leave the longhouse temporarily was a culturally institutionalized custom that was reinforced by the females' subsistence activities in the village and was based on the long-established division of labor between the sexes. In addition, in the early twentieth century Iban society experienced the shift to a monetary economy with the introduction of rubber planting. In that sense, the increase in the number of males who worked away from home did not disturb the socio-economic structure of the village community. When we examine the rural changes in terms of migration studies, it is clear that what is more important is the recent phenomenon of female out-migration brought about by the diversification and stabilization of the males' employment situation. Considering the important roles of married women in the maintenance of the subsistence economy and in social relationships in particular, the drift of these females should be noted as a significant factor in the acceleration of the degradation of the longhouse community in terms of weakened solidarity of the ageing *bilek*-family, stagnation of subsistence activities, and the malfunction in the inheritance of tradition.

The changes observed in this chapter may be an example of the general transformation of indigenous societies in the interior of Sarawak, but for Iban society dwelling in the low and middle reaches of the large rivers where it is comparatively easy to access urban areas, these changes can be commonly observed. However, the Iban are still behind the Chinese and Malay in terms of their economic situation, and those who fail to find work or reach retirement age without taking up steadier residence in town return to the longhouse to dispose of their free time. In other words, the longhouse community means 'insurance' to the urban dwellers, and it can be paradoxically but safely said, that although the longhouse community has been declining, it still provides assurance of the Iban's urban life. In this sense, the longhouse preserves its reason for existence and is taking on a different meaning in the lifecycle of those Iban who move between the rural and the urban. Concerning their movement between the two locations, it is also necessary to investigate changing ethnic relations and interaction with the macro-society that surround the increasingly urban Iban, as well as the political and economic influences of retired people in their longhouse community in the village.

5
The Living Strategy of Urban Iban

Introduction

In Chapter 4, we discussed one of the primary factors of structural change occurring in rural communities in Sarawak, most notably the trend in recent years, of more females leaving their village to follow their husbands who are employed in urban areas. This change has meant that while Iban migration patterns are more difficult to describe within the traditional framework of *bejalai*, it does not follow that they have cut their ties completely with the rural community. As will be discussed at a later point, most of the urban sojourners claim that in the future, after retirement, they will return home to their village. Considering that changes in the structure of the rural community have been largely affected by these new migration patterns, it is important to clarify why the Iban stay in a 'local town' such as Sibu, for a relatively long period of time. Moreover, to the Iban, Sibu is not necessarily a step for further migration to a larger city, but rather it seems to be the terminus or end point of the process of family migration. In other words, Sibu is the most important urban center that is equipped with the desired 'urban essentials.'

In this study, as mentioned in Chapter 1, I do not attach much importance to the scale of cities nor population size as a determining factor for migration. These days, rural–urban migrants are not only in search of better economic opportunities, but are also attracted to cities for a wide range of options, including consumption, education and life style. What is more important for them, I believe, is to view the migrants as actors and systems that can mediate between macro-societies and rural communities (Yoneyama 1987; Wazaki 1988). The town of Sibu provides the Iban in the area with these factors. In this sense, Sibu as a town is an appropriate research site worthy of consideration, and one in which we can examine the urban life of Iban migrants from rural areas in the Rajang Basin.

From the viewpoint of urban administration, on the other hand, Iban in-migration has been a cause of social problems. Family migration not only affects the structural changes in the rural community, but also is vital for urban population increase. Whether they stay in illegal settlements or legal apartments, those who are accompanied by their family are likely to stay longer compared to those who leave their family in the village. The urban administration, however, regards such in-migrants as the urban poor and does not hold the view that the migrants are important actors who may assist in the articulation of urban and rural areas. This study, based on the premise that the Iban migrants may become catalytic agents who bring about rural–urban interactions, attempts to undertake an extensive examination of their living strategies in the city.

Therefore, in the following sections we will examine three main issues that effect rural-to-urban migrants: firstly, the emergence of squatter settlements and housing problems in relation to the urban administration; secondly, migration patterns between rural areas and the regional center, Sibu; and finally, migrants' strategies to keep their bonds with the rural communities. These three themes reflect the political, economic and social aspects of rural–urban migrants' activities. Each of them, indeed, is a very important subject, but for the urban poor from rural areas, these issues relate to each other and form the core of their strategies to keep rural–urban relations strong. Having noted their importance, it is surprising that there are very few comprehensive studies of these themes. This chapter hopes to provide new material for consideration; it is a case study devoted to their exploration and elucidation, particularly from the viewpoint of the migrants themselves.

Squatter settlements and the growth of local towns

The urban poor in a local town

The emergence of squatter settlements or spontaneous settlements[1] has been one of the major phenomena associated with rapid population increase in Southeast Asian cities. For this reason a great deal of attention has been directed to these kinds of settlements in urban centers, especially in 'primate cities,' deepening our understanding of urban poverty.[2] For example, the formation of home-based social networks in urban areas (Hugo 1981; Kato 1986) and their close relations to chain migration (Butterworth 1970; Yamazaki 1978; Niitsu 1989) are important. The higher rate of employment in the informal sector (Hart 1973; Tokman 1978; Jagannathan 1987; Nakanishi 1988a, b; Kumagai 1990) is also considered to be a common characteristic of the urban poor. Based on these understandings of the actual conditions of urban poverty, there also have been lively discussions on the concepts of 'shared poverty' or 'urban involution' (McGee 1971).

Most of the early studies of squatters or the urban poor[3] described the urban in-migrants themselves and their many social problems (Perlman 1976; Yonemura 1991a). Since the 1970s, however, the emergence of the urban poor began to be discussed in the context of marginality theory,[4] which was based on dependency theory. Marginality theory argued that the urban poor were victims of a newly structured relation between the central capitalist world as the ruler and the marginal capitalist world as the ruled.[5] This argument has been very influential in the studies of Southeast Asian cities, paralleling the ideas of the modern world system theory presented by Immanuel Wallerstein.

The discussion on urban in-migrants has not been completely free from the tendency to define them as poor, stagnant and marginalized people.[6] On the contrary, recent empirical studies are much more positive, highlighting the initiative of urban in-migrants and their diverse living strategies. These recent studies touch on various topics such as the interaction with other (ethnic) groups in urban areas and administrative bodies, their practical use of their connection with social organizations in the village of origin and their contribution to the urban economy.[7]

Much of this research is on the urban poor in large cities. It was only in 1975 that Dwyer pointed out the fact that not only primate cities but all smaller cities and towns in Southeast Asia have squatters or spontaneous settlements mainly composed of rural-to-urban migrants (Dwyer 1975). It is unfortunate, therefore, that so little attention has been paid to the in-migrants in these local cities or towns. There may be some conceivable reasons for this.

Firstly, there are statistical problems. Many scholars find even the official data and statistics of Third World countries are limited. This is particularly the case with statistical data on local cities or towns. These data are more difficult to use because of the indistinct administrative boundaries, frequent expansion of urban areas and the lack of a consistent concept of 'urban' even within the same country.

Secondly, the scope of the problems in local towns hardly motivates scholars to explore them further. Individually speaking, every local town has problems of urban poverty and a housing shortage. Such problems, however, are not often recognized as emergency issues partly because of their peripheral location. If compared to the larger cities that often have substantial squatter problems even in the cores of the cities, spontaneous settlements in local towns tend to emerge on the fringe, even in the early stage where the commuter distance is not so important because of the small scale of these secondary centers.

Thirdly, the understanding of migration as an economic activity leads to a neglect in analyzing local towns. Previous studies have attached more importance to larger cities regarding them as the final destination for migration, where migrants are supposed to enjoy more job opportunities and higher wages, while local towns are often considered to be relay points for migrants before reaching these larger cities.

Finally, these emphases upon migration to larger cities seem to satisfy a more macro viewpoint, which gives priority to large urban centers. Consequently, the study of migration to smaller cities and towns has been little researched and now needs more attention.

Here, we can emphasize the significance of conducting this research in Sibu. It may be true that, from the national viewpoint, squatters in this town represent a trivial housing problem, but nevertheless it is one of the vital issues for the town's urban administration. The influx of rural indigenous peoples may change the town's ethnic composition and thus transform regional political balances in the town and its hinterland. This is why local political leaders pay attention to the in-migrants from rural areas and their squatter settlements. From the viewpoint of the Iban, on the other hand, Sibu is almost the final point of their destination. Although small in scale and population size, Sibu is relatively near to their home village and also embodies the sense of 'urbanness,' which is very important for people who continuously move between rural and urban locations and maintain a living base in both places.

Local towns in Sarawak and the situation of the Iban

So far, the Malaysian government has developed few clear policies for urbanization of local towns.[8] This is also true in Sarawak and as long as we refer only to population size, urban centers in Sarawak may be typical of local cities or towns in Malaysia. However, the focus here is not to look at Sibu in accordance with population ranking in the state, but rather it should be noted that in Malaysia, the Sarawak state has been peripheral both economically and politically on account of its historical background and geographical isolation.[9] In particular, despite the Malaysian national target to promote industrialization and information technology, Sarawak is still dependent on the production and export of raw materials such as oil, gas and timber. This imbalance in the economy has effected the employment structure, especially that of in-migrants from rural areas.

Another important point is that the ethnic composition in Sarawak is very different from that of Peninsular Malaysia. According to the 1991 Census, the population of Sarawak was 1 642 771, consisting of various ethnic groups such as the Iban, Chinese, Malay, Bidayuh, Melanau and other smaller groups (Department of Statistics Malaysia 1995b). In Malaysia, there is another unique 'ethnic' category called '*bumiputera* (literally sons of the soil),' which is an administrative and political term to clearly distinguish the 'indigenous' peoples from the 'non-natives,' such as the Chinese or the Indian who have mostly migrated into Malaysia since the colonial period.

In Peninsular Malaysia, the term *bumiputera* is normally used for the Malay and Orang Asli groups. In Sarawak, on the other hand, it includes the Malay, Iban, Bidayuh and all other small ethnic groups in the interior. The *bumiputera* policy,[10] which came into force in 1971, is an affirmative action plan to propel poorer indigenous people into the economic mainstream. In the context of Sarawak politics, however, the priority as the *bumiputera* is undoubtedly given to the Muslim-*bumiputera*. Therefore, it is useful to classify the population into three categories, namely, Muslim *bumiputera*, non-Muslim *bumiputera* and non-*bumiputera*. In Sarawak, if categorized in accordance with this criterion, Muslim *bumiputera* comprises 27.4 percent, non-Muslim *bumiputera* 43.2 percent, and non-*bumiputera* 29.2 percent. In urban areas, however, non-*bumiputera* outnumbers the other two groups, comprising 50.7 percent, compared to 28.9 percent Muslim and 19.9 percent non-Muslim *bumiputera*.

This Chapter while drawing on the previous sections, which described rural Iban communities, now focuses more specifically on in-migrants in the urban areas, particularly the squatters and their resettled community of Iban. As the dominant ethnic group within the category of non-Muslim *bumiputera*, and despite their predominance as the largest single ethnic group in Sarawak, the relative economic situation of the Iban seems to be becoming harsher. This observation is with respect to employment opportunities, housing policy, and loan treatment in comparison to the Muslims who have been given preferential treatment since 1963 when Sarawak joined Malaysia. The process of marginalization of the Iban is closely related to the so-called 'federal factor.' In addition, as will be discussed in Chapter 6, the Iban have been recognized as a 'rural people' who have been left behind in national and state development. Thus, despite a strong sense of their own cultural identity, the Iban have been excluded from the mainstream of government development programs. In short, as 'Sarawakians,' as non-Muslim *bumiputera*, and as a rural populace, the Iban are burdened with a multi-layered marginality.[11] Examining this situation is essential to an understanding of the pattern of internal migration.

Setting

As previously discussed, the field research of this study was undertaken in Sibu, the regional center of the Rajang Basin (see Figure 2.5). Mainly owing to its timber-based industry, it has become the second largest urban center in Sarawak (Department of Statistics Malaysia 1995b) (see Table 2.4). Chapter 4 described the out-migration of the Iban from the longhouses and its impact on their communities in the middle reaches of the Rajang where there is a large population of Iban. What was clarified in Chapter 4 was that the family out-migration from rural areas has been steadily increasing and their most important destination was neither the metropolis nor the state capital, but the neighboring local town of Sibu.

The reason why Sibu was chosen as the research site is not just because of its economic and social importance for the Iban who live in the Rajang Basin, but also because the town has become a place where the Iban are experiencing a sense of their marginality through their interactions with other ethnic groups and the urban administration. Sibu has a significant community of Chinese. In 1901 the Foochow group from China began to migrate into Sibu under the sponsorship of the Brooke Government because the area was expected to become a paddy-planting center. Until the present, Sibu has been known as a Foochow dominated area.

In 1925 the Sibu Municipal Board (SMB) was formed and the town was defined as a regional center of the then third division (which included the present Sibu Division). The defunct SMB was taken over by Sibu Urban District Council (SUDC) and became autonomous in 1952. The area of SUDC was then about 7.8 square kilometers. The 1947 Census indicated a population of 9983 in the Sibu Municipal District. In 1957 the Sibu Urban District boundary was extended and contained a total area of approximately 51.8 square kilometers. The population was 29 630 as of 1960, according to the 1960 Census. In 1981 the SUDC was restructured and upgraded to Sibu Municipal Council with areas extended to 129.5 square kilometers. According to the 1991 Census, the population of Sibu was 126 381, consisting of Chinese (66.7 percent), Iban (13.4 percent), Malay (10.5 percent), Melanau (7.1 percent), Bidayuh (0.7 percent) and others (0.6 percent).

In Sarawak there is a belief in the stereotype about the correlation between ethnicity and the employment sector. It is as follows: the business sector for the Chinese (non-*bumiputera*), the government sector for the Malay/Melanau (Muslim *bumiputera*), and the informal sector or unskilled labor sector for all other indigenes (non-Muslim *bumiputera*). Ethnic composition in Sibu[12] apparently coincides with this stereotype. On this point, too, squatters in Sibu could be a focus of inquiry, in order to explore the marginal situation of Iban in-migrants into urban areas.[13]

Squatters, migrants and housing

Squatter settlements in the town of Sibu

In Sibu, the number of squatters are said to have rapidly increased since the end of the 1970s and up to the 1980s (Sutlive 1992). According to research conducted by the Land and Survey Department, at least seven major squatter

Figure 5.1 The town of Sibu

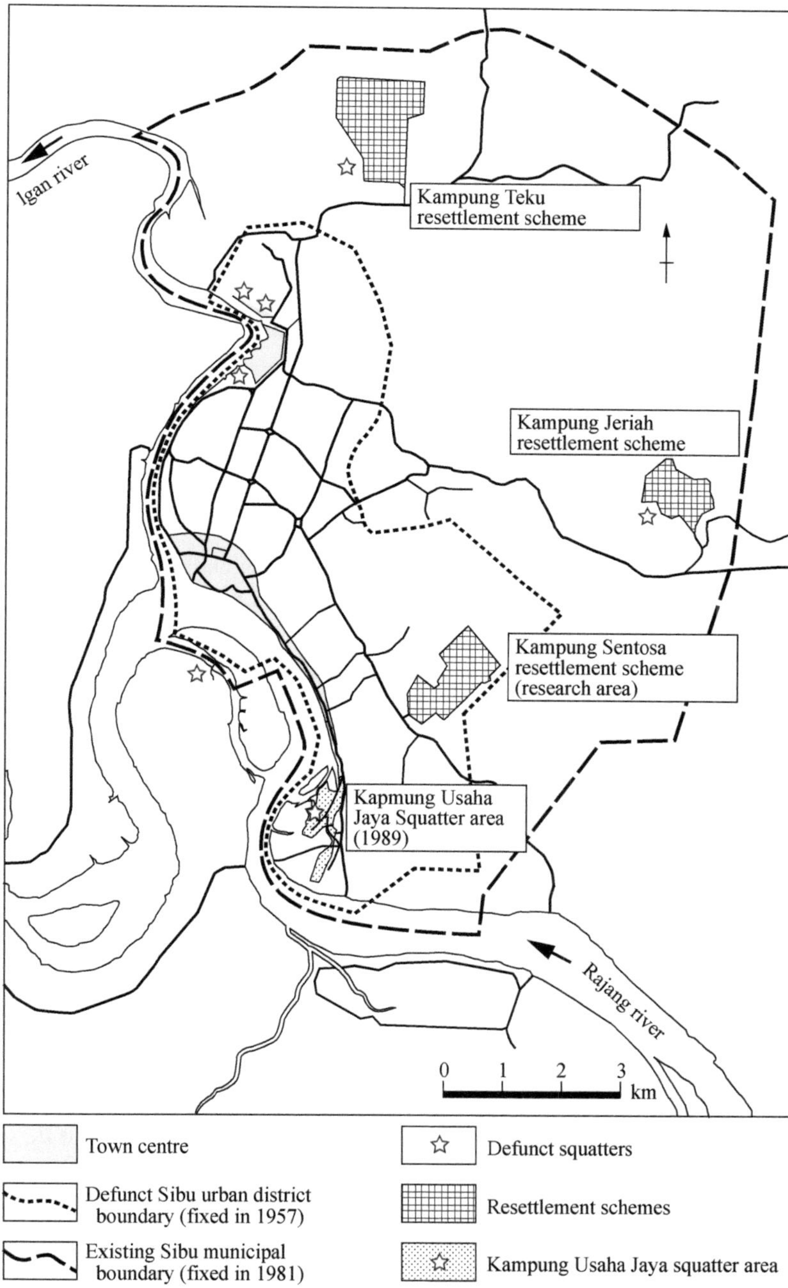

Table 5.1 Number of buildings in squatter areas in the town of Sibu

SQUATTERS AREA	MALAY/ MELANAU[a]	IBAN[b]	CHINESE[c]	TOTAL
Kampung Usaha Jaya, Upper Lanang	633	605	172	1,410
Sungai Pakan, Loba Kerto	5	18	0	23
Batu 6, Jalan Sibu/Oya	311	121	6	438
Sungai Antu	6	125	1	132
Sungai Teku	5	0	0	5
Kampung Nyamuk, Jalan Igan	103	3	14	120
Rumah Eroke	0	32	0	32
Total	1,063	904	193	2,160

Notes.

a: equivalent to Muslim *bumiputera*

b: equivalent to Non-Muslim *bumiputera*

c: equivalent to Non-*bumiputera*

Source: Land and Survey Department, Sibu Division

settlements have emerged within Sibu since the second half of the 1970s (Land and Survey Department, Sibu Branch 1984). Figure 5.1 illustrates the locations of the settlements, most of which are situated near the town boundary, and Table 5.1 shows the estimated number of illegal houses and the approximate ethnic composition in each settlement.

The increase in squatter numbers provoked the Sarawak Government to action and in the 1980s and early 1990s their main response was to issue Temporary Occupation Licenses (TOLs) to the squatters and the urban poor. This license permitted these people to occupy a piece of land in a resettlement area for up to a sixty-year time limit. In Sibu there are now three resettlement areas where TOLs were issued (Figure 5.1).

In the Kampung Jeriah Resettlement Scheme, TOLs were given to those people who had already squatted there. Without adequate readjustment of allotments or segregation planning, Muslims and non-Muslims were mixed in the area, leading to complaints among the residents.[14]

Kampung Teku Resettlement Scheme is a planned settlement constructed to provide segregation areas for the three groups: Muslim *bumiputera*, non-Muslim *bumiputera* and non-*bumiputera*. The area includes not only former squatters from various areas in Sibu, but also new migrants from the neighboring villages.

The newest resettlement area is Kampung Sentosa. This scheme also has a deliberate policy of ethnic segregation and almost all of its residents are former

Plate 5.1 Kampung Usaha Jaya squatter settlement (1996)[15]

Plate 5.2 Squatters' huts in Kampung Usaha Jaya (1996) [16]

squatters from Kampung Usaha Jaya area, which was the largest squatter settlement in Sibu.

According to the report of the Land and Survey Department, in these three resettlement schemes a total of 2394 lots were already allocated by 1998 and an additional 368 lots were supposed to be allocated in the future.

Plate 5.3 Hanging wet clothes in a squatter settlement (1996)

The argument about the present situation of the Iban that follows below is mainly based on data, which was gathered through interviews with Kampung Sentosa residents. All the registered household heads that were interviewed were non-Muslim *bumiputera* (mostly Iban). Although the number of interviewees was limited because of various restrictions, the data shown here are believed to represent the general features of the Iban 'urban poor' who migrated from rural areas and remained with their families in the town.

Growth of Kampung Usaha Jaya and its population composition

Kampung Usaha Jaya squatter settlement (hereafter called Kg. UJ) came to be established on the bank of the Rajang River. It was said that in the second half of the 1970s some Malays and Melanaus (Muslim *bumiputera*) began to squat in this area, and were followed by the Iban particularly in the early 1980s, when the squatter area had already expanded considerably (Figure 5.2).

There is no accurate data on the growth of the settlement except for the occasional reports by the Land and Survey Department. According to research by the Department in September 1982, Kg. UJ settlement was made-up of the Malay/Melanau (193 households), Iban (101 households) and Chinese (105 households), while the annual report of 1989 showed the ethnic composition of the households as 621 Malay/Melanau, 438 Iban and 158 Chinese. The population composition immediately before the resettlement scheme of 1991 was 633: 605: 172 respectively.

Figure 5.2 Expansion of Kampung Usaha Jaya squatter areas

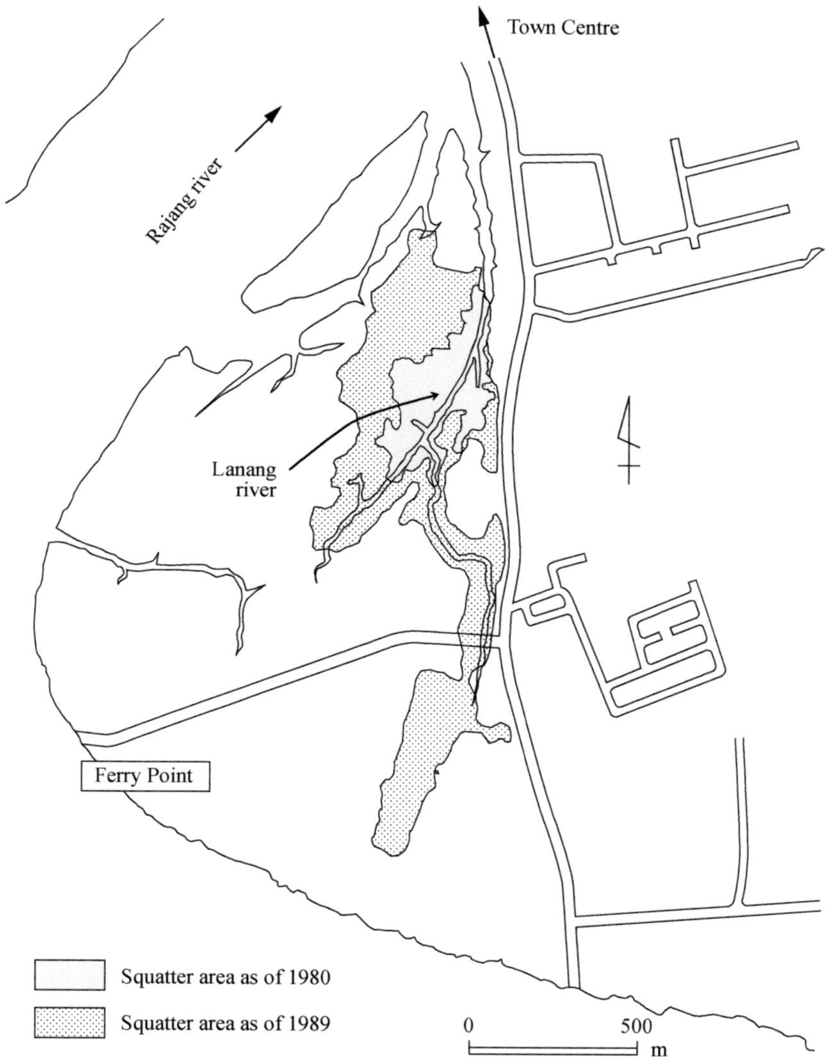

Source: Aerial photographs, Sibu Town, Sortie 8/80, Scale 1:10 000, 1980. Aerial photographs, Sibu Town, Sortie 3/89, Scale 1:10 000, 1989

As for the Iban, Table 5.2 indicates that most of them came to Kg. UJ in the 1980s. It should be noted that 57.6 percent of the registered household heads of Kampung Sentosa, when interviewed, reported that they had lived in rented rooms or houses in Sibu before moving to this settlement. According to this table,

Table 5.2 Year when interviewees moved to Kampung Usaha Jaya and their previous residence

Year moved to Kampung Usaha Jaya	Previous place of residence									
	Sibu Town					Longhouse				
	Rented room	Government quarters	Company barracks	Relative's house	Others/ unknown	Sibu district	Other districts	Other towns	Unknown	Total
Before 1979	2	2		1		1				6
1980	8				3					11
1981	15	4			3	2				24
1982	9	2		1	1	3				16
1983	3	1	1	1	1	1	2			10
1984	11				1	2				14
1985	8	4	1	1						14
1986	5		1			1				7
1987	5			1	2	3				11
1988	3				1		1	1		6
1989	4									4
1990	2									2
After 1991					1			2		3
Unknown	1								3	4
Total	76	13	3	5	13	13	3	3	3	132

Source: Author's field survey 1999

Table 5.3 Year when the Kampung Sentosa residents came to Sibu and their working situation at the time

	Government sector	Private Sector & Self-employed	Unemployed	Others/ Unknown	Total
Before 1960	1	3	0	0	4
1961–1970	14	10	0	0	24
1971–1980	25	36 (1)	4	0	65
1981–1990	6	21 (1)	3	0	30
After 1991	1	2	0	0	3
Unknown	2	0	0	4	6
Total	49	72	7	4	132

Note. The numbers in brackeys = self-employed
Source: Author's field survey 1999.

some 83.3 percent of them had already been in Sibu before coming to Kg. UJ. Those who came to the settlement directly from longhouses and from towns in other districts comprised only 12.1 percent and 2.3 percent respectively. Their average age at the time of first migrating into Sibu was 26.0 years old, while their average age at the time of moving to Kg. UJ was 32.9 years old, and 90.9 percent of them were married and accompanied by their family.

The employment rate of the household heads when they first came to Sibu was 91.7 percent, of which government employees occupied 37.1 percent. The employment rate slightly rose to 93.2 percent—59.8 percent of government employees—when they moved to Kg. UJ (Table 5.3).[17] These figures indicate that most of the squatters in Kg. UJ did not necessarily suffer extreme poverty, but had already experienced relatively stable urban lives in other locations.

According to the interviews, they expressed three major reasons for their move from rented rooms (or houses) to the squatter area. Firstly, the rate of rent increase for their room exceeded that of their wage rise. Secondly, the increase in family members resulting from marriage and childbirth meant that their living space became too small. Thirdly, the growth of their children began to burden them with food and educational expenses, alongside that of the cost of rent for their rooms. In addition, those who were then government employees discussed the shortage of government quarters for them.

To illustrate their situation, let us present the case of a man who migrated to Kg. UJ in 1982. He was born in 1958 in a longhouse in Durin, just thirty kilometers southeast of the town of Sibu, but gave up living in the longhouse in 1980 and migrated with his family to Sibu to take up a wage-earning job. At first, he worked for a private company as a security guard and remained in the company until 1982. At that time, he lived in an apartment in the town with his wife and two children. In 1982 he began to work for the Forest Department, Sibu Branch, as a driver of official vehicles. Although he wanted to live in the government quarters as a government employee, there was no room in the quarters for 'lower-level' officials. When he entered the government sector he heard a rumor that those who had established illegal houses in squatter areas would be provided with a legal lot by the government in the near future. He constructed a hut in Kg. UJ, and gradually made it habitable, but in 1984 was transferred to the Sarikei Branch, about fifty kilometers southwest of Sibu. In Sarikei, he could live in government housing, and fortunately, he found a friend who wanted to rent his squatter house in Kg. UJ. During his stay in Sarikei for twelve years between 1984 and 1995, he obtained extra income by renting his illegal house to somebody else. He explained that in Sibu, poor people had difficulty in finding a reasonable room in the town center and many people wanted to rent even an illegal house.

Compared to other squatters in Southeast Asian countries, those who lived in Kg. UJ were notable for their higher employment rate, especially in the government sector. The large number of government employees seemed to be related to the so-called '*bumiputera* policy.' This policy is a popular name for the 'New Economic Policy (NEP)' formulated under the Second Malaysian Plan (1971–1975), which was a type of affirmative action intended to raise the economic standard of vulnerable indigenous peoples in Malaysia. Although the quota system, at the lower echelons of the administration, is not institutionalized, there are many Iban who perceive that they have had the benefit of the *bumiputera* policy, which helped them to gain positions as government employees. This perception may be based on the fact that from the 1970s to the 1980s, the working rate of Ibans in the study area had improved particularly in the government sector (Table 5.4).

However, the Iban are also aware that they are provided with employment opportunities only in the non-clerical or blue-collar sections, and that the Malay/Melanau (Muslim *bumiputera*) are given preference in government jobs, despite their similar educational background and work experience. Most of the Iban express their grievance—sometimes with resignation—against the discrimination between Muslim and non-Muslim even within the *bumiputera* status.

In urban centers in Sarawak, strategies to improve the supply of housing for these low-income groups has had very little emphasis, compared to job creation. While the fruit of the *bumiputera* policy, at least in the study area, has been reflected in the expansion of employment opportunities in the government sector, the supply of government housing has been so poor that lower-class

Table 5.4 Working situation of household heads in Kampung Sentosa at each period

PERIOD	GOVERNMENT SECTOR	PRIVATE SECTOR	SELF-EMPLOYED	UNEMPLOYED	UNKNOWN	TOTAL
When came to Sibu	49	70	2	7	4	132
When came to Kampung Usaha Jaya	79	41	3	5	4	132
When came to Kampung Sentosa	83[a]	35[b]	6	5	3	132

Notes.
a: including 5 pensioners and 1 deceased
b: including 2 deceased
Source: Author's field survey 1999.

government employees rarely obtain the chance to be provided with dwellings. Since non-clerical work, in particular, is dominated by non-Muslim *bumiputera* in-migrants, such as the Iban from the interior, job creation and housing supply should be considered as an interrelated problem. In short, as is pointed out by the former Kg. UJ residents themselves, it can safely be said that the squatter settlements in Sibu resulted from the imbalance between job-creation and housing policies.

The actors who formulated the resettlement plan

In the latter half of the 1980s the Sarawak government had a policy of squatter removal whereby the government provided the squatters with housing lots in new resettlement areas and issued them with a provisional land title called a 'Temporary Occupation License (TOL).'[18] In order to obtain a new lot and its TOL in a resettlement area, each squatter was required to make an application by himself and had to meet specific conditions as indicated in Table 5.5.[19]

On acquisition of a new lot, the applicants were required to pay a handling charge (called a 'premium') by installments. Though the premium ranged from 4900 *Ringgit* Malaysia[20] (400 square meters) to 14 210 *Ringgit* (1160 square meters), according to the area of the lots, these prices were extremely low in comparison with ordinary purchase prices of land. Moreover, they were supposed to be given formal land titles[21] after paying 10 percent of the premium.

In the mid-1980s seven squatter areas were observed in Sibu. The Land and Survey Department proposed resettlement schemes of some squatter communities, and in 1984 the scheme presented to the Kg. UJ residents was

Table 5.5 Prerequisites to apply for a lot in the resettlement area

	CONDITION
1	An applicant must be acknowledged as a squatter by the staff of the enforcement section of the Land and Survey Department.
2	The hut of the applicant concerned must have been examined and registered by the Land and Survey Department.
3	The hut concerned must be possessed by the applicant himself.
4	An applicant who has long rented a hut in the squatter area and has lived there has rights to apply for a lot in the resettlement area.
5	An applicant must meet the condition that (s)he has no land suitable for residence within a 3 miles radius from the resettlement area provided by the Land and Survey Department.
6	An applicant must have Malaysian citizenship.
7	An applicant must have a family.
8	A female squatter must be over 21 years old and has children even though she has been divorced from or bereaved from her husband.

Source: Land and Survey Department, Sibu Division.

for them to move to Kampung Jeriah (hereafter called Kg. Jeriah) Resettlement Scheme. It is noteworthy that the residents were united in refusing to resettle at the new settlement, because it was farther away from the town center. Although the Sarawak government had intended to make residents from Kg. UJ and those who had already squatted in nearby Kg. Jeriah, resettle in Kg. Jeriah; the consensus of the residents led the government to withdraw their initial plan. Consequently, the government issued TOLs only to those who had already squatted in nearby Kg. Jeriah without any systematic readjustment of the lots.

It is interesting to note that an alternative resettlement plan was submitted in 1988 by the residents themselves, not by the government.[22] When the residents refused the government's initial scheme and afterwards presented the new plan to move to Bukit Lima (existing Kampung Sentosa), a major role was played by the then informal organization called '*Jawatankuasa*' (literally committee). *Jawatankuasa* had been organized among each group of Muslim *bumiputera*, non-Muslim *bumiputera* and non-*bumiputera*. The committee members of each *Jawatankuasa* group had cooperated with each other in meetings on their resettlement scheme.

This organizational ability of the squatters deserves attention. While there are many studies of informal organizations of the urban poor (or squatters), most of them point out the importance of homeland-based organizations for mutual aid. Some of the studies even declare that the foundation of the associations organized by the urban in-migrants can be attributed to common backgrounds or their shared kinship, and not just ethnicity. But the importance of homeland-based or kinship-based organizations is tacitly emphasized on the premise that there is a considerably large population in the original villages of squatter residents. As for the case of the Iban or other non-Muslim *bumiputera* in Sarawak, however, the scale of their village is rather small because their communities are usually organized in the form of a 'longhouse,' a kind of communal house.[23] The small population of the home village (longhouse) hardly gives them the opportunity to compose homeland-based associations in urban areas.

Actually, although the Iban of Kg. UJ did not have any strong ethnic-based or homeland-based organizations, they did have the means to achieve collective support of the Iban residents through the loosely organized *Jawatankuasa* committee. Moreover, through each *Jawatankuasa* organization of the Malay/Melanau (Muslim *bumiputera*), the Chinese (non-*bumiputera*) and the Iban (non-Muslim *bumiputera*), there was cooperation between them, which functioned to coalesce agreement on the issue of the resettlement scheme, considered to be of primary importance by the Kg. UJ residents themselves. Particularly from the standpoint of the Iban (non-Muslim *bumiputera*), inter-ethnic cooperation was indispensable. One of the then committee members of *Jawatankuasa* asserted that, under the conditions of the Muslim preferential policy in the national context and the predominance of the Chinese in Sibu, the Iban had a consensus view that it would be very difficult for them to advance their own interests without cooperation and compromise with other ethnic groups. It can be safely said that this view on ethnic composition was a factor that enabled the solidarity of different ethnic groups in Kg. UJ.

Another remarkable point mentioned earlier, was the large number of government employees among the *bumiputera* in Kg. UJ, including staff of the Land and Survey Department, the Public Works Department, the Sibu Municipal Council and other related government agencies. According to a then *Jawatankuasa* committee member, they could obtain sufficient information through these government staff to search for a suitable area for the construction of a new resettlement area and estimate its feasibility. What is more, most migrants to Kg. UJ since 1985 had already acquired some information about the proposed resettlement project and moved into Kg. UJ in the expectation of the possibility of being given new lots free of charge by the government.[24]

In short, although they were not formally organized, Kg. UJ residents were endowed with considerable organizational ability and information gathering. And furthermore, *Jawatankuasa* committee members obtained a chance to reach the negotiation table directly with the then Land Minister of Sarawak and made a political deal prior to the implementation of the resettlement scheme. One of the then committee members boastfully showed me a picture in which the delegates of Kg. UJ residents and the then Land Minister were seated at a round table, and asserted that by discussing their collective support of local political leaders in Sibu, they carried the negotiations to a successful conclusion.

Their interaction with the government and the administration shows their diverse strategies to realize stable urban lives. In the following section, details of their present urban lives will be explored.

Economic aspects of migration for the local town

Origins of Kampung Sentosa residents and their working situation

The new resettlement area, Kampung Sentosa (hereafter called Kg. Sentosa) has two phases of implementation. According to the Temporary Occupation Licenses (TOLs) that were issued, Phase 1 was composed of 246 households of Malay/Melanau (Muslim *bumiputera*), 151 of Iban (non-Muslim *bumiputera*) and 94 of Chinese (non- *bumiputera*), while in Phase 2, there were 247, 268 and 71 households of each. In both phases, residential areas of each ethnic group were segregated as shown in Figure 5.3.

In 1991 the resettlement of those people who had obtained TOLs in Phase 1 was implemented and is now almost complete. As of 2003, resettlement in Phase 2 that was brought into effect in 1996 has not yet been accomplished, and some houses are still under construction.[25] Besides these houses, there are still lots, which have not yet been allocated, as well as land for the government reserve.

Through personal interviews in the non-Muslim *bumiputera* area, data were obtained for 132 households (85 households in Phase 1 and 47 in Phase 2). Figure 5.4 shows the age structure of the interviewed household heads and their current family members, according to which the average age of the household heads was 48.1 years old. The average number of household members was 6.0 including 52.3 percent of conjugal (or nuclear) families, 30.3 percent of stem families, 12.9 percent of joint families and 4.5 percent of other types.[26]

Figure 5.5 shows the route taken by the registered household heads and their spouses from their home to Sibu. The figure indicates that their home places are dispersed in rural areas around Sibu and not necessarily concentrated in a specific region. Most of their home places, however, are located within a 100 kilometer radius from the town of Sibu. It can be inferred that Sibu does not draw long-range migration from distant rural areas but exists as a regional center in the Rajang Basin.

The main purpose of the first migration into Sibu was to seek jobs.[27] But unlike the squatters studied in other Third World countries, most of the

Figure 5.3 Plan view of Kampung Sentosa resettlement area

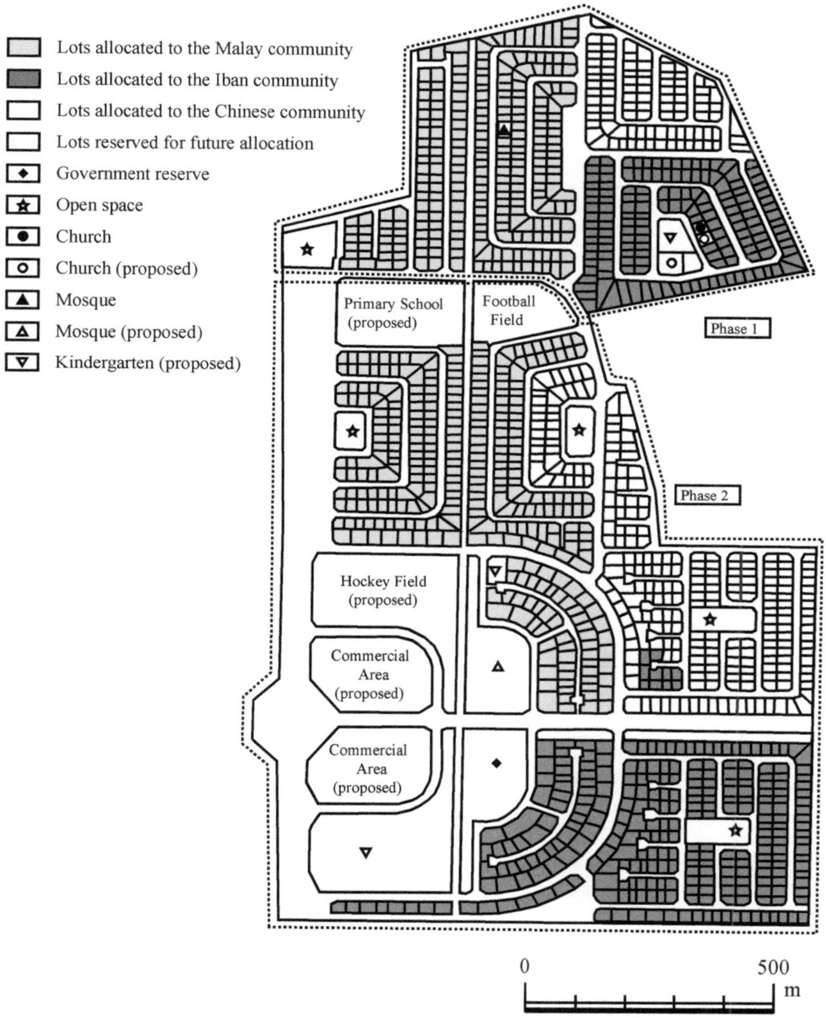

Source: Land and Survey Department, Sibu Branch, modified by the author

Iban of Kg. Sentosa responded to the question by stating that before their move into Sibu they had already been assured of a job on the introduction of their acquaintance, or at prior interviews with their employers. The working situation of registered household heads when they first came to Sibu is shown in Table 5.3. 37.1 percent had obtained jobs in the government sector and those

Plate 5.4 Kampung Sentosa resettlement area

in the private sector, including self-employed comprised 54.5 percent, of which 23.5 percent were contract workers.

The job situation of registered household heads in the research period ending in September 1999 indicates the relative increase of employees (including pensioners) in the government sector (see Table 5.4). As for the occupations of current household members, as is indicated in Table 5.6,[28] those who work in the government sector account for 39.5 percent (male: 43.3

Plate 5.5 Houses under construction in Kampung Sentosa (1999)

percent; female: 28.8 percent), while the major occupations in the private sector are factory workers, various kinds of drivers and construction laborers, and those in the category of self-employment are mostly taxi drivers and food sellers.

Those who are categorized in the government sector are mostly engaged in non-clerical work such as garbage collecting, grass cutting (gardener), road repairing, driver of official vehicles and office cleaning. As mentioned earlier, the Iban in Sibu are convinced that they receive the benefit of the diverse job opportunities under the so-called *bumiputera* policy. However, they also hold

Figure 5.4 Age structure in Kampung Sentosa (interviewed households)

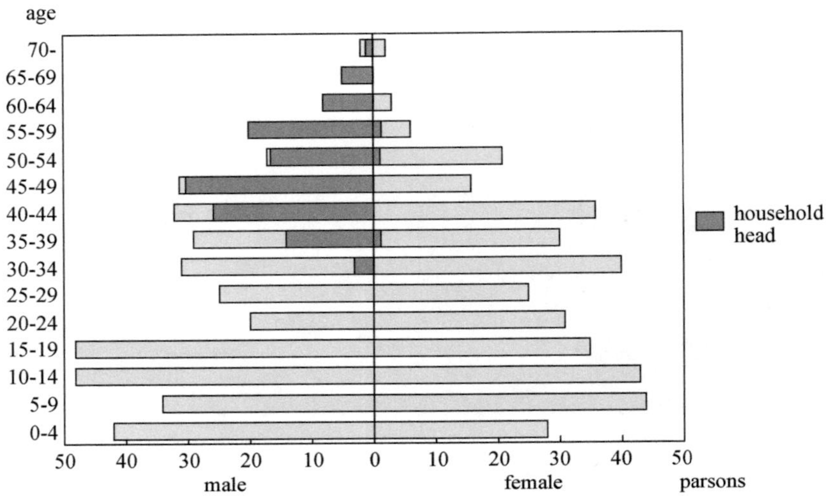

Source: Author's field survey 1999

a grievance against the Muslim-preference policy, which seems to prevent the Iban from being promoted. Therefore, although the majority of the Iban in Kg. Sentosa are involved in formal sectors, especially in the government sector as lower-grade laborers, there is no doubt that they are part of the low-income group in the town.

The status as government employees, however, ensures a stable income and a pension after retirement. It seems that one of their long-term living strategies for establishing their lives in the town, is to try to obtain steadier jobs as lower-level government employees, even with some discontent, rather than to seek short-term higher wage contract work, which is unstable and sometimes involves risks.

Staying rooted in a local town?

Those who had experienced heavy labor in logging camps or other short-term contract work in distant places before settling down in Sibu comprise 45.5 percent of registered household heads. These workers were usually provided with shelter and food, and in most cases they went back to their home places when the contract expired. As was pointed out in previous studies (Jayum 1991) and in Chapter 4 of this book, it is possible for the Iban to live at a subsistence level in the rural longhouse communities, if they engage in

Figure 5.5 Cluster of home places of Kampung Sentosa residents

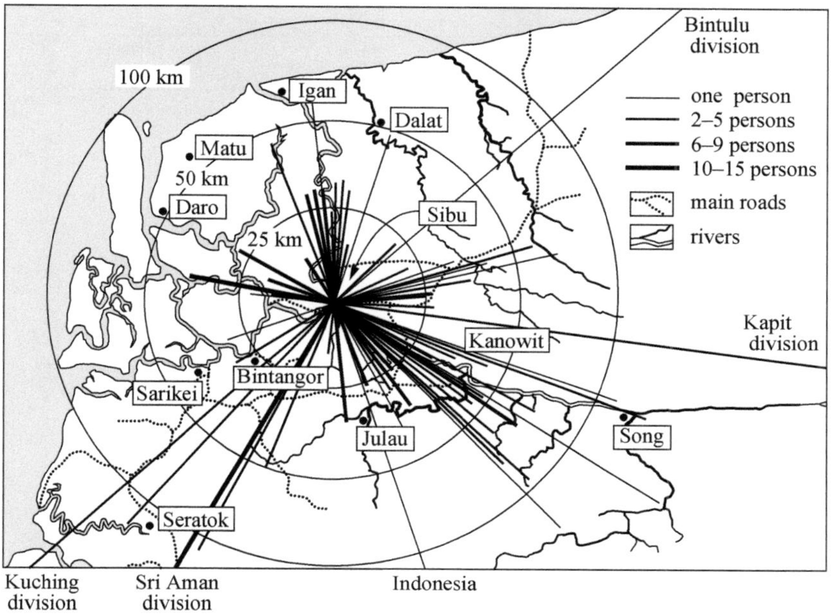

Source: Author's field survey 1999.

small-scale agriculture such as paddy planting. Therefore, there were very few people who continued to stay in urban areas without any employment, and most of the jobless used to stay in the longhouses until new work had been definitely arranged. This occurred whether they sought informal jobs through acquaintances that lived in urban areas, or tried to find formal occupations, which needed written applications or personal interviews. This is largely different from the situation of urban unemployment shown by the Todaro (1969) model, which explained that 'expected earnings' allowed rural people to come to the city and led to over-population without satisfactory job opportunities. In terms of employment, the Iban in the Rajang area usually make thoroughgoing preparations before coming to Sibu. However, once they obtain stable jobs in Sibu, they then faced the need to find housing.

Though the squatters of the defunct Kg. UJ were symbolic of the insecurity of housing in Sibu, they also displayed certain shrewdness, as stated above; in their interaction with the administration so as to make their urban lives more stable. Moreover, their more secure urban lives in the resettlement area have been reinforced by the improvement of the infrastructure such as the supply of

Table 5.6 Working situation of household members in Kampung Sentosa

	AGE															
	15–19		20–29		30–39		40–49		50–59		60–		UNKNOWN		TOTAL	
TYPE OF JOB	M	F	M	F	M	F	M	F	M	F	M	F	M	F	M	F
Government Sector																
Office worker				2	1	3	3	1						1	4	7
Teacher			2	2	2	2									4	4
Post Office/Telekom/ Library assistant			1				3		2				1		7	
Hospital attendant/Nurse				1			6	2	2	1					8	4
Medical assistant							4		2						6	
Public Works Dept./Land & Survey Dept.			1		2		8								11	
Electricity/Waterworks			2		1		1								4	
Mechanic							2		1						3	
Police/Army	1		1		1		4		1						8	
Port Authority/Bomba					4		2		1						7	
Driver					2		2								4	
Cleaner/Charwoman				1		2		1								4
Cook							2	1						1	2	2
Laborer of various government office					6		4		4		1		1		16	
(Longhouse head)									3		1				4	
(Pensioner)									5		4				9	
Subtotal (government sector)	1	0	7	6	19	7	41	5	21	1	6	0	2	2	97	21
Private Sector																
Office worker		1	2	3	2										4	4
Social welfare/Missionary work					1	2	1		2						4	2
Salesperson/Service trade		1		9		1					1				1	11
Factory laborer	2	1	5		2	7		4							9	12
Sawmill	2		2	1		1									4	2
Engineer/Mechanic/Welder			3		8		2								13	
Carrier/Conveyer			3		2										5	
Driver			3		10		3		1						17	
Security guard					1		1								2	
Housekeeper/Cleaner					2		1					1				4
Cook assistant		1						1								2
Physical laborer			7		2		1								10	
Contract laborer	1		3	2	6	3	5	1	4		1				20	6
Self-employed																
Taxi driver					1		2		2		1				6	
Storekeeper/Hawker					1	4	2	2	3	1					6	7
Carpenter					1		1								2	
Subtotal (private sector/ self-employed)	5	4	28	17	37	19	18	8	12	1	3	1			103	50

Table 5.6 Continued

	AGE															
	15–19		20–29		30–39		40–49		50–59		60–		UNKNOWN		TOTAL	
TYPE OF JOB	M	F	M	F	M	F	M	F	M	F	M	F	M	F	M	F
Housewife		4		22		45		38		23		4		7		143
Farmer										1	3	1			3	2
Unemployed	6	1	8	4	2		1		3		4				24	5
Total	12	9	43	49	58	71	60	51	36	26	16	6	2	9	227	221

Source: Author's field survey 1999

water, electricity and a telephone line at every door or by the public services such as garbage collection or bus routes.

In addition to these improvements, the Iban were also involved in the informal organizations. The previous informal people's organizations were reformed to become 'Village Security and Development Committees (*Jawatankuasa Keselamatan dan Kemajuan Kampung*: JKKK)' authorized by the federal government, and each chairperson of the committee was formally registered as a 'community chief.'[29] While it cannot necessarily be said that the formation of a formal organization directly affects the integration of all the residents, it does play an important role, at least, to involve the community members more effectively and to keep in contact with the administration.

Thus, by virtue of steadier jobs, living quarters and the urban public services, or through the formation of formal organizations, the Iban seem to live in Sibu as 'urbanized people,' not as 'urban villagers.' However, when we reflect on the tendency in studies of rural–urban migration, to disregard the movement of migrants into local towns, we have to question again why the migrants have endeavored to settle into such locations. Why is it that the nearest regional center, Sibu, does not have importance, at least for the Iban, as a transit place to migrate further to a larger city? To answer this, the following section will return to the question of whether the stability of their jobs and residence can be a definitive factor in their choice to settle in Sibu.

Migrant strategies to maintain rural–urban linkages

Intention to return to the village of origin

According to personal interviews with the registered household heads who had been successful in obtaining stable residence in Sibu, 55.3 percent of them revealed their clear intention to return to their home longhouse after retirement, and 14.4 percent answered that they would enjoy 'double residence' by spending some of their time in Sibu and some of it in the longhouse. On the other hand, only 17.4 percent specified that they had no intention to return to the home village and would stay in Sibu even in their old age, while 12.9 percent had not yet decided or were reluctant to answer about their future plans.

The reason for the return to their home is clear. Since they expect that their income will decrease after retirement, it will make it more difficult for them to remain in town. They therefore intend to transfer their base back to the longhouse and to make a living by small-scale agriculture. To illustrate this trajectory, let us cite a narrative as an example. A lower level government employee stated:

> It costs us a lot of money to live in Sibu. We have to pay for electricity, piped water and telephone, all of which are much cheaper or unnecessary in the longhouse. When we go to town by bus, we need to pay 60 cents for one-way. Having a bowl of noodles and a cup of coffee cost 3 *Ringgit* and 1 *Ringgit*, respectively, this cost only half in the town of Kanowit. Now it is somehow OK because I have a job in the government sector, but after retirement we cannot live here without enough income. So, I would like to go back to the longhouse to spend time by planting a small acreage of paddy, and live with a small amount of pension as a supplementary income.

Many household heads in Kg. UJ answered in a similar way. However, do they really have a place to return to in their original longhouse? To estimate their access to property in their longhouse communities, questions were asked as to whether they had their own '*bilek* (family room),' which is a domestic, separate room to maintain each stem-family and is one of the inherited properties in a longhouse community. The result of the interviews was that 82.6 percent of them replied that they do have a *bilek* in either their own or their spouses' longhouse. Regarding the current dwellers in a *bilek*, however, there is some variety as is shown in Table 5.7. Those who have exclusive ownership of a *bilek* through inheritance, from their late parents or by constructing a new *bilek* by themselves, comprise 36.4 percent, and most of these *bilek* are empty at present (29.5 percent). The *bilek* in which at least one of their parents lives are 36.4 percent, while those occupied by their siblings are 8.3 percent, and other relatives 1.5 percent.

If a married brother (or sister) lives in a *bilek*, it is quite likely that he or she will inherit it, whether his (her) parents are still alive or not. On the other hand, if only parents or their unmarried children are left in a *bilek*, the heir to the *bilek* generally has not yet been determined. Although most of the respondents gave me an immediate answer that they had a *bilek* in a longhouse, my further questions

Table 5.7 State of original *bilek* of Kampung Sentosa residents

State of original *bilek*	Household
Occupants of original bilek	
Empty	39
Double residence	9
Parent	48
Brother/Sister	11
Other relative	2
Having no bilek in the longhouse	17
Others/Unknown	6
Total	132

Source: Author's field survey 1999

made some of them profess their anxiety that their parents and siblings had not yet decided who would succeed the *bilek*. One of the respondents replied:

> Yes, I have a *bilek* to return to in my original longhouse. But at present, one of my sisters currently lives with my parents in the *bilek*. She has already married and has a child, so it is probable that she will be given the proprietorship of the *bilek* by our parents. If she and her family remain in the *bilek* after the death of our parents, I have to make a new *bilek* attached to the longhouse before returning to the home village.

Inheritance of land in the home village

Besides the issue of *bilek* succession, there is also the question of inheritance of land in the home village in relation to the inheritance of the *bilek*. To my question, most of the registered household heads (77.3 percent) answered that they have some parcels of land[30] either in their own or their spouses' home village. It should be noted, however, that if their parents are still alive, this land still belongs to their parents in most cases, and the children are not necessarily guaranteed to inherit their parents' land.

A number of previous studies on the Iban's system of land tenure have pointed out the loosely disciplined land holding practices connected to the 'egalitarianism' of their society. For example, the problem of each household's unequal land holdings has not brought about stratification in Iban society. Padoch (1982a) explained that this situation could be attributed, not only to ecological factors such as relatively low population density and the tradition of shifting cultivation, but also to their egalitarianism, which was reflected in frequent land borrowing free of charge. Land borrowing between *bilek*-families is a good indication of the looseness of their land usufruct and land inheritance practices. According to customary law (*adat*) of the Iban, those who have left their original *bilek* for matrimony (*ngugi/nguai*) cannot claim the *bilek* or the land of their parents. This does not mean, however, that they entirely lose the chance to inherit land. They are still allowed to ask for pieces of land, and the decision of whether or not they are given any parcel of land, and if so how large a piece of land, depends on their parents and original *bilek*-family members (*se-bilek*). This '*se-bilek*' entails a family that consists of those people who have not left the *bilek* for marriage and still belong to it regardless of their current place of residence. However, Kg. Sentosa residents pointed out that in general those who remain in the longhouse to look after their aged parents will most probably inherit a larger tract of land.

On the other hand, even those who have left the *bilek* for marriage can seek approval to return to the original longhouse or *bilek* as long as they pay a fine. In addition, if they are considered to have contributed enough to maintain their original *bilek* or look after their parents instead of their brothers (or sisters) who live outside the longhouse, it will be easier for them to return to the *bilek* or claim a relatively larger tract of land without feeling alienated.

Thus, the customs of the Iban are flexible and this is useful for the urban dwellers. However, because of their long-term absence from a longhouse community they can incur a weakening of their various rights as a *bilek*-family member. At the same time, they can preserve the possibility of returning to a *bilek* and of inheriting land regardless of their current place of residence. What is important is for them to maintain intimate and sympathetic relations with the longhouse community and *bilek*-family. This may include a tacit long-term contract between the parents living in a village and the children residing in town, where economic aid such as remittances are provided to the parents (Stark and Lucas 1988; Hoddinott 1994).

Maintaining relationships with the longhouse

Remittances are one of the essential topics raised when the relationship between urban sojourners and village residents is discussed. Even in Sarawak, many longhouse dwellers are economically dependent on their children who are working in the urban areas. According to the personal interviews with Kg. Sentosa residents, sixty-three household heads still had at least one parent in a longhouse. In my survey fifty-two persons (82.5 percent) answered that they gave economic assistance to their parents in the longhouse; those who send remittance periodically make up only 15.9 percent (ten persons). This means

Plate 5.6 Sunday market at Jalan Pedada, Sibu

that most household heads give cash directly to their parents either when they went back home or when their parents came to town to visit them.

There are many opportunities for urban dwellers to go back to the longhouse. During the annual festival, *Gawai*,[32] most town dwellers return to the village and to their longhouse.

Apart from *Gawai*, there are many other reasons, such as funerals, the end of the mourning period, engagement ceremonies, wedding receptions and exorcism ceremonies. Some people go back to the longhouse on the weekend or sometimes take leave to join large-scale group work, attend important meetings, or help their family during the busy farming season. Thus the circulatory movement of people is very common.

Plate 5.7 An event in a village[33]

The urban-rural relationship is not just developed by urban dwellers. Rituals and other gatherings held in Kg. Sentosa are also, in most cases, communicated to relatives and friends in the longhouse. During the agricultural off-season, longhouse people sometimes spend their spare time with their children in town. It is much more important for the people from the longhouse to go to town to see a doctor at a hospital, visit public offices, draw pensions and utilize their bank accounts. Therefore, it is crucial for them to have a close relative in town that provides them with an urban base and makes it easier to visit and stay in town for these various purposes.

Through these frequent and mutual movements between urban and rural communities, the children have many opportunities to give their parents money; this seems to leave an impression of their sympathetic ties rather than of remittance activities per se.

Apart from relationships between the *bilek*-family members, town dwellers also have some obligation to remain as a longhouse community member. As indicated above, those who have an exclusive ownership of a *bilek* make up 36.4 percent of the registered household heads in Kg. Sentosa. Indeed, these people have already been assured of future residence in the longhouse; nevertheless they are also obliged to go back frequently to their longhouse. This is because

Plate 5.8 New Year celebration in Kampung Sentosa[34]

the custom of the Iban does not allow the *bilek* to be empty for a long period of time. According to customary law, each household is obliged to use the kitchen in their own *bilek* (called *nungkun dapur*). When they cannot discharge this duty, they are compelled to pay a penalty to the head of the longhouse community. Although the penalty varies from one longhouse to another, they are usually fined ten to fifty *Ringgit* Malaysia and a chicken. The size of the fine is small, but the Iban say that those fined by the head of a longhouse feel deeply ashamed (*malu*) as a community member.

These ways of keeping rural–urban relations connected can be considered as an extremely important strategy by the town dwellers that plan to return to the longhouse after retirement. In sum, it is necessary for them to remain accepted as a core member of the longhouse community by giving a clear indication that they can contribute to the maintenance of the *bilek* and the community as well.

With regard to the issue of a breakaway from a *bilek*, he or she is considered to have become 'independent (*kediri*)' of his (her) parents if they have constructed a new *bilek* after his (her) marriage. While to acquire a house in town can be recognized either as 'independent' or still belonging to a *bilek* according to the consensus between the parents and the children. If they have a stable residence in an urban area, they are said to be '*idup kediri*,' which means 'to make one's own living' or 'to live independently economically.' However, this does not necessarily mean their secession from their original *bilek*-family (*se-bilek*).

The opinion as to whether they are independent of their parents' *bilek* or not, may be strongly influenced by their intention to return home or to remain in town in the future.

In short, a migrants' choice to secure a residence in Sibu was based on careful consideration of their position in both the rural and urban setting, as a strategy for their future life.

Conclusion

To the Iban, in the regional context of the Rajang basin, the town of Sibu is a place for the Chinese. At the same time within the national context of Malaysia or Sarawak, it is a place where they first feel frustrated by government policies that give preference to the Muslims.

In Sarawak, the non-Muslim indigenes are regarded as 'unfortunate poor people who are never able to develop by themselves' as long as they live in villages. Once they migrate into urban areas, the same people are perceived and responded to as 'problem people who bring rural poverty into urban areas.' Thus the Iban see themselves as 'the urban poor.'

In these situations, however, they always seek strategies to make their lives in town more stable. For example, they prefer to get a steadier job in the government sector, even a relatively unskilled job, squat on government land to obtain a new legal lot, make use of their status as government employees to have access to useful information, compromise with other ethnic groups, and make political bargains with local politicians.

Their long-term stay in the urban area, however, does not mean a rupture with the longhouse community, but rather the preparation for a more comfortable future life in the longhouse. In this chapter, we have discussed the manner in which they keep a balance between rural and urban life, and remain involved in the *bilek*-family and the longhouse communities.

These can be said to be the long-term strategies of 'the urban poor' who do not necessarily consider their urban base permanent, but try to establish their homes in different places with an eye to the life cycle. In this sense, it was significant for them to make a choice of their urban residence in a local town, which is relatively near to their longhouse of origin. Thus, the meaning of their urban residence is very different from that of the '*bejalai*' custom (male's journey to obtain wealth or fame by himself or in a small group).

So far, there has been little research on poor in-migrants in local towns. If the characteristic of a local town can be attributed to a part of its population who sustain solid connections with the communities in the hinterland, and maintain frequent and mutual mobility between urban and rural areas, it becomes more important to see a local town and its hinterland as a unit. This can be said to be a living space for movers.[35] In other words, treating the rural and urban together as a unit is possible by observing various aspects of the activities of the urban poor in a local town, or by clarifying their living strategies which reinforce rural–urban relations, both of which have been ignored by research conducted in larger urban areas.

It will be also necessary for the urban administration to take a wider view of a local town and its hinterland and to present comprehensive development programs designed to bring about closer integration between the two areas, the urban and the rural.

In the study area of Sibu, the squatter problem seems to have been resolved at present because of the large-scale resettlement schemes put in place since the 1980s. The administration, however, does not deny that the numbers of squatters may probably increase again in the near future, and feels challenged by this prospect.

The Sarawak government has already disclosed that it will stop giving out land lots with TOL through its resettlement scheme during the 8th Malaysia Plan, and instead will give priority to the construction of low-cost housing schemes. However, the standard price of a low-cost house recently offered for sale in Sibu is 32 000 *Ringgit* Malaysia and above, which is still so expensive that lower-income people such as the Iban could not afford such a house. This policy shift by the Sarawak government is noteworthy, and may well repeat the failure of the housing policy of the 1970s that occurred in Peninsular Malaysia. Although the Iban in town grasp aspects of the government policy, they are not necessarily aware of its entirety. It is possible that the mobility and living strategies of the Iban in town could develop new dimensions if they were able to obtain information about the government's proposed development policy.

6
Development Policy and Human Mobility: The Iban's Voting Strategy

Introduction

Rural–urban relations have conventionally been understood in terms of the social and economic interactions and linkages between two distinct modes of production and reproduction (Potter and Unwin 1989). Kelly (1998) remarks that most of the literature has essentially overlooked the politics of rural–urban relations, both in terms of the policy choices that are made with regard to land use and the political processes (broadly conceived) that facilitate land conversion. Although Kelly's comment was drawn from research undertaken in the metropolitan area of Manila, it can be applied in general to other primate cities, and intermediate and local cities and towns in Southeast Asian countries. In Sarawak, too, the politics of rural–urban relations include rural land development. Moreover, the struggle for power is often reflected in human mobility between rural and urban areas. This power struggle is not limited to the national political arena. Observation on the balance of power at the micro-level, such as the relations between village members and even household members concerning land use may provide us with a clue as to how to understand the political influence on human mobility.

Previous chapters observed the Iban's mobility and living strategies mainly from socio-economic and cultural points of view. However, rural–urban relations—more specifically, mobility patterns between rural and urban areas—are significantly affected by a development-biased political system, the central theme of this chapter.

Iban studies have seldom considered the impact of politics on rural–urban migration even though the pattern of Iban migration cannot be understood simply from a socio-cultural perspective. As discussed in the previous chapters, the Iban have been politically marginalized even though they are the majority of Sarawak's population. While Iban politics have been examined by many researchers, such as Leigh (1974), Jayum (1994) and Searle (1983), observing collective action and reaction of the Iban in state politics, does not take into account how and why 'ordinary people' move in response to the politics within and between rural and urban locations.

In Sarawak, government-led development projects sometimes directly affect the livelihoods of rural residents. As mentioned in Chapter 1, the longhouse is recognized as the smallest unit of rural development. Considering the small size in population of a longhouse community, an individual's action may be perceived as a significant political factor. Therefore, it is reasonable to regard rural residents as important actors who may affect the government's rural development policy, but as will be discussed later, in many situations we see the intervention of urban sojourners in rural development. With the election, in particular, urban sojourners return to the longhouse, and attempt to influence public opinion in the rural regions by taking part in campaigning and voting activities. The result of the elections in the longhouse is seen to have a considerable affect on development politics in the rural sector. Thus, this chapter describes Iban mobility between and around rural and urban locations in relation to this political trend, and especially with regard to rural development policy in Sarawak. When we deal with development policy in relation to the activities of minority groups, we need to take notice of at least two points: firstly, the relations between the nation-state and ethnicity; and secondly, the negotiation between actors who participate in the management of land and resources.

There has been an extensive discussion about the reactions and responses of particular ethnic and minority groups to political decisions in a wide range of settings and in a variety of countries. A classic example is the rainbow theory of machine politics and its refutations, which attempted to show how ethnic minorities achieve varying degrees of influence and recognition in city politics in the United States (Erie 1988; Inglot and Pelissero 1993). But when discussing the relationship between the nation-state and ethnicity in the context of Southeast Asia, there are a number of questions that must be addressed. These include the arbitrary drawing and control of ethnic boundaries by the government (in many cases, a relic from the colonial period), and the extreme vulnerability of indigenous minorities to the power of the political majority. Moreover, the emphasis on development policy in the post-colonial period and the recent trend of rural-to-urban migration of indigenous peoples, has made the relationship between the developmental state and ethnicity even more complicated.

Since the 1980s, empirical studies on the interaction between the nation-state and ethnicity have critically examined the historical process in which ethnic categories have been created and settled by the colonial and post-colonial governments. These studies have revealed the vagueness of such categories and their findings have deepened our understanding of 'ethnicity' and its relationship to the nation-state.[1]

Going beyond the concept of 'ethnicity' itself, recent studies have dealt with the 'vulnerability' of ethnic minorities or indigenous peoples. 'Vulnerability theory' often discusses the conflicts between nation-states and indigenous peoples over the distribution of resources, and criticizes the marginalization or exclusion of vulnerable peoples. Some scholars such as Hong (1987) and Inoue (2002) see themselves as benevolent advocates of people who are politically tyrannized in the name of development policy.[2]

We can see these two trends of study as closely related research fields, if we consider the features of locality and regionality imposed on particular ethnic groups. In post-colonial Southeast Asia, an image has been created, whether appropriate or not, of the juxtaposition between the ethnic (or political) majority who live in the plains or urban areas and the ethnic minorities who subsist in the interior or on the periphery (see Figure 2.1, Chapter 2).[3] After gaining independence, Southeast Asian countries have attached much importance to economic and industrial development, especially in urban districts, by largely relying on foreign trade and investment from developed countries (Armstrong and McGee 1985). Rural development policy, on the other hand, has been driven by two basic objectives. One objective has been to find ways to fully utilize rural resources and land, which are often considered by the urban dweller and the political majority to lie 'idle.' The other has been to try to prevent rural (indigenous) peasants from migrating into the cities and to somehow encourage them to remain on the 'periphery;' goals that are reflected in the expedient policy of promoting rural agriculture.[4]

In the case of Sarawak, the Malay/Melanau (Muslim *bumiputera*), who mainly live in the coastal plains, are considered a political beneficiary group in the context of the Muslim-preferred policy, and the Chinese are widely considered to enjoy a monopoly on the urban economy. On the other hand, the 'Dayak' (often regarded as synonymous with non-Muslim *bumiputera*) have often been regarded as indigenous groups who live in the interior and subsist on traditional shifting cultivation (King and Jayum 1996). At the same time, there seems to be a conscious effort by politicians—not only Malay and Chinese, but Dayak politicians as well—to frame the problem of regional disparities between urban and rural, or the advanced plains and the underdeveloped interior, as the result of the relationship between the politico-economic majority and the minorities. Although it is obvious that these two dichotomies cannot be considered strictly the same, politicians have often tried to identify regional disparities with ethnic differences—as the Dayak-based party did in the 1980s and 90s—in order to promote rural development. It is also expedient to attribute ethnic problems to regional disparities and it is a favorite device of the developmental state for securing a national consensus over the need for 'balanced development.' In such situations, how do indigenous peoples (who are often regarded as 'vulnerable peasants') perceive themselves in the context of the nation-state, and how do they take part in the politics of development? In order to reconsider these dichotomies, this chapter analyzes the voting activities of rural–urban migrants in relation to the politics of development in Sarawak. Elections are a highly visible political stage-show, where rural proprietors can more easily interact with the nation-state over the allocation of resources, and rural–urban migrants also appear on the scene as very important actors. As will be shown later, rural–urban migrants, who frequently go back and forth between these two locations, are influential in resource management in their home communities and in order to maximize their impact, their mobility often reaches a peak during election periods. By considering this mobility as a catalyst for involving rural populations in the politics of development, we may provide an alternative approach to the usual discussion of the interaction between the nation-state and the 'vulnerable peasants.'

In the following section, I will firstly explain the establishment of the Dayak-based political party, the *Parti Bansa Dayak Sarawak* or PBDS, and its advocacy of rural development. The third section will examine how the Iban in urban areas participate in rural development, especially in view of their voting activities. The fourth section will describe an election campaign where one of the main issues involved the establishment of a large-scale commercial plantation. This example illustrates the Iban's perspective on resource management in rural areas. Finally, we will examine the significance of the Iban's migration strategy in so far as it relates to rural development.

Mechanism of development policy in 'underdeveloped' areas

Complexity of ethnic categories in Sarawak

Since the 1980s, family migration from rural to urban areas has increased among the Iban. While the proportion of urban dwellers in the total Iban population was only 4.8 percent in 1980, it grew to 18 percent in 1991 (Table 6.1), and is expected to increase further in the years ahead. This chapter examines the relationship between the 'living strategy' of the indigenous people and the government's development policy, by taking into account some issues of ethnicity in Malaysia.

The category of population classified as 'Iban,' apart from the question of its origin, invokes a rather clear ethnic boundary at present and their identity

Table 6.1 Population rate in urban and rural areas by ethnic group

ETHNIC GROUP	1947		1960		1970		1980		1991	
	URBAN	RURAL	URBAN	RURAL	URBAN	RURAL	URBAN	RURAL	URBAN	RURAL
Iban	0.6	99.4	0.9	99.1	2.3	97.7	4.8	95.2	17.9	82.1
Chinese	24.0	76.0	29.4	70.6	34.7	65.3	38.4	61.6	67.0	33.0
Malay	20.2	79.8	14.3	85.7	17.6	82.4	17.8	82.2	43.0	57.0
Bidayuh	0.6	99.4	1.4	98.6	2.5	97.5	4.9	95.1	19.0	81.0
Melanau	2.4	97.6	4.3	95.7	6.7	93.3	14.0	86.0	28.5	71.5
Other indigenous	0.3	99.7	0.6	99.4	2.6	97.4	5.3	94.7	13.9	86.1
Total	10.8	89.2	12.6	87.4	15.5	84.5	18.0	82.0	37.5	62.5

Source: Masing (1988) and Department of Statistics Malaysia (1995b)

as Iban also tends to be attributed to relatively simple criteria.[5] What matters more for the Iban themselves are the concepts of Dayak and *bumiputera*, terms bestowed by politicians and the nation-state on collective ethnic groups.[6] These obscure terms are often colored by politics and tend to create confusion.

Another point is the gap between the preconceived attitudes of the Dayak and their actual situation. Although the growing number of Dayak people who reside in cities indicates that 'Dayak' cannot be equated with 'rural' or 'interior' people, the Sarawak government nevertheless tends to substitute the terms 'rural populace' and 'interior community' for the term 'Dayak community.' This substitution of nomenclature is carried out to justify the country's development policy by replacing the interests of specific ethnic groups with a national interest in reducing regional disparities.

Before we proceed, it is necessary to clarify the complexity of ethnic categories in Sarawak. According to Jayum (1994) and Jayum and King (1997), the term Dayak, in the strict sense, comprises the Sea Dayak (Iban) and the Land Dayak (*Bidayuh*), but since the late 1980s, it has become increasingly common to refer to the Iban, Bidayuh, and Orang Ulu (various smaller non-Muslim indigenous groups) as Dayak. Although these groups share certain similarities in their physical outlook, longhouse living, languages, and customs (Kedit 1989), Dayak as a collective term does not represent a single undifferentiated ethnic entity.[7] Rather, the term is only meaningful when political propaganda is required, for instance, in advocating development projects for rural areas or in promoting the unity of non-Muslim indigenous groups.

In the national context of Malaysia, the general term *bumiputera* is well known. This is a political term that was created to group together all indigenous peoples into one category. However, in terms of the beneficiaries of the New Economic Policy, priority is clearly given to the Muslim *bumiputera*, while the Dayak, mostly non-Muslim *bumiputera*, are relegated to a 'second class' status (Chin 1996). Thus, in the context of Sarawak politics, we have to consider the three categories that make up the total population (1 642 771): Muslim *bumiputera* (27.4 percent), non-Muslim *bumiputera* (43.2 percent), and non-*bumiputera* (29.2 percent) (Department of Statistics Malaysia 1995b).

Based on these categories, the Iban are the largest group among both the Dayak and the non-Muslim *bumiputera*. Particularly in the middle and lower Rajang, where the Iban are the predominant indigenous people, the terms Iban, Dayak, and non-Muslim *bumiputera* are sometimes regarded as synonymous.[8]

Dayakism and ruralism

In examining the relationship between ethnic categories and Sarawak development policy, it is common knowledge that the government's development projects are only provided to supporters of the parties in power (Mason 1995; Aeria 1997). This is most apparent in small-scale projects in 'underdeveloped' rural areas.

Politicians in Sarawak refer to this rural-biased development policy as 'ruralism.' This policy is related to the political term 'Dayakism,' which was advocated as the party's doctrine by a Dayak-based party, the *Parti Bansa Dayak Sarawak* (PBDS).

The PBDS was formed in 1983 when it split from the Sarawak National Party (SNAP). The SNAP had been part of a coalition government (Sarawak *Barisan*) and represented the interests of the Dayak community. However, in 1980, a dispute arose over who would succeed President Datuk Dunstan Endawie when he resigned. The most likely candidate was the then Deputy President, Datuk James Wong (a Chinese), but a faction of young highly educated Iban members protested and argued that SNAP, as a Dayak-based party, should nominate a Dayak as President. The senior Iban members, whose educational level was relatively low, supported the Chinese candidate because they did not want to see their influence in the party challenged by the young and educated generation.[9] This incident was seen as a confrontation between 'multi-racialism' promoters and Dayak sympathizers on the one hand, and as friction between the different generations on the other. In short, it was a combination of political and ethnic tension within the party that led to a confrontation among the Dayak (mostly Iban) members. As a result, at the party's general meeting in 1981, the faction favoring the Chinese candidate defeated the young Iban members. In 1983, the younger members broke away from SNAP to organize a new Dayak-based party, the PBDS.

The principles of the newly established PBDS may be summarized as follows:

> SNAP no longer plays its original role of helping to alleviate rural poverty in the Dayak community, even though the socio-economic status of the Dayak is well below the national average. In the context of the New Economic Policy, the government should consider how to eradicate poverty among the Dayak who live in remote rural areas. The PBDS seeks to ensure that the voice and the interests of the Dayak are reflected in national policy.

Although the principle of the PBDS to pursue benefits for the Dayak community and its slogan of Dayakism were often criticized as 'chauvinistic,' the PBDS adopted the slogan not in opposition to other groups, but rather as an affirmative political label envisaging the unity of disparate non-Muslim indigenous groups under one political party (Mason 1995). Jayum appreciates that it was not a chauvinistic slogan but rather a 'communal' one with a goal that was similar to other parties such as Malay/Melanau-led *Parti Pesaka Bumiputera Bersatu* (PBB) and the Chinese-led Sarawak United Peoples Party (SUPP). Yet the formation of the PBDS clearly posed a threat to the stability of both the PBB and the SUPP in the Sarawak *Barisan* (Jayum 1993).

The term 'Dayakism' was mainly adopted as a deliberate attempt to emphasize the unity of the Dayak, or the non-Muslim *bumiputera*, and for the development or alleviation of poverty among the Dayak in rural areas. By stressing that most of the Dayak still live in the interior, the PBDS advocated investment in rural development. Thus, during the election campaigns of 1987 and 1991 for the State Assemblymen, 'rural development' became the main theme of PBDS, and the term 'ruralism' emerged in Sarawak in this political context.

Immediately before the 1987 state election, the PBDS left the state coalition government (though not the federal coalition) in order to challenge the Sarawak *Barisan* state coalition. When the polls closed, of the forty-eight allotted seats, the *Barisan* parties secured twenty-eight of them, the PBDS fifteen, and the *Parti Rakyat Malaysia Sarawak* (PERMAS, a Muslim-based opposition party) five seats. After the election, the PBDS lost considerable power when eight of its State Assemblymen defected to the *Barisan* parties. In the 1991 state election, the PBDS candidates were returned in seven out of fifty-six constituencies. Immediately after this election, the PBDS applied to rejoin the state coalition.

The PBDS decision to rejoin the coalition was based on the realization that, as long as they were part of the opposition, their constituencies could never benefit from the subsidies made available for development. After the 1987 and 1991 elections, those constituencies, which had voted for the opposition, were in fact not allocated any development funds, and numerous rural communities that had supported the PBDS were excluded from the government development plans. In short, the retaliatory measures taken by the *Barisan* government made it very clear that the PBDS could never realize its goal of 'ruralism' so long as it remained in the opposition. As another condition of rejoining the state coalition government, the PBDS was forced to declare its commitment to a 'multi-ethnic party,' and could therefore no longer advocate 'Dayakism.'

The Dayak community was reluctant to support the PBDS partly because of its reputation for intractability,[10] and also because it was generally recognized that Dayakism was ultimately an Iban-centric idea.[11] Beyond that, the lukewarm attitude of the Dayak also reflected their misgivings over the practicability of the PBDS's ideals. In other words, the Dayak themselves were keenly aware that the whole notion of 'ruralism'—priority on rural areas in the allocation of development funds—was something that the PBDS could not deliver on, as long as they kept out of the coalition, for the simple reason that they lacked any source of funds.

Distribution of development projects and the 'subsidy syndrome'

It is true that in Sarawak, over the last two decades, a large sum of money has been invested in rural development projects under the name of 'ruralism' (Chin 1996). To the extent that this funding can be attributed to a new awareness on the part of the government of the importance of the Dayak for political stability, perhaps the recent up-and-down behavior of the PBDS (part of the coalition, opposed to the coalition, then back to being part of the coalition) did have some significance after all. In this sub-section we examine the process of budget distribution for rural development schemes over the last few decades and the reality of the so-called 'subsidy syndrome' among the Iban.

Among the many kinds of development projects provided by the government, the indigenous peoples in rural areas are primarily interested in 'Minor Rural Projects' (MRPs); subsidies made available to improve rural infrastructure such as the repair of longhouses, distribution of generators, supply of water and electricity, construction of jetties and bathing places, and the extension and repair of minor feeder roads. These MRPs are generally undertaken at the request of the rural residents themselves. For those who live in the interior, filing an application to request an MRP is a useful measure for it permits the local residents to express their urgent demands immediately.

In the name of 'ruralism,' the Sarawak government has invested a great deal of money to comply with these requests by rural residents. Observing this response has made residents keenly aware that demanding subsidies from the government is the quickest and easiest way to fund minor development schemes or improvements in living conditions. Ngidang (1995) and Aeria (1997) refer to this typical attitude of rural inhabitants as the 'subsidy syndrome.'

However, the prospect of a favorable response to an MRP petition is largely dependent on whether the petitioners have access to politicians. The government claims that it receives MRP requests from any rural constituent, but it is clear that there is political manipulation involved in determining which requests are accepted to become projects. Indeed, the decision-making process of approving MRPs and allocating funds is so unclear, that ordinary people really never know the status of a request or whether funding is likely to be approved. This opacity is related to the fact that Divisional Residents (hereafter, Residents) and District Officers (DOs) have little influence on the state government in the planning of development projects, which is described as follows.

In 1987, Prime Minister Mahatir directed each DO to prepare a 'District Development Plan' (DDP), and most of the DOs from Peninsular Malaysia responded positively. Since the DOs themselves prepared the DDPs with the assistance of consultants and various kinds of committees, the DOs could strengthen their influence on the development schemes in their own districts by assuming the status of Chief Planning Officer or Chief Development Administrator (Solhee 1994: 10).

In contrast, no district in Sarawak submitted a DDP. According to Solhee, the Sarawak government did not issue a directive to the DOs to prepare DDPs, because the government sought to strengthen centralization at the state government level and keep the decision-making authority concerning development issues to itself. In effect, as Solhee points out, the authority and influence of the Residents and the DOs in development activities have been gradually eroded over the last decade. In some cases, the Residents and DOs are not even officially informed of the development activities taking place within the boundaries of their areas (Solhee 1994: 13).

In Sarawak, even the authority to approve farm subsidy programs or minor projects such as MRPs is not vested in the Resident or DO; rather, the individuals filling these positions are relegated to the role of mediator between the ministries or agencies and rural residents, or at most, they are given figurehead positions such as the Chairman of Development. Consequently, rural residents also tend to neglect the DOs. Although MRP requests are supposed to be submitted to the local DO, most rural residents bypass this formal procedure and try to submit their requests directly to the elected leaders in their areas or to the local branch offices of the Government parties. Their behavior in this instance is based on the recognition that the DO has little influence on the decision-making process of authorizing rural development projects. The longhouse communities with access to politicians in particular, have found that it is faster and more reliable to approach politicians directly than to go through the formal process with the DO to get an application accepted. This weak position of the DO in planning minor projects is even more apparent for larger-scale schemes such as the development of plantations and major road construction, where they have practically no influence at all.

By reducing the power of administrative officials, the Sarawak government has succeeded in consolidating the direct influence of government parties over the rural population. In other words, the enhancement of the doctrine of rural development and the rise of the subsidy syndrome paralleled the establishment of patron-client relations between assemblymen and the constituents of rural regions. One interesting aspect of this development that is very rarely noted is that urban residents often intervene in the patron-client relations in rural areas. In the following sections, we will discuss this issue on the basis of data obtained through field research both in Kanowit, a rural area, and in the communities of urban migrants living in Sibu.

Development fund distribution and voting activities among urban residents

The ballot-counting system in Sarawak

When the *Parti Bansa Dayak Sarawak* was established in 1983, its advocacy of 'Dayakism' and 'ruralism' seemed to be based on the recognition that the Dayak were economically disadvantaged because they lived in remote rural areas. However, this sense of being marginalized in society and the notion of social entitlement developed not only among the rural Dayak but also just as strongly among the Dayak living in urban areas. In particular, the Dayak—most of whom are non-Muslim *bumiputera*—feel very strongly that the privileges extended to the *bumiputera*, as part of the New Economic Policy, go overwhelmingly to the Muslim *bumiputera* and the Dayak have been largely excluded from the socio-economic mainstream. This perception was discussed in Chapter 5, which described the living strategies of the Iban in Sibu. Here we reexamine their strategy, but this time primarily from the political point of view.

In this section we investigate how the 'urban poor' participate politically in rural development projects, based on the data obtained through field research in Sibu and Kanowit. The main issue is the voting activity of the Iban, which can be considered as a form of preparation for their return to the longhouse.

In Sarawak, there are two types of public elections; one is the general election for the Parliament of the Federation, and the other is the State Assembly. Both adopt a single-member constituency system. In these elections all people twenty-one years and over are qualified to vote and they can choose their polling place regardless of their current residence.

The voting activity of the Iban in the Rajang area is closely related to development politics in Sarawak. Although the government budget for rural development has been increasing in the last two decades, it has not been distributed impartially to each district. The fact that the development funds were not allocated to the constituencies, in which an opposition candidate was elected in past elections, indicates the government's discriminatory treatment between constituencies (Mason 1995). This punitive decision by the government on funds distribution is common knowledge among the Iban in the Rajang area. They are well aware that their support for the Government parties can make sure that they obtain government subsidies or rural development projects. Moreover, since the 1991 election for the State Assembly the government began to adopt a new ballot-counting system, which can find out details of the results in each longhouse (Mason 1995).

In rural areas in Sarawak, ballot boxes are usually set up in government schools and other public facilities. Some boxes are placed in the *ruai* of the longhouse if there are no public buildings around the village.

After the voting time is complete, the election administration immediately opens the boxes at the polling station. When I was undertaking participatory observation in Rantau Kemiding in 1996, when the election for the state assemblymen was held, a lot of voters surrounded the polling station in the village, a classroom of the village government school, and carefully looked at the process in which the election staff opened the ballot box.

Thus, voters can immediately check the approval rate for the government among the village people. This voting rate is also officially recorded. As a consequence, it is inevitable for a longhouse community to increase the voting rate for the Government parties if they really want to obtain rural development projects, such as the supply of water and electricity, the construction of rural roads, minor bridge-building, or the provision of various kinds of building materials, all of which are indispensable for the improvement of living conditions in the longhouse.

Urban residents' participation in rural development projects

Considering the decision-making processes, mentioned above, on the funds distribution for rural development, most of the residents in Kg. Sentosa, Sibu, chose to vote in a longhouse in order to prepare for a more comfortable life in their future retirement. However, they also paid attention to the expansion of urban amenities or infrastructure in their current residence, Kg. Sentosa. For example, improvement of public transportation, road-pavement in the settlement, construction of an assembly hall and religious places (mosques or churches), establishment of a primary school and kindergarten, are all dependent on approval and subsidies from the government. It is therefore important for them to show their support of Government parties even in the urban area.

Table 6.2 shows the variation of the registered polling places of Kg. Sentosa residents in 1999. As mentioned in Chapter 5, I conducted interviews with one hundred and thirty-two Iban household heads that were previously squatters but currently live in the resettlement area, Kg. Sentosa. According to the interviews, forty-four household heads (33.3 percent) stated that all of the household members registered their votes at the polling place in their home villages, not in the town of Sibu. In addition, some thirty-one other households (23.5 percent) were divided with some members of the household registering their votes in their home villages and other members in the same household registering their votes in Sibu. Altogether, seventy-five households (56.8 percent) included members who registered their votes in rural constituencies.

This behavior by the Iban people who are resettled in the city, of registering their polling places back in their home villages, can be called 'return voting,' which is based on careful consideration and planning for the stability of their future life. The Iban in the study area have acquired legal residential lots in the resettlement district and appeared to be leading fairly stable lives in the city, but they have recent memories and experience of being squatters. They remained very much in the lower class in Sibu, and most Iban in Sibu anticipated a substantial fall in income after retirement, making it difficult for them to stay

Table 6.2 Distribution of registered polling places among each household

	VOTING DISTRIBUTION				
PLAN FOR THE FUTURE	A	B	C	OTHERS/ UNKNOWN	TOTAL
Return to the longhouse after retirement	38	16	14	5	73
'Double residence'	6	12	1	0	19
Stay in town	0	0	23	0	23
Undecided/Unknown	0	3	9	5	17
Total	44	31	47	10	132

Notes.

A: Whole membership of household vote at longhouse.

B: Some household members vote at longhouse and others in Sibu.

C: Whole membership of household vote in Sibu.

Source: Author's field survey 1999

in the city. As mentioned previously, many Iban planned to move back to their rural subsistence agriculture-based communities where it is far cheaper to live. This lifecycle pattern in which urban Iban anticipate going back to their longhouses in later life, accounts for their 'return voting' behavior of going back to one's home village to vote.

On the other hand, those who attach importance to the improvement of their urban lives think it necessary to also vote in the urban constituency. This resulted in 23.5 percent of all households having a strategy to disperse their voting places in Sibu and a longhouse, between husband and wife or parents and children within a household. In short, their considerable concern, both for the present urban life and their future life in a longhouse community, is clearly reflected in their voting activities.

Indeed, voting is the easiest way for the populace (including the poorest people) to participate in politics in Sarawak, but in every election over the past decade or so, the Government parties have been almost guaranteed to win a sweeping victory. Thus the Iban of the study area do not view elections as a way to make their opinions reflected in Parliament or the State Assembly, but rather as an opportunity to demonstrate their pro-government support in order to extract economic benefits.

This strategy is based on their perception of themselves as marginalized people. Many of the Iban in urban areas hold a view that can be summarized as follows: the Chinese can acquire the necessary know-how to accumulate wealth through various kinds of networks, and the Malay (Muslim *bumiputera*) have practically unconditional access to government subsidies because of the government's policy of Muslim bias and preference. However, it is practically impossible for the Dayak and the Iban to improve their situation through their own efforts because they lack both the know-how and funds. Moreover, the Dayak have been politically marginalized after a series of political defeats and splits in the Dayak-based parties. This perception has led the Iban to conclude that in order to obtain their share of subsidies and public funding they must assume a subservient attitude toward the government. In other words, they think that applications for development projects require a demonstration of pro-government sentiment, which is often manifested by 'return voting' for the government in power. This behavior should be understood as the result of deliberate decision-making through a process of elimination accompanied by a certain degree of resignation, rather than interpreting their perception and actions as a 'subsidy syndrome.' The resignation comes from the fact that the Iban recognize that their influence on state level politics is limited and they also lack common political objectives (Jayum and King 1997). Their votes can be readily swayed by local issues affecting their everyday lives as they tend to be more interested in personal or regional issues (Jayum and King 1997: 55). This tendency is reflected in the diversity of the Iban voting record, which will be discussed in the remainder of this chapter.

Diversity of the voting record among the urban poor

In the Kanowit district, located in the middle reaches of the Rajang Basin, the number of registered voters greatly exceeds the resident voting age (twenty years and older in the Census) population as shown by the 1991 Census (Table 6.3).

This means that a sizable number of people return to the district from urban areas during elections, a movement that is indicative of 'return voting.' However, a closer examination of the situation, based on extensive interviews with the Iban, revealed that the urban dwellers did not necessarily 'return' to their own home villages during election time, and their voting behavior actually included a number of different patterns. Here we will consider some typical cases that highlight the active and strategic aspects of their voting behavior.

The first case illustrates the 'return voting' pattern described above where voters are thinking ahead to their future life in the longhouse community. Yet even among the seventy-three out of one hundred and thirty-two households whose heads stated their intention to return home after retirement, some sixteen households (21.9 percent) split their registered voting places between the parents and children or between husband and wife. There are two main reasons behind this pattern of behavior. The first is closely related to the way in which they acquired legal residence in Sibu. In the late 1980s when they were still squatting on a riverbank in the southern part of Sibu,[12] the Iban struck a deal with

Table 6.3 Number of registered voters and Census population of 20-year-old and over in the Kanowit District

		ETHNIC DISTRIBUTION (PERCENT)			
	TOTAL	MALAY/MELANAU	CHINESE	IBAN	OTHERS
1987 Election for the State Assembly	13,936	2.65	14.98	82.38[a]	-
1990 Election for the Parliament	16,154	1.58	12.85	85.11	0.45
1991 Election for the State Assembly	16,154	2.06	14.67	82.92	0.34
1995 Election for the Parliament	18,049	5.00	20.00	75.00	-
1996 Election for the State Assembly	17,513	1.70	13.52	83.93	0.85
Census population of 20-year-old and over (1991)	13,027	-	-	-	-

Note. a: Dayak

Source: New Straits Times, Borneo Post, and Department of Statistics Malaysia (1995b)

locally elected officials; they could obtain legal residential lots within the new resettlement area in exchange for their votes cast for the Government parties. These people were thus faced with a dilemma, they consider it important to register their votes in their home village to promote local development, but at the same time they feel obligated to vote for Sibu leaders for their help in obtaining legal lots. Consequently, a few members of these conflicted households register at a polling place in Sibu. Of course another reason for voting in town is that they live there, so naturally they are concerned with the improvement of their living conditions in the resettlement area. Just as in the rural areas, the development of urban infrastructure in Sibu—putting in drainage systems, paving roads, installing telephones in each household, extending regular bus routes and so on—is achieved by submitting petitions to the politicians in power. It is for this reason that some in the Iban community consider it important to express pro-government sentiment by voting in Sibu. At the same time, these people acknowledge that they might transfer their voter registration place somewhere else, as their strategic needs change in the future.

The second case exploits the fact that, under the existing system, voters can choose any polling place irrespective of where they actually live. In effect, this makes it possible for those in power to redistribute votes from one constituency to another. For example, residents in a district where the candidate from the Government party is sure to be elected may be requested to vote in a different district where the opposition party is influential. In the course of my research, I found three household heads that registered their voting places not in Sibu or their home village, but in other districts purely at the request of powerful leaders. Maintaining and cultivating connections with influential politicians is a way to secure development projects for one's home village. Cooperation may have other benefits as well, such as an appointment to the post of *penghulu* and district councilor, enabling a more active role in politics.

The third case revolves around the fact mentioned earlier that rural development funds are unequally distributed to rural constituencies according to political decisions made by Government parties. Furthermore, the amount of money and materials dispersed in a constituency largely depends on the local candidate's competence in procuring funds. With this situation in mind, four household heads stated that they often transferred their voting registration to a constituency where it was easier to obtain development projects. Under the terms of the Minor Rural Projects (MRPs), the applicants can demand the provisioning of actual goods (electric generators, building materials, outboard motors, and so on) from the local Government party branch. Indeed, some cases have been reported where the applicants have been able to acquire cash income through illegal channels. Even in these cases, the critical factors are one's connections with influential people in the local party branch, and whether these political patrons come from the same ethnic background.

As I have demonstrated, the 'return voting' and other voting behavior of the Iban represents a deliberate and straightforward strategy to improve the stability of their lives.[13] It was shown that even those who had secured a legal residence in the city often transferred their voting registration and distributed the household members' votes to different registration sites. It is apparent that the Iban in the study area keep a constant watch for any opportunity to leverage the power of their voter registration to win concessions from patrons. This strategy aims to improve their living conditions not only in their urban neighborhoods but also back in their home villages where they are likely to retire later in life.

Large-scale development and land resource management

The behavior of the Iban calculated to gain Minor Rural Projects (MRPs) described in the previous section was predicated on an overwhelming victory at the polls by the Government parties. In 1996 for instance, the parties in the alliance captured fifty-seven of the sixty-two seats when the election for the Sarawak State Assembly was held.[14] This sweeping victory by the alliance had been expected before the election, so controversy over policy occurred in very few constituencies. One rare instance where a dispute did occur in the 1996 election was in the Machan constituency in the Kanowit District. The point at issue was relatively clear and involved land resource management of a newly planned oil-palm plantation in the area. In this section, we examine the trends of the 1996 election, particularly as it pertains to large-scale developments.

Dispute over the opening of a large-scale plantation

In the Machan constituency in the Kanowit District, the 1996 election was the de facto battleground between two candidates, the incumbent assemblyman from the *Parti Pesaka Bumiputera Bersatu* (in the alliance), who forcefully advocated the oil-palm plantation project, and a new independent candidate who had a very different view on how the plantation should be constructed.[15] The independent candidate had a difficult time getting his views expressed in the mass media, but based on a personal interview with the candidate his basic contentions can be summarized as follows:

> The oil-palm plantation scheme promoted by the third sector or by a Joint Venture Company wants to utilize Native Customary Land[16] over which the Iban have already established usufruct based on history and customary usage even though no legal

title have yet been issued. The Joint Venture Company is to 'lease' the native land and return a part of the profits earned by the plantation management to the Iban 'landowners' (Figure 6.1). However, the scheme requires the Iban to recognize that

Figure 6.1 Joint venture model of an oil-palm plantation

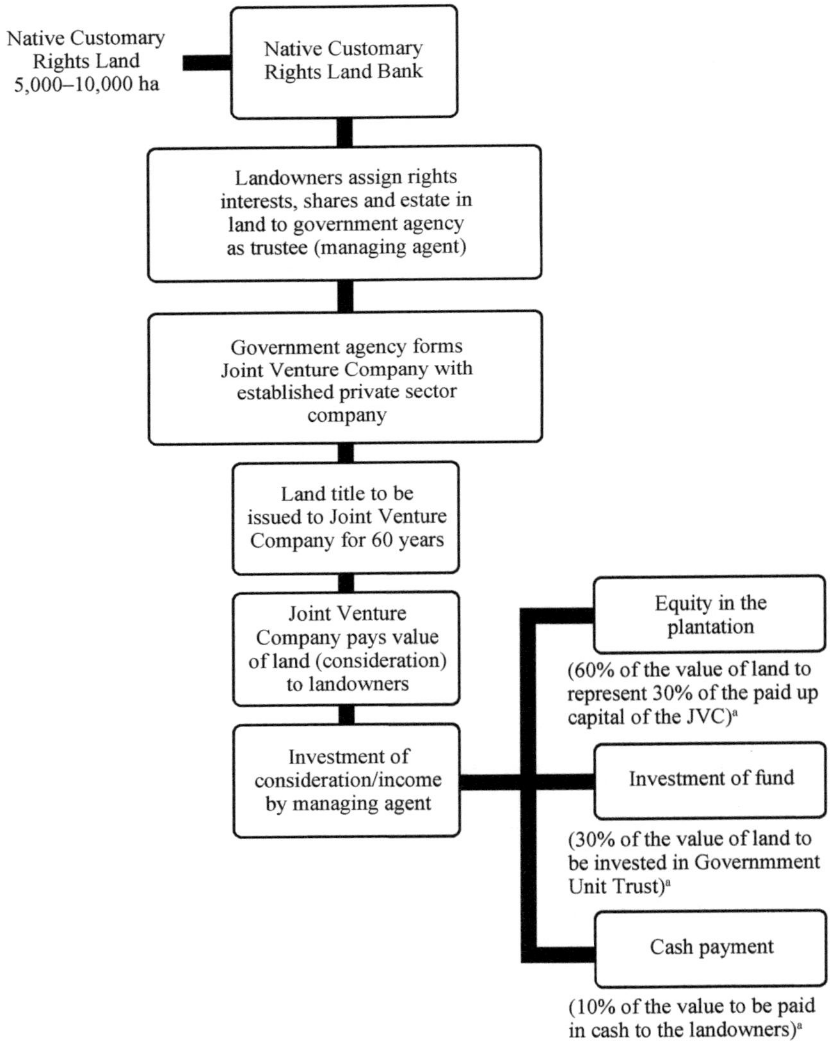

Note. a: The percentage of distribution indicated above may vary according to the value of the land, the cost of the project and its debt ratio.
Source: Department of Land Development

Plate 6.1 Oil-palm plantation under construction (1997)

Top: After felling and burning the secondary forests, the developers make terraces on the steep land to plant the oil palm seedlings. Bottom: Nurseries of oil palm seedlings are made on flat land.

the title to the native land would be issued in the name of the Joint Venture Company. Although the title is limited to a set term of sixty years, this seems like too long a period considering that oil palms only produce oil for twenty-five to thirty years. I feel that, since the land is valuable property for the Iban, the management of land resources should be put into their hands. The proposed scheme could very well end up depriving the Iban of their land. All ambiguity regarding the land's management should be scrupulously eliminated from the plantation scheme, and it should be modified to clearly stipulate the rights of landholders.

Plate 6.2 *Anjong nama* (Going to the District Office to file candidacy for the State Assembly at the Kanowit District Office) (1996)[17]

In the view of the Iban, most large-scale development projects have been closely related to land problems. Aside from their infrastructural benefits, large-scale projects such as irrigation systems and commercial plantations, involve sensitive issues of land management, which almost inevitably cause conflicts between residents and developers, or sometimes even among the local residents themselves.

Most of the land in the interior of Sarawak is categorized as Native Customary Land, where no legal land title is issued. Indeed, indigenous peoples are allowed to utilize a parcel of land based on *adat* (custom), so long as they can prove that the land was cleared by themselves or by their ancestors before 1958. These customary rights notwithstanding, the land law of Sarawak provides that native land 'legally' belongs to the Sarawak government. There is a general feeling of unrest among the Iban over this situation of dual land 'ownership.' They worry that the government, in the name of development projects might unfairly utilize 'their' land, or that their customary rights to use the land, might even be taken away from them. Plantation projects, in particular, exacerbate this feeling of unease because of the requirement that the land title be issued in the name of the Joint Venture Company. Thus the independent candidate's articulation of these issues accurately represents the vague feeling of unease over the security of the Iban's land rights.[18]

Meanwhile in the government-controlled press, the independent candidate was portrayed as objecting to the plantation scheme and of interfering with the

Plate 6.3 Going home by car at big events (1996)[19]

economic development of rural areas.[20] This of course was a distortion because the candidate was never against the plantation scheme itself. Indeed, he had tried to promote a commercial oil-palm plantation in the same area in cooperation with a private developer, instead of depending on a government agency. From the latter part of 1993 and into 1994, the independent candidate gathered people from the longhouses in the affected area to discuss the land issue.[21]

Although the independent candidate of the Machan constituency was considered an exceptional person who could challenge the incumbent on even terms, he lost by a majority of 4619 to 2389.[22] For the indigenous voters in the Machan area, the 1996 election seemed to offer two choices; they could either support the independent candidate and remain in relative poverty, unless they

Plate 6.4 Election campaign posters on the wall of the *ruai* in Longhouse A (1996)

Plate 6.5 Voting in the village (1996)[23]

themselves found a way to pursue the 'development' without any government subsidy, or they could vote for the incumbent from the party in power knowing that without any government subsidy they would face economic stagnation, even though many voters were suspicious of the government. One can interpret that the defeat of the independent candidate was simply because the people selected the latter choice. But the question now arises, did they really have a choice?

Another interpretation emerged from interviews with those who favored the independent candidate. Some of the people who voted for this candidate did not see a clear separation between the Government party and the opposition. Indeed, some of the people who supported the independent candidate half expected that if he had won the election, the party in power would have invited him to join their party in a few years, and in that position he would have been able to deliver government patronage to his supporters. This view was held by a supporter of this candidate, who when interviewed stated:

> Even if our candidate loses the election, we will be treated coldly by the government, only for a few years until the next election period. If he wins this election, on the other hand, he will be invited to align with a party in the alliance, in which case our 'return' will be bigger.

There had been other similar instances where an independent candidate joined the parties in power after being elected. During my interview with those close to the independent candidate, they mentioned another oil-palm plantation in the Sarikei district where (according to them) the local residents had been able to establish land ownership after the land had been developed by the government agencies, and they believed that the plantation in their district could very well follow this precedent. Aside from the issue of land ownership, they contended that there was not much difference between their attitude towards land development and the government policy. This reinforced their belief that the independent candidate would have probably joined the party in power.

My interviews revealed that the supporters of the independent candidate were not just expressing their opposition to the government policy or throwing their votes away on a candidate who could not possibly win; rather, they regarded their action as a pragmatic and expedient method of defiance against the government in order to make inroads into the power structure and derive greater benefits from the government in the near future. It can be said, however, that their attitude made the incumbent candidate feel insecure about his seat, thus forcing him to negotiate and offer concessions to the voters.

Management of land resources

The political episode described in the previous sub-section is very revealing from the perspective of understanding land management and urban-rural relations. The incident provides a window through which we can clearly observe the Iban's changing perception of land management. This event raised the Iban's awareness of land 'ownership.' Most of the Iban who stood behind the independent candidate were not against the plantation scheme itself, but were ready to approve the scheme only if land title could have been issued to individual landowners. During the election campaign there was no discussion at all regarding land resources from the viewpoint of conserving the natural environment. I also found very few people who objected to the scheme on the basis of wanting to conserve their own farmland.[24]

In addition to Soda (1999), Chapter 4 described how the residents in the longhouse communities of the Kanowit district utilize their land for planting

Plate 6.6 A Longhouse meeting in the *ruai* (1997)

paddies within very narrow spaces, and the rubber trees covering all the hilly areas have been left untapped for many years. Currently, very few people earn their livelihood by small-scale agriculture alone. Most people rely on their modest pensions, occasional contract work, and financial assistance from their children. Planting oil-palm trees on their 'underutilized' land would therefore not immediately threaten their livelihood. Indeed, many Iban concede that it is unproductive to leave their land idle.

The idea that their land is 'underutilized' seems incompatible with the organic cycle of traditional shifting cultivation that requires a fairly long fallow period.[25] Regarding land utilization, the residents seem to place more emphasis on the economic value of their land in the modern sense. If that is the case, it is only natural that they would attempt to establish a legal basis for their occupation or ownership based on customary law, before agreeing to a large-scale development project on the land. This attitude can be considered to be a manifestation of their heightened awareness about notions of land ownership.

The second point that needs to be made in this context is that those playing a leading role in the management of land or in the decision-making that is involved in the disposal of land are not necessarily the longhouse dwellers. Even though some parcels of land in the villages around the town of Kanowit are already registered in the names of individual villagers, the actual title deeds are often kept by their children, who live in the cities, not by the villagers themselves.

This accounts for the fact that when important meetings are held in the villages regarding the disposition of land, one can observe many town dwellers present at the 'longhouse meetings.'[26]

In 1998, when questionnaires regarding the disposition of land were distributed to individual villagers, or when villagers were considering whether to sign contracts permitting development of land for the oil-palm plantation, most of them called their relatives or children in the city to ask their advice. These relatives who reside in urban areas are very influential in the decision-making process of longhouse communities, as will be illustrated in the next section.

Leadership of longhouse communities and rural–urban interactions

Town dwellers as opinion leaders

The independent candidate for the assemblyman position of the Machan constituency in the 1996 election was an executive in a foreign-affiliated company in the town of Miri. During the election campaign he established his headquarters in Longhouse A in Rantau Kemiding, Kanowit District and set out on a campaign tour throughout the constituency. His important supporters were retired officials (former teachers, policemen, soldiers, and so on) in the longhouses and clerks in private companies who, though they generally lived in urban areas, took time off to come back to the village during the campaign. Working behind the scenes were low-ranking government officials on active duty in urban areas.[27] Although these people do not hold any positions in political parties, the villagers nevertheless expect them to provide informal connections with the political network. Under the direction of these people, the canvassing tour for the independent candidate was arranged.

In short, during the 1996 election period, the urban dwellers from the longhouses and the villagers, who had lived in urban areas for prolonged periods, played a critical role as opinion leaders in the longhouse communities. Indeed, the influence of these people in rural communities extends beyond the occasional events such as elections. Their influence is apparent from the fact that the head of a longhouse community (*tuai rumah*) is sometimes found to reside not in the longhouse but in an adjacent city.

My interviews with one hundred and thirty-two household heads in the resettlement area in Sibu (Kg. Sentosa) revealed the presence of six incumbent *tuai rumahs*[28] and two ex-*penghulus* (chief of a certain domain). These people make frequent trips back and forth between Sibu and their longhouse in the country. During their periods of absence from the longhouse, their duties are taken over by an official in the rural branch of the party, a local teacher,[29] a councilor in the district, or by an ex-*penghulu*. This is partly because in rural areas even capable people or those with good education have little access to job opportunities in the private sector, but only in the public sector. Another reason is that those who are in the public sector for example public servants, *penghulus*, and local councilors, come under the control of the government. At present this also means that they are actually appointed by the Sarawak government, and not surprisingly, most of them are proponents of the government.[30] From the village standpoint, these people represent channels of access to the government, or at least to the local branches of Government parties. These locally influential people also move regularly between town and country in much the same way as the *tuai rumahs*.

The longhouse community in Rantau Kemiding, which served as the base for the independent candidate during the 1996 election period, was branded as anti-government. Within the community there was divided opinion about whether or not to support him. When the then *tuai rumah* handed over his position to the defeated independent in 1999, the new leader tried to reunify the community and resume access to the government by emphasizing the proportion of pro-government supporters within the community and by allotting important roles to those who could maintain close ties with the wider society beyond the village. Among the reassembled members of the JKKK or Village Development and Safety Committee, the chairperson of the committee (*tuai rumah*) was the head of a company who usually lived in the town of Miri, the vice-chairperson was a one-time schoolmaster, the secretary was a teacher still actively teaching, and the treasurer was a public servant (a driver for a state-operated hospital). Other positions including chairmanships of seven bureaus[31] were assigned to two government employees (a soldier and a staff member of the Public Works Department), two former government employees (a policeman and a staff member of the Agriculture Department), two former teachers (one of whom had also served as a councilor of the Kanowit District), and one woman without any previous work experience (her late husband had been a state assemblyman, and she herself chaired the women's committee of the Kanowit Catholic Church).

As observed above, community leaders do not necessarily stay in their longhouse all of the time. The key qualities of a leader are not only their ability to maintain harmony within the community but also to maintain close connections in the society, especially to the parties in power.[32] Thus, longhouse communities do not necessarily choose their leaders from among the longhouse dwellers. They tend to support leaders—regardless of their current place of residence—who can link the rural to the urban, or the longhouse community to the local assemblymen.

Moving between rural and urban areas

Early in this chapter it was mentioned that among the one hundred and thirty-two interviewed household heads, seventy-three persons (55.3 percent) stated their intention to retire in the longhouse, and nineteen persons (14.4 percent) wished to maintain their residence both in the longhouse and in town, and more than half of these already enjoyed this 'double residence' status. Among these one hundred and thirty-two household heads, 75 percent visit their home village at least once a year, and 34.8 percent come back to the village almost every month.

It is easy to understand that these tendencies are a reflection of the Iban's migratory or nomadic traditions. Yet they also emphasize that it is important for them to establish residences in both urban areas and the longhouse community in order to participate in various kinds of activities and to assert their rights on behalf of the village. In other words, their frequent movement back and forth between the town and the longhouse is motivated by a desire to make their lives, to some degree, more stable, and to also link their urban activities with those of the longhouse at the level of ordinary life.

Most interior areas of Sarawak still have no telephone or newspaper delivery service. Even though television sets are becoming increasingly popular with the diffusion of power generators, there is no Sarawak-based TV station. Except for message-exchanging programs provided by local radio stations, there is no form of mass media that provides information relevant to the daily lives of people in the interior. Therefore, the frequent return of urban dwellers to the village provides valuable opportunities for the longhouse communities to acquire information about what is going on in the wider world. The return of those with political access is especially important considering the central role of the Government parties in authorizing rural development projects that are crucial to the development of the longhouse communities.

Over the last decade, the Sarawak government has frequently emphasized its goal of distributing funds not with an 'urban bias' but to support rural development, a message that is directed specifically toward the non-Muslim *bumiputera*, who make up the vast majority of the inhabitants in the interior. In other words, the government is acknowledging those excluded from the earlier urban-biased development policy and is attempting to quell discontent through the distribution of government subsidies to the rural population. Some Iban are forgiving and appreciate the government's attitude. Yet considering that many Iban intend to establish homes in both urban and rural regions and constantly move back and forth between city and country in a never-ending quest for development funds and subsidies, it is almost meaningless to sort out winners (beneficiaries) from losers in the 'development game' in relation to rural–urban disequilibrium.

Although acquisition of a legal lot in Sibu guarantees their right to permanent residence in the city, many Iban in the research area feel it would be difficult to continue to live in town after retirement, and expect to move back to the longhouse. This perception reinforces their political behavior in maintaining both a current residence in town and a future living base back in the longhouse. Their mobility such as manifested in return voting from urban to rural areas and their ingratiating behavior toward the Government parties can be viewed as deliberate strategies for securing government subsidies and funding for development projects. Even when they appeared to challenge the party in power, the intention of the Iban was to make inroads into the power structure and derive certain benefits from this greater access. Thus it is inappropriate and a gross simplification to consider the Iban's 'fawning attitude' (which Ngidang (1995) refers to as a 'subsidy syndrome') as nothing but a blind and haphazard pursuit of subsidies.

Conclusion

Since the 1970s, Southeast Asian countries have been trying to replace class struggles or conflicts over the distribution of resources with a 'national consensus of economic growth' by emphasizing the priority of 'development' (Shiraishi 1994). In order to grasp the meaning of development policy in the context of Southeast Asia, where countries typically have multi-ethnic societies, it is also important to focus on the response of each ethnic group to the politics of development.

The political behavior of the Iban regarding development projects seems to be a pragmatic response calculated to obtain optimal economic benefit. It may be possible to explain their behavior with the concept of 'everyday forms of resistance' conceived by Scott (1985), however, I would argue that Iban behavior, as described in this chapter, differs from Scott's concept in at least two respects. Firstly, the objectives of Iban activities go well beyond the mere level of subsistence. Rather than viewing their activities as passive and low profile tactics to minimize their disadvantage, I see their behavior in a more positive light as a struggle to maximize their own interests, albeit within a limited range of choices. Secondly, although they may exhibit some signs of resistance in their day-to-day efforts to gain benefits, it is clear that their primary efforts to gain advantages are through legitimate political means such as influencing elections.

Their strategies are not limited to such low-profile techniques as dissimilation, foot-dragging, pilfering, and feigned ignorance. Rather, their strategies are both more active and more varied; they sometimes act in compliance with government policies, they sometimes withdraw economic benefits from unconnected constituencies by moving their voter registration place, and they sometimes show temporary defiance towards the government in order to penetrate the power structure. These strategies take on a very different aspect from 'everyday forms of resistance.'

What should be emphasized here is that the key actors of these various efforts are mobile urban dwellers that frequently move back and forth between the town and the village. Their proactive efforts to secure economic benefits are sometimes reflected in the transfer of their voting registration from one constituency to another. This act could have an impact on the allocation of development funds that are politically motivated to redress regional disparity.

These urban Iban, as a result of their great mobility and their role as opinion leaders in the longhouse communities, act as intermediaries between longhouse residents and politicians or between 'vulnerable peasants' and development politics. In this sense, the urban dwellers play a pivotal role by involving the longhouse communities in political interaction. At the same time we cannot simply regard the longhouse residents as passive observers of the political scene. As mentioned in the previous sections, the longhouse residents themselves choose their leaders from among those who live in urban areas and have access to politicians. Thus, indirectly the local rural folk also take some initiative in trying to involve themselves in the politics of development .

In this chapter, I have discussed the issue of resource distribution in Sarawak, by using the indigenous people residing in urban areas as the focus of analysis. Regarding these people as the intermediary between urban and rural areas was useful for reconsidering the dichotomy between notions of the development state and 'vulnerable peasants,' and between urban-biased development and 'ruralism.'

It is certain that this population has been increasing along with economic growth, promotion of development projects, and the spread of urbanization. Although the Iban are still in a marginalized position in Malaysian society, the range of their social and political activities is constantly expanding. It will thus become increasingly important to focus greater attention on the political roles of marginalized peoples in urban areas—ethnic minorities, the urban poor, the so-called urban villagers, and so on—in the years ahead. This is all the more pressing considering that rural development is held up as one of the important political goals of the nation-state in many Third World countries. A deeper understanding of this subject is also essential in discussing the relationship between development policy and ethnicity in the Third World.

7
Iban City Dwellers and Rural Property

Introduction

As has been mentioned, the prevailing image of the Iban is as a people who live in the forests of Sarawak and practice slash-and-burn agriculture. Their traditional residence, the longhouse, has also attracted the attention of both tourists and scholars alike. In recent years, however, the number of Iban residing in cities has rapidly increased, and it is reasonable to assume that the proportion of Iban people living in urban areas has risen over the last few years (Figure 7.1).

As mentioned previously, the Iban began to migrate out of villages in significant numbers in the 1960s, when the timber and oil industries were undergoing rapid growth. During this period the first waves of Iban men left the village in pursuit of wage-earning jobs in these sectors (Sutlive 1992; Kedit 1993; Morrison 1993) and a considerable number of the migrants began to stay in the cities. The 1980s saw a major change in these labor migration trends, single men continued to leave, but a growing number of them began moving to the cities in family units rather than on their own—that is, the men started taking their wives and children with them. At the same time, job opportunities in the cities began to diversify. This trend has been described in some detail in the previous chapters.

Building on this discussion, Chapter 5 utilized data collected in Kg. Sentosa Resettlement Scheme, Sibu, to examine and elucidate how the urban Iban have maintained their ties with their longhouse communities. The Iban living in Kg. Sentosa mostly migrated to the town of Sibu in the 1970s and the 1980s from neighboring districts and divisions. Most of the people interviewed had stable jobs—especially in the government sector—although some were engaged in side businesses in the informal sector. They had seemingly adapted to urban life. As we observed in Chapter 6, however, the Iban in Kg. Sentosa kept moving back and forth between Sibu and surrounding rural areas, and planned to return to the original village or longhouse in the future. The political bargaining processes relating to rural development also motivated those who moved back and forth between the locations frequently. Since most of the government-led development projects need important rural property, land and its transfer and redistribution have become significant issues for the Iban.

Figure 7.1 Population rate of Iban in the urban areas

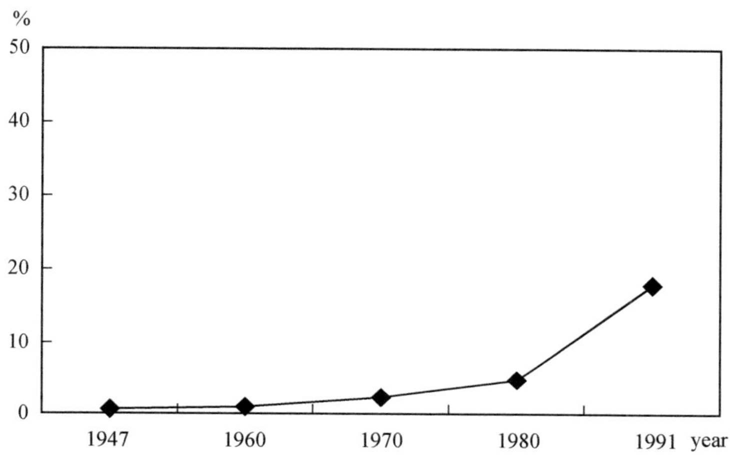

In recent years, the Iban have developed a sharper sense of land ownership and become more aware of development policy. Even those who now reside in the cities but plan to return to their longhouse after retirement, are paying more attention to the recent rise in the economic value of land, as land inheritance and *bilek* succession are closely related. As discussed in Chapter 6, however, many of them have not yet decided whether they will return to the original longhouse of the husband or the wife. Some interviewees intended to choose a 'double residence' to maintain a base both in Sibu and in their original longhouse. How is this noncommittal sense of belonging among urban Iban related to land development in rural areas? This chapter clarifies these points by examining the Iban's broad interpretation of the *bilek*-family and the changes in their concept of land ownership.

Noncommittal sense of belonging

Belonging to the longhouse community?

In Sarawak, the smaller units of administrative organization, such as the longhouse and the village, are based on personal principles. Each village and longhouse does not have a clear administrative boundary of its territory, and is not subordinate to administrative demarcation. The affiliation of a person to a specific community is relatively dependent on his or her relationship to the household head and the longhouse head. Moreover, in the case of the Iban, the name of a village (longhouse) changes frequently because a longhouse is usually named after its head.[1] In this sense, personal principles are more important than territorial or spatial ones in the administration of Sarawak.

Malaysia does not have a system of family registration or resident cards. Each adult resident is supposed to possess an identification card (ID card) that shows an address, but this does not restrain a person from living at a different address. They can also change their voting place regardless of their address on their ID card. In this sense, it is difficult to define which administrative unit people actually belong to.

In Sarawak, the largest territorial unit of administration is the division, and this unit is divided into districts, some of which have sub-districts within the territory. Divisions, districts, and sub-districts all have geographical boundaries. Conversely, the smallest unit of administrative organization has as its head either a *tuai rumah* (the head of an Iban longhouse), a *ketua kampung* (the head of a Malay village), or a *kapitan Cina* (the head of a Chinese community in certain regions). These so-called villages are components of a larger unit under the chief of a particular domain, such as a *penghulu* or *pemanca*. However, the heads and chiefs at these levels do not necessarily preside over a well-defined geographical territory. Indeed, most villages and longhouse communities are aware of the village territory and have established a rough consensus on their boundaries with neighboring villages, but there are no administrative records of these boundaries. Therefore, if different ethnic groups coexist in a certain area, each group is administered by a head from the same ethnic group. In some cases, the *penghulu* or *pemanca* administers a wide range of communities across district boundaries. Thus, the head of a village or the chief of a certain area is not necessarily subordinate to the administrative district.

Conversely, an Iban can 'belong to a longhouse community' or 'be under a *tuai rumah*' even if he or she actually resides a long way from the longhouse or the village. Iban people can remain as a member of their longhouse community regardless of their current residence as long as they meet specific conditions. Those who do not plan to live permanently in the cities are, to a greater or lesser extent, in preparation for shifting their main living base back to the longhouse community. Among the Iban, *bilek* is a property that is inherited by lineal descendants. It is not only a living space of a stem family but also the home to which to return when urban dwellers give up living in the city. Even if an Iban lives in the city, he or she can remain a member of a longhouse community so long as he or she maintains a *bilek* as a place to which to return.

In order to secure this living base in a longhouse, urban dwellers are expected to abide by Iban customs under the control of the head of the longhouse. According to Iban custom in the Rajang Basin, for example, if all members of a *bilek*-family reside in the city, they must return to the longhouse at least once a month and use the fire in the kitchen of their currently 'empty' *bilek*. If they are unable to do this for over a month, they have to pay a penalty—usually some fowls or a small amount of money—to the head of the longhouse. In other words, even if the whole *bilek*-family lived in the city, the members of the family could retain their membership of the longhouse community by abiding by the customary obligations.

Villagers in the city?

Since those who live in urban areas can remain members of the longhouse community as long as they meet certain specified conditions, these people could be termed 'villagers in the cities.' This term is reminiscent of the concept of 'urban villagers' coined by Gans (1962), but the use of the term has the connotation that rural-to-urban migrants and their settlements, are a major source of social problems (Fujimaki 1993). This represents a biased view that is supportive of the urban administration. The Iban in Sibu did indeed live in squatter settlements, but in cooperation with other ethnic groups such as Malay, Melanau, and Chinese, they obtained 'legal' lots in the suburbs of Sibu through political negotiation with the urban administration and local political leaders. As for the jobs they hold in Sibu, many of them are engaged in the formal sector as government employees, policemen, company workers, and taxi drivers. In this sense, they are seemingly successful in adapting to urban life and behave like 'urbanites.' However, this study has not attempted to measure the degree of adaptability of these rural-to-urban migrants. The concept of 'villager' is raised in this chapter only to emphasize the viewpoint of those who remain in the rural villages. In other words, the issue in question is whether or not urban dwellers are recognized as community members by the longhouse residents.

Most of the Iban living in Kg. Sentosa, Sibu, maintain their membership of the longhouse community and also belong to the Kg. Sentosa JKKK (Village Development and Safety Committee). The JKKK is a people's organization that exists in every village in rural regions. In the case of the Iban community along the Rajang River, JKKK is usually composed of a longhouse community[2] and plays a role as the smallest unit in the administrative organization of the country. In urban settings, some residential areas such as Kg. Sentosa also have JKKKs, which function as neighborhood associations.

Iban people living in Kg. Sentosa belong to both the JKKK for their original longhouse and the JKKK for their current residence in Sibu; this dual membership is perhaps a reflection of their ambiguous sense of belonging. Their 'double belonging' could be interpreted as an opportunistic strategy for their own convenience. However, these apparently different identities may be very compatible for the Iban in Kg. Sentosa. Since this theme of identity and belonging is closely related to the broad interpretation of *bilek*-family by the Iban, it is discussed in more detail later in this chapter.

'Occupation' of land and 'land ownership'

Before examining the relationship between the Iban concept of *bilek*-family and their sense of belonging, I will present an overview of land issues in rural areas. This is important because the nature of Iban attachment to rural land seems to influence their sense of belonging.

Land ownership

In the last section, the noncommittal or flexible sense of belonging among the Iban in Kg. Sentosa was emphasized. In this section, we will outline the process that has resulted in the emergence of strained relations among the Iban over ownership and use of land in the rural area.

It can be safely said that the most important rural property for the Iban—both for longhouse residents and urban sojourners—is land usufruct or the possessory right to land. Why is land so important to them, especially to urban dwellers? To answer this question, we have to take into consideration the processes and related concepts of modernization. I previously examined the evolving concept of land ownership among the Iban in Rantau Kemiding in the Kanowit District, and pointed out that their concept is now confusing because of the co-existence of different land institutions; that is, traditional customary land tenure and the modern land registration system (Soda 1999). According to Iban customary law, the first person to clear an area of primary forest was allowed to claim the right to use that parcel of land, and this preferential usufruct could be inherited by their lineal descendants. But now, a modern system of land registration has been partly introduced even in rural areas such as Rantau Kemiding (Figure 7.2), and this has stimulated awareness, among the Iban, of the economic value of land.

In recent years, substantial use of land for agriculture has been limited to smaller areas because of the reduction in dry paddy cultivation and rubber tapping. In Rantau Kemiding in Kanowit, for example, I conducted research on their socio-economic activities and found that in 1996 less than fifty percent of the working population was engaged in rice farming. As for rubber tapping, only a few *bilek*-families produced rubber sheets to earn cash money, and most of the rubber gardens in the area had been left unused for many years. In other words, longhouse residents have become less dependent on land in terms of subsistence, and more dependent on non-agricultural economic activities. When asked about land use, an old man in Rantau Kemiding, made a self deprecating comment:

Figure 7.2 State of registered and surveyed land in and around Rantau Kemiding Village

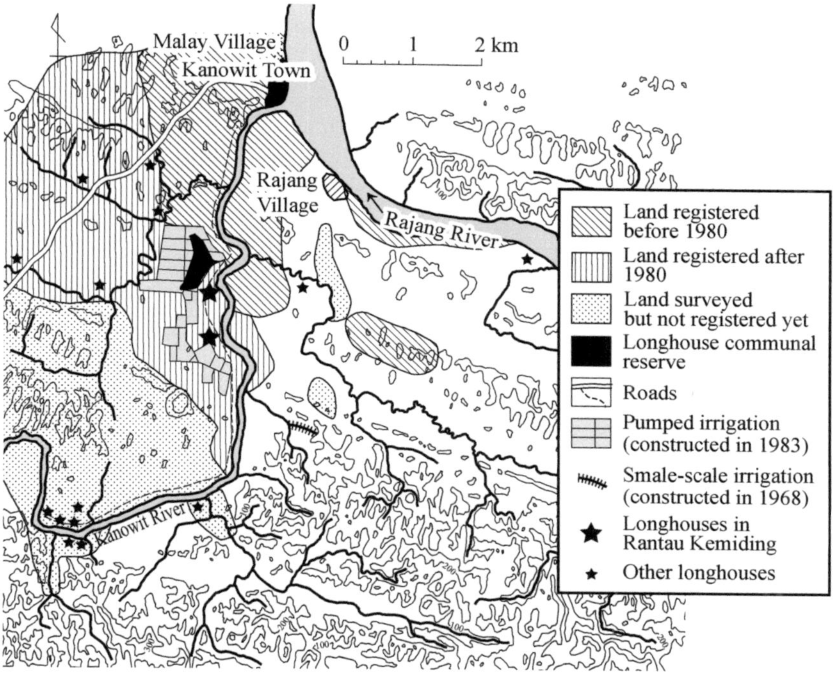

Source: Land and Survey Department, Sibu Branch, Sarawak

> We Iban are very rich in land, but we do not know how to use the land. We just planted paddies and rubber trees on our land, but after the market price of rubber fell down, we just left them untapped. Nowadays, secondary forests are also seldom used because we are largely dependent on wet paddy planting. Our land is left idle. What a waste! How can we catch up with the Chinese?

According to the Iban's traditional agricultural cycle, the land left unused was significant as fallow land, a process that would restore the fertility to the soil. However, even Iban people in rural areas have become aware of the economic value of land and now tend to see unused land as 'wasteful.'

In addition, when feeder roads were built to the area and an irrigation system was introduced in the village in the 1980s (see Figure 7.2), many of the Rantau Kemiding residents obtained cash money in compensation for land development and became aware that land can generate cash through selling and leasing. They also know that recent land development projects—large-scale plantations in particular—have accelerated the move to commercial land use, even on Native Customary Land[3] in the interior. According to this trend, in recent years, the Iban in Rantau Kemiding have become conscious of land ownership in the modern sense—instead of traditional and loose possessory rights to land—which they think is useful for securing exclusive rights to land and for the potential of making a profit through future land development. In other words, the Iban concept of land 'usufruct' has changed and is moving towards a narrower concept of 'ownership.'

Land registration

The difference between land 'usufruct' and 'ownership' is defined in this book as follows: land usufruct is the right to use, manage, and inherit a parcel of land based on Iban customary law. Under the Land Code 1958, indigenous people are allowed to follow their customary land law to maintain their rights to customary land that was cleared before 1958, while they are prohibited from transferring or granting the land to non-indigenous people. This land is called 'Native Customary Land' in the Land Code. On the other hand, 'land ownership' is guaranteed by registering a parcel of land in the name of individuals or associations at the Land and Survey Department. Land ownership in this sense includes the right to dispose of the land concerned. In short, to acquire ownership of a parcel of land, the Iban have to register it in accordance with the modern land law of Sarawak.[4]

The Iban recognize at least two effects of land registration. Firstly, they think that they can protect their own land from land disputes between longhouse communities or between *bilek*-families by clearly demarcating individual lots through the land registration process. Secondly, they believe that they can avoid forfeiture of land rights, even when government-led development projects are carried out in the area.

Recently, not only minor rural development projects but also a number of large-scale development projects have been promoted in the Rajang Basin. Indeed, many Iban in the area expect development projects to trigger improvements in rural life, while others distrust the Government and the developers, believing that they are likely to use vast tracts of land inappropriately. Some people know successful development cases such as the oil-palm plantations in Seratok, and hope for the implementation of large-scale plantation developments in their own area. However, the lack of accurate and trustworthy information among the Iban has often caused some confusion. The Iban in the mid-Rajang area are now afraid that under the name of a 'development project' they may be deprived of unregistered land that is still categorized as Native Customary Land. In this context, they consider that land title deeds will provide a shield against forfeiture of their land.

If a parcel of land deemed Native Customary Land is to be registered, the category of the land must be converted. Actually, the legal procedures required in these cases may discourage the Iban from registering the land. But what is more troubling for them is fixing the name of the landowner of this parcel of land. As was described above, the *bilek* order of succession and the inheritance of land often involve considerable ambiguity. This ambiguity has often functioned in a way that avoids succession disputes, from at least appearing on the surface. However, recent developments make it more difficult to leave this ambiguity unresolved.

Who is the landowner?

As mentioned above, some parcels of land in the hilly interior areas have already been registered at the Land and Survey Department. Obviously, those who have acquired land titles are keenly aware of the economic value of land and the concept of land ownership. However, nowadays even those who do not have title are forced to be sensitive to vagaries of land ownership.

There have been recent proposals for several large-scale plantations—mainly oil palm—in the Rajang area. In the planned plantation areas in Kanowit, for example, the Government carried out a survey of landholdings and customary usufruct prior to the implementation of the development project. However, the land survey undertaken was not for the purpose of issuing land titles in the rural residents' names. In Kanowit, the development companies are supposed to become the titleholders of the plantation and a portion of the interest will be distributed to the original 'usufruct' holders (see Figure 6.1 in Chapter 6). The main purpose of the land survey was to determine the compensation for land development and the dividend of future profit.

In the research undertaken for this work, the questionnaires distributed to every *bilek*-family during the survey required them to enter the names of individuals (or joint names) to show the current occupier of each parcel of land. In doing so, the Iban were forced to reconfirm who were the occupiers of the land in question, as many of them had left the land of their parents or *bilek*-family undivided among their siblings. In other words, family members were forced to reach a consensus on the division and inheritance of their parents' land. When the questionnaires were distributed in the research area, many town dwellers were summoned home for family meetings on the subject. They also spent a lot of time involved in the longhouse meetings.

The participants of the survey were required to fill in a questionnaire for each parcel of land, describing its location, approximate area, year opened, present usage, and the name of the occupier. Many *bilek*-families were perplexed about how to deal with the land of people who had died. Some *bilek*-families had not yet divided the land that had been opened up several generations ago and tracing the history of this land involved more than one *bilek*-family. Confirming the ownership of each parcel of land was thus a confusing and difficult process. As discussed above, however, a more modern concept of land ownership has recently been adopted by the Iban. Therefore, most of them thought it necessary to cope with the task of filling in the questionnaires, recognizing that their current loose and ambiguous concept of land usufruct—which sometimes belongs to the *bilek*-family—may be inadequate to maintain their land rights in the contemporary nation state. At present, the Iban require a clearer definition of an 'individual's land.' Thus, in contrast to their 'traditional' custom, which has been regarded as loose and vague on this concept, rigid perceptions about landholding and ownership have emerged and this change is affecting relationships between *bilek*-family members.

Ambiguity and rigidity of family membership

In order to continue with our exploration of the sense of belonging, concept of land ownership and land use and relationship to family, this section discusses the changing meaning of the 'family' and the 'household' in Iban society.

Various fields of research have long been interested in and explored the notion of rural space. Within the past decade or so, various disciplines have reexamined the concepts of 'rural village,' 'peasantry,' and the 'rural household.' One of the most important questions is whether urban sojourners can be regarded as members of the original household in their home village.[5] In relation to Iban society, we can use the so-called *bilek*-family (*se-bilek*) as a unit of analysis to reconsider the concepts of family and household. A *se-bilek* is usually composed of people who 'live together' in a *bilek* and it is recognized as a managing unit in swidden agriculture. Previous studies called this unit the *bilek*-family. However, with the increase in the number of urban sojourners, the Iban have begun to interpret the concept of *se-bilek* more broadly.

Chapters 5 and 6 described the lives of those Iban who migrated to Sibu, obtained legal residential lots, and established stable residences in a resettlement scheme. This indicated that they had set up households independently of their parents in the home village. This unit is indeed calculated as a household in official statistics. In Iban language, this unit is also often called a *se-bilek*. However, many urban Ibans are not independent of the parent *bilek* in the customary sense. In this case, parents may consider that a child's household in the city is still part of the parent's *se-bilek* in the longhouse.

The *se-bilek* is principally composed of a stem family and each generation includes only one married couple (Figure 7.3).

Figure 7.3 Conventional reproduction of a *bilek*

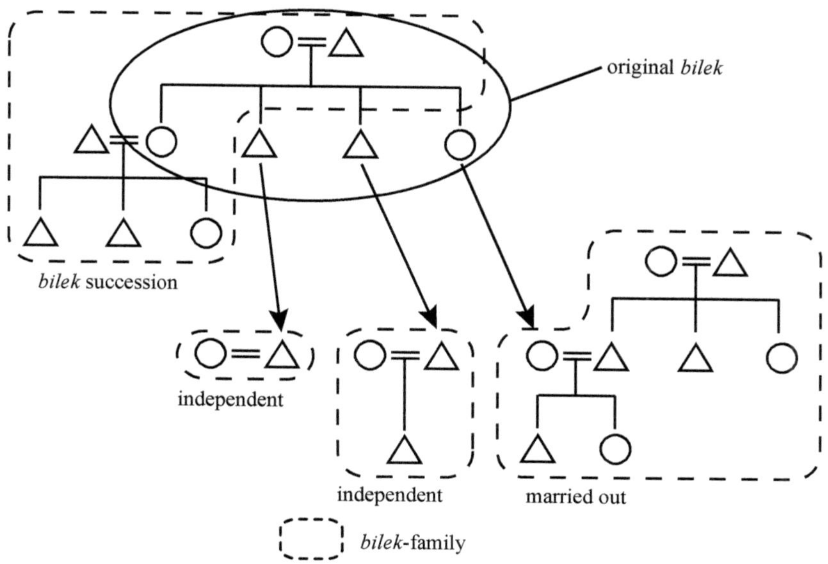

In other words, the parent *bilek* is supposed to be succeeded by a married couple that remains in the *bilek*. In Iban language, leaving home and moving to the spouse's *bilek* on marriage is called *ngugi* or *nguai*. When adult children leave the original *bilek* to get married and set up home on their own, they are considered to be independent (*kediri*). When this occurs, the person marrying out ceases to be a member of the original *bilek*-family. However, it is often unclear whether married couples in the cities are now affiliated to, or independent of the parent *bilek*. From the viewpoint of the parents, multiple households set up by their children can be included in the parent *bilek* (Figure 7.4a). Conversely, it is considered that married couples in the cities retain the potential to inherit the parent *bilek* on either the husband or wife's side (Figure 7.4b).

Thus, although many urban Ibans intend to return to the village after retirement, they take an equivocal attitude towards their affiliation and put off making a decision about whether to succeed to the parent *bilek*. In this sense, their lives in the cities represent a kind of 'moratorium' or 'reprieve' before making a decision about the succession order of the parent *bilek* and the inheritance of rural property. If they return to the village, they have to decide whether to stay in the parent *bilek* or set up a new *bilek* of their own. However, while they are living outside their villages, the Iban do not have to relinquish membership of the parent *bilek* on either the husband's or wife's side; they

Figure 7.4 Broad interpretation of *se-bilek*

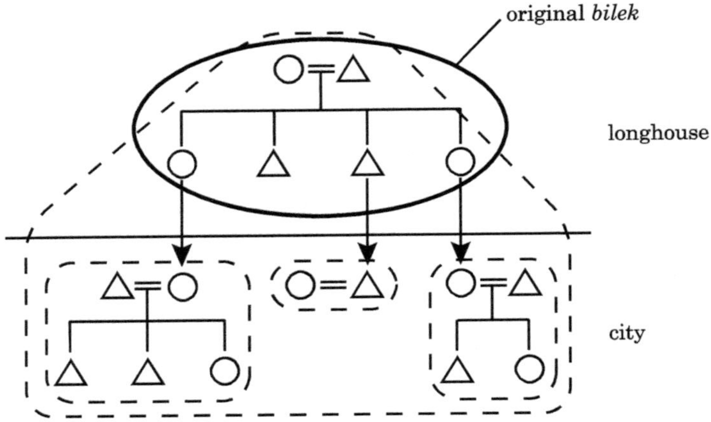

Fig. 7.4a From the parent's view

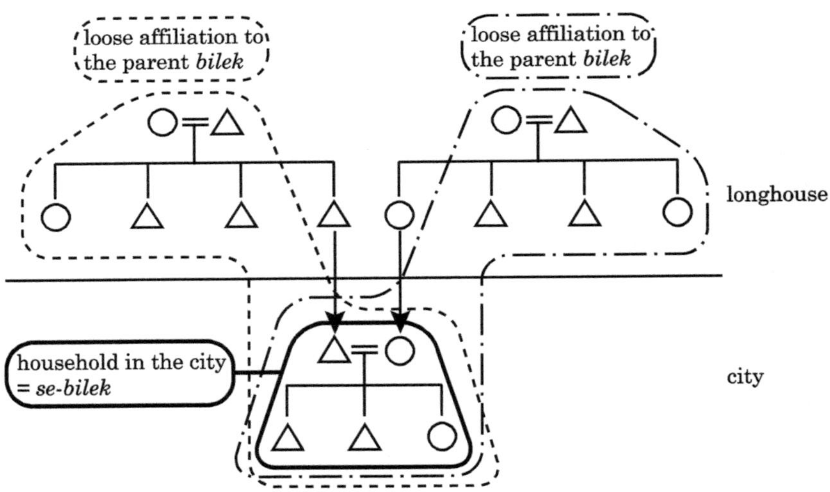

Fig. 7.4b From the child's view

remain loosely affiliated to both. During the long 'reprieve' in the cities, they can consider what position they should choose in their *bilek*-families and villages of origin. In other words, they have tended to broadly interpret their customary structures to suit their own needs.

These loose and ambiguous relationships between family members, however, are gradually becoming more difficult to maintain—a situation closely related to the changing attitudes and processes of defining land ownership. With part of the land in the village being registered, the Iban have begun to be aware of land ownership in the modern sense; moreover, recent development programs have required them to develop a more rigid concept of an 'individual's land.' The Iban often decide who should succeed their parents' *bilek* or how to portion out their parents' land among the children in the last stage of their parents' lives (Uchibori 1996). This ambiguity underlies their urban living patterns and their broad interpretation of the *bilek*-family. However, the task of defining a portion of land and its ownership has forced them to confirm individual inheritance rights among family members. Because of this, some urban Iban feel pressured to seriously consider their future plans or to decide where to affiliate after retirement resulting in a more pressured and stressful encounter for some of them.

Thus, as was described in Chapters 5 and 6, we could conclude that urban Iban have developed a long-term life plan based on a broad interpretation of their tradition and customs. However, rural development programs and the modern concepts of land ownership make such a broad interpretation untenable and their opportunistic attempts to maintain convenient relationships with the parent *bilek* may come to naught. The surfacing of family succession and land inheritance problems is straining kinship relations between parents and adult children and between siblings within the Iban population, which is now split between those still living in rural communities and those living in the cities.

Conclusion

It is easy to foresee a rising trend in the size of the Iban urban population. The functions of kinship ties are still essential factors in explaining their rural-to-urban migration, their lives in the cities, and their relations with the longhouse communities. It is also true that, relations between family or household members and their meaning for individuals are gradually changing, largely influenced by contemporary political and economic factors. This change is affecting the decision-making process of the Iban in relation to migration and their urban lives.

When we look at changes in the pattern of Iban migration between rural and urban areas in recent years, they do not fit neatly within the old framework of 'rural-to-urban migration' and 'return migration,' nor are they easily understood from the viewpoint of the migration decision-making process or 'push/pull factors.'

This chapter has described the changing ties between rural and urban dwellers, focusing on the administration of rural property, that is, the *bilek* and the land. Iban city dwellers are seeking and exploring 'better' relations with their parents and siblings not only to improve their current urban existence but also to secure a future life in the village. They constantly re-interpret family relations and revise their life plans to improve their living environment in both settings. This is reflected in the urban Iban's 'double residence,' 'double belonging,' or noncommittal sense of belonging. In this sense, their living strategies can be seen as an attempt to expand their living space between the two areas, the rural and the urban.

This potential expansion of living space is based on the ambiguity of relations between urban sojourners and the longhouse community of their origin. However, the expansion in a modern sense of land ownership and a rise in the economic value of land may create strains in their family relations, which are incompatible with the 'flexibility' of Iban society. What is important here is that the Iban in the study area clearly recognize the effectiveness of modern land ownership and try to incorporate these modern concepts into their traditional custom. In this sense, the discordance between the modern and traditional concepts of land within the Iban population is one of the inevitabilities of the modernization process and may present a temporary challenge for them.

Part III

8
A Focus on the Movers: Research Trends in Rural–Urban Relations in the Third World

Part II of this book presented a new ethnography of the Iban in the contemporary context by describing their mobility and living strategies from both a rural and urban perspective. What was elucidated in these chapters can be summarized as follows: 1) with regards to the Iban of the research area, their out-migration significantly affected changes in their agricultural practice as well as the structure of their longhouse community; 2) the Iban in Sibu maintained their ties with the longhouse community of their origin in order to prepare for their future return upon retirement; 3) rural-to-urban migrants have realized, to some extent, the improvement of their urban lives in the town of Sibu through their interaction with other ethnic groups and with the urban administration; 4) urban dwellers illustrated various patterns of movement, especially during election periods, for the purpose of improving the economic situation of their village of origin; 5) intervention of urban dwellers in rural development led to changes in family relations and more broadly in rural society itself; and 6) the Iban in the research area endeavored to expand their living space and embody a rural/urban continuum at the individual level. All of these features were directly or indirectly connected to urban society, national politics and the world economy.

The description of their lives in both rural and urban areas has significance as a new ethnography of the Iban in the contemporary context. However, this case study should be reexamined within a theoretical framework, through which the Iban case can provide a key to articulate rural and urban perspectives beyond the dichotomy evident in many studies previously conducted. Chapter 1 in Part I, presented both an outline of the composition of this book as well as a brief introduction to the theoretical exploration of rural–urban relations. A more comprehensive description of Iban life in the modern context brings to our awareness that an extensive examination is required to explain the significance of this study within the body of literature on migration.

This chapter appraises the literature, focusing particularly on those studies that analyze topics related to migration in developing countries, and those works that have been written from rural and urban perspectives. These works reconfirm the significance of this study and we assert that the Iban case illustrates the articulation of rural and urban studies on migration.

Literature on rural change and the experience of the Iban

Diversification of lifestyles in rural areas

Rural change in the Third World has been the subject of a large number of studies in a range of academic disciplines. Topics have included urbanization and industrialization in rural areas, innovation in agricultural technology, changes in the distribution of rural products, and the deagrarianization of rural society. Most of these studies have made it clear that the penetration of capitalism and global economic systems in the post-colonial period have both directly and indirectly brought about socio-economic transformation of the rural sector in these societies. In general, field research on rural change has focused on the modernization of rural economies and the diversification of the means of earning a livelihood for rural households.

Although some historical studies on rural change in the Third World have been pessimistic about the vulnerability of rural peasants, resulting from the infiltration of world capitalism (Frank 1967), more recently a number of scholars have described the alternatives adopted by rural residents to improve their circumstances (Leones and Feldman 1998). Since the 1980s, in particular, researchers have attached importance to non-farm, off-farm or non-agricultural activities and have put a positive value on rural diversification (Shand 1986; Ranis and Stewart 1993; Leones and Feldman 1998; Lanjouw and Lanjouw 2001; Adams 2002). These researchers conclude that economic activity in rural areas has expanded beyond subsistence agriculture.

As for the Iban research case, in the process of settling down, wet paddy and other cash crops, especially rubber, were introduced into the longhouse community; developments which were both the cause and result of interaction with other ethnic groups such as the 'Whites' (the Catholic Church) and Chinese merchants. In rural areas in Sarawak, however, the opportunity for cash income in the non-farm sector has been very limited, encouraging the Iban to look for wage-earning jobs away from the village. In this sense, the increase in out-migration of the Iban in the 1960s can be considered as part of the same trend that occurred in general in many Southeast Asian countries. Therefore, whilst out-migration has been observed since this time in rural Southeast Asia, including the Iban longhouse communities, it was only in the 1980s that rural studies began to pay attention to the non-farm activities occurring outside of the villages.

While non-farm activity became a major theme of rural studies, Rigg (1998) pointed out that there was substantial diversification that occurred in rural economies at the time. Traditionally, rural activities were largely agricultural and even non-agricultural endeavors were based in and around the village. But today, the search for income diversity increasingly takes rural people out of farming and into locations 'beyond the village.' In the 1980s, when the 'green revolution' in the Third World attracted researchers' attention, it was thought that only wealthy farmers could take advantage of the new agricultural technology, and that the gap between rich and poor farmers would rapidly widen (Cederroth and Gerdin 1986). In many regions, however, these pessimistic expectations were not realized. Instead, scholars discovered that the diversification of village and household economies had allowed small farmers and small landowners to survive by achieving subsistence incomes both within and outside of the village (Rigg 1998).[1] Rigg also suggested that inequality of rural incomes in developing countries was not so much an outcome of the 'agrarian revolution' but rather a product of differential access to non-farm earnings.

As for the so-called Iban studies, researchers have paid considerable attention for some time now, to the custom of *bejalai*, and several scholars (for example Kedit 1993) examined the effects of *bejalai* activities on rural communities. However, as Iban *bejalai* was often described by emphasizing its cultural aspect, the discussion of their livelihood in relation to non-farm activities was not adequately explored or elaborated. In this sense, and perhaps not surprisingly, studies about the Iban share the same problems with the general area of study about rural livelihood in the Third World.

Non-farm activities outside of the village have become important characteristics of rural society in developing countries. Thus, the participation of the rural population in work away from the farm, often at a great distance, has been a major research topic in rural studies (Elmhirst 2002; Bounthong et al. 2004). In other words, recent rural changes cannot be adequately explained without paying attention to the livelihood strategies of individual rural households, which include non-farm activities in and beyond the village. What should be noticed in this research trend is that it has become difficult to define the rural population or household and assume the village boundary as a spatial unit of analysis.

Peasantry, farm village, rural household: rethinking existing concepts

Recent changes in rural society challenge us to reconsider the analytical unit used to evaluate socio-economic activities in rural areas. In the field of rural studies, a 'household' has long been perceived as the basic unit of agricultural activity and the basis for analyzing rural livelihoods. However, the concept of the household economy has been reconsidered by different disciplines that deal with the farm village (Wilk 1989; Koppel and Hawkins 1994).

In the latter half of the 1980s, population and family economics began to look at 'household resource allocation' in the rural Third World with the major theme being the effect of remittances from urban migrants on members of the rural household. For example, Lucas and Stark (1985) tried to assess the altruistic and selfish motives for these payments. In other studies, remittances were regarded as a long-term contract between parents and adult children, which took future inheritance into account (Stark and Lucas 1988; Hoddinott 1994).[2]

These studies emerged as a critique of 'unitary models.' For neoclassical economists, the significance of the farm household lay in its role as a unit of production, consumption and migration decision-making. Within such models, the household was viewed as having only one set of preferences and treated as a solid unit, undifferentiated by gender or age. The assumption of the joint utility function of the household has become the focus of growing criticism. For example, some economists have drawn on the game theory to construct 'bargaining models' of the household that incorporate both cooperation and conflict among household members. Other approaches, described as 'collective models' by Alderman et al. (1995), focused on the individuality of the household members and addressed the question of how individual preferences lead to collective choice, using cooperative and non-cooperative game theory, and theories based on the concept of a 'sharing rule' (Hart 1992, 1995; Haddad et al. 1997; Maggs and Hoddinott 1999). These studies have stimulated scholars to reconsider household and family models in the rural Third World. The problem is however, that attempts to develop new models of intra-household resource allocation have exceeded satisfactory empirical research.

In the field of cultural anthropology, too, the concept of the rural farm household has been reconsidered in the context of a growing demand for non-agricultural work as a sub-livelihood. Takada (1991) reviewed rural studies of the developing world, especially in relation to Bangladesh, and pointed out two problems. Firstly, he criticized previous studies for regarding the 'labor force in a farm village' as equal to the 'working population in the agricultural sector.'[3] This is because greater importance was attached to selective indices of the peasant stratum such as land holdings, land rights and agricultural output. Non-agricultural work and other side business of rural household members were unreasonably neglected. Secondly, the geographical range of research sites has been a priori limited to the village territory. Since the villagers are regarded as those people living in the village, individuals engaged in non-agricultural work, outside the village, are often neglected from the analysis.[4] However, most poor households cannot make a living without income from non-agricultural work or remittances from urban migrants (Takada 1991: 32).

In relation to the use of ambiguous concepts such as 'peasantry,' 'rural household' and 'farm village,' Koppel and Hawkins (1994) not only criticized scholars' preconceptions and biased views, but also pointed out different ways of classifying the statistics of these categories in different countries. Meanwhile, Hart (1992, 1995) questioned the notion of the farm household as a unit of production and consumption, and suggested an alternative, politicized approach, focusing on gender and generational relations within and among households. By stressing the role of poor women, she also implied that alternative work groups and institutions outside the household could become important mechanisms for resource transfer and consumption guarantees (Hart 1992, 1995).

Criticism and questions on such conventional concepts as 'peasantry,' 'rural household' and 'farm village' have also been presented by many other researchers (Elson 1997; de Haan 1999; Adams 2002; de Haan et al. 2002; Bounthong et al. 2004). Thus, different disciplines have suggested that even the smallest social unit (for example the household) is not confined within the village but has the potential to expand into the wider world. In other words, these studies urge us to pay attention to the geographical expansion of social networks and to develop a broader perspective on aspects of the macro-society that are projected onto rural society.

Deagrarianization and spatial expansion of household economies

Non-agricultural work can be a crucial factor in understanding rural–urban relations comprehensively, because those who work temporarily outside the village are thought to mediate between rural and urban societies. Deborah Fahy Bryceson tried to illustrate rural–urban interactions in terms of the increasing non-agricultural (or non-farm/off-farm) activities. The emerging importance of non-agricultural activities is termed 'deagrarianization.' It has been defined as a long-term process of occupational adjustment, income-earning reorientation, social re-identification, and spatial relocation of rural dwellers, away from strictly agricultural-based modes of livelihood (Bryceson 1996, 1997, 2000, 2002). In addition to these four perspectives, Rigg (2001) and Rigg and Nattapoolwat (2001) presented a fifth feature, 'spatial interpenetration,' and they wrote that: 'taken together, these processes describe a profound shift in rural economies and in rural people's concerns out of farming and into non-farm activities' (Rigg 2001: 6–7; Rigg and Nattapoolwat 2001: 949–950).

As mentioned in Chapter 4, acquiring wage-earning jobs has been one of the most important issues for the Iban in the research area; that is, the Iban's concerns have also shifted to non-farm work outside of the village. This trend has been accelerated by the out-migration of Iban females. Considering the division of labor between the sexes in the village, it can be safely said that the management of the agricultural cycle by females enabled the males to go for *bejalai* or work away from home. In the 1980s the Iban males became eager to engage in more stable wage labor, affected by the increase in job opportunities in urban areas. They began to attach more importance to the regular job, *kerja*, rather than *bejalai* and *bekuli*, which consequently resulted in the out-migration of females who followed their husbands. This change in the migration unit among the Iban population has definitely accelerated the deagrarianization of the longhouse community. In this process, key factors and features of deagrarianization presented by Bryceson (2002) and Rigg and Nattapoolwat (2001) are apparent.

Rigg (1998) also emphasized the significance of the remarkable diversification that has occurred in both the household and in rural economies, and focused more attention on the household because, while the rural economy is spatially designated, the household economy often crosses spatial boundaries. The frequent movement of household members between rural and urban localities brought about spatial expansion of the household. In this sense, the Iban household typically has the feature of spatial expansion, because even a family living in the city retains the membership of the parent household (*bilek*-family) in the longhouse by frequently returning to the original village. This high mobility makes it difficult to assign discrete spatial addresses to the movers. As Rigg remarked, livelihoods in Southeast Asia cannot be simply divided into rural/urban or agriculture/industry. In other words, the increased mobility of people and the expansion of households are blurring the rural/urban distinctions (Champion and Hugo 2001). This means that the affiliation of a person to a specific household or community is largely dependent on his or her own sense of belonging. Research in Rantau Kemiding inevitably deals with village members including those who currently live in the city, because many of them are recognized as household members by the head of the *bilek*-family (*tuai bilek*) (Chapter 5). As discussed in Chapter 7, however, changes in the sense of belonging among these movers may affect the solidarity of the household. In this sense, examining the meaning of the spatial expansion of the household in relation to the mobility of its members has the potential to add a new dimension to previous studies on rural-to-urban migration.

Rural-to-urban migrants: from the urban perspective

Most research on the diversification of livelihoods has focused on households whose members divide their economic activities between the village and the city. This means that the diversification and spatial expansion of the rural household economy is closely related to the increase in rural-to-urban migration. However, there seems to have been an assumption that income diversification is usually realized by unmarried youths, who engage in relatively short-term non-agricultural wage labor outside the village, and who are also thought to be 'circular migrants.' This premise probably arose because most studies were conducted from the rural perspective. In other words, the research foci have been on the livelihood strategies of 'farm households,' the stratification of rural residents, and the changes in the social structure of the village. However, with the considerable increase in the number of those who leave home, the migratory unit has also been changing. Not only unmarried individuals, but also married couples and even whole households began to migrate to the cities. This change is worthy of some consideration (Smith et al. 1984; Williams 1989; Root and de Jong 1991). Furthermore, despite the increase in out-migration and the extended period of the city sojourn, the occasional return of urban sojourners to their home community is becoming more important in that they induce a variety of flows and interactions between the rural and the urban areas. However, there are few studies that describe these relations from the perspective of rural–urban migration. A difficult question remains as to how to conduct a tracing survey on those people who left the village for an urban area. Therefore, most research has had no choice but to focus on urban 'in-migrants' from the viewpoint of the destination (urban) area. Conversely, rural studies have tended to regard the increase in out-migration as the diversification of cash income, and thought little of the migrants' socio-political concern for the village of origin. This section describes the literature on these themes and questions in relation to the Iban case.

An emerging and positive view of the urban poor

Traditional approaches to the study of migration have relied on the notion of 'push/pull' factors as the main explanation as to why people move (Tacoli 1998). In relation to rural-to-urban migration in the Third World in the 1960s, it was often pointed out that decisions to migrate were more strongly affected by hardships in the source areas (the 'push' factors) than by perceived advantages in the destination areas (the 'pull' factors) (Niitsu 1973).

In place of this naïve theory, in the 1970s, in relation to patterns of labor migration, we saw a lively discussion about the informal employment sector, such as seasonal and circular migration (Papanek 1975; Murai 1978; Niitsu 1973, 1989; Kumagai 1990; Fujimaki 1993; Mosse et al. 2002). Since the informal labor market absorbed a large number of the poorer labor force that were unable to enter the formal market, the urban informal sector was considered to have prepared for an inflow of the rural population. The argument about the informal sector developed into theories such as 'over-urbanization,' 'subsistence urbanization,' and 'pseudo urbanization.'[5] There was a certain amount of veracity in these theories that explained why the poorest people from rural areas could survive in Third World cities. Studies of the urban informal sector also presented new notions such as 'shared poverty in the cities' (McGee 1971), 're-creation of villages' (Mountjoy 1976) and 'enclaves of peasant society' (Yamazaki 1977: 20), most of which were described in terms of the pastoral landscape, countrified human relations, and the 'rurality' of in-migrants in the cities.

Studies of rural-to-urban migrants, however, had long been conducted within the framework of 'urban villagers,' 'ethnic villagers' (Gans 1962), 'peasants in cities' (Mangin 1970), or the 'urban village (*kampung*)' (Papanek 1975). These ideas were fundamentally based on discussions of the 'rural/urban dichotomy' and Louis Wirth's 'theory of urbanism,' both of which emerged from the Chicago School of Sociology. Fujimaki (1993) criticized these perspectives as being too static to take into account the lifecycle of migrants and the process of their adaptation to the cities. Furthermore, most of these studies tackled the migration issue from the point of view that the rapid inflow of the rural population into cities presented obstacles for appropriate urban planning and development.

Structuralist and world-system approaches to migration, on the other hand, tended to portray rural-to-urban migrants or the urban poor as victims rather than rational decision makers (Matsuda 1990; Yonemura 1991a, b; Tacoli 1998). Their movement was determined by macro-social, historical and dialectic processes such as the socio-spatial restructuring of production at national and global levels.

Thus, rural-to-urban migrants have often been described from a perspective at the macro-level such as urban society, national politics and the world economy. Recent research, however, has tended to appraise the response and resistance of the urban poor to a dependency structure in more affirmative terms (Matsuda 1996, 1998). Although, it is difficult to absolutely discount the validity of dependency theory and structuralist explanations, the initiative shown by the urban poor and the dynamism of their communities have become major themes for examination. In the chapters in Part II of this book, instead of regarding migrants as the source of social problems and describing them as victims and marginal sojourners, or judging their adaptability to urban life and distinguishing between the push and pull factors that drive migration, I preferred to describe the initiative of the Iban people who devised various kinds of living strategies. It is considered to be more important to take this approach in describing their urban lives as they are, and to clarify the strategies they activate, in order to remain and reestablish substantial relationships with the rural community. From the Iban case it is obvious that migrants' interaction with the macro-society, including other groups in the city, and the rural community of their origin, may often be a prime mover of rural changes.

The meaning of the village for urban residents

Some urban anthropologists have focused on the identity of rural-to-urban migrants in relation to their ethnicity and home village society. They found that the ethnic identity of migrants was reconstructed in a different form from that observed in the village. The question of 'urban ethnicity' was raised in the late 1960s and generated a lively debate (Cohen 1969; Epstein 1981). Paradoxical concepts and new terms such as 're-tribalization,' 'ethnic re-identification,' and 're-creation of folk,' were coined to describe the changing identity of rural-to-urban migrants. This provoked a discussion on how migrants revised or broadly re-interpreted the folk culture of their rural society and the traditional values of their ethnic group in the context of their urban lives.[6]

Rural characteristics were often observed in migrant communities in the cities. Studies of urban ethnicity, for example, closely observed the process by which neighborhood organizations, common-villagers' societies, or locality-based mutual-aid associations were established in many Third World cities (Hugo 1981, 1992; Kato 1983, 1986; Matsuda 1998; Hataya 1998). These informal associations in the cities provided rural-to-urban migrants with temporary accommodation, job opportunities, low-interest funds for business, and financial contributions in the event of a death or accident. Since most migrants, whose urban lives are quite unstable, are largely dependent—not only economically but also socially and culturally—on these informal associations, researchers have examined their mutual-aid functions.

These researchers, instead of dealing with migrants in the narrow context of urban studies, tried to understand the nature of migrant communities in terms of the traditions of their home place or their ethnic customary law. The most important factor here was to clarify the meaningful relationships that exist between rural and urban societies from the perspective of migrants.

Previous studies argued about the formation of migrant communities in the cities and cultural changes in relation to the rural societies from which they had originated. These studies, however, paid little attention to the meaning of rural transformation for rural-to-urban migrants. As described in the chapters in Part II of this book, the Iban in Sibu began to recognize the increase in the economic value of rural properties and were keen to participate in the decision-making of using resources for rural development. These examples highlight the idea that changes in the management of resources in the home village is an important issue for urban dwellers.

There have been several reports which note that financial aid from rural-to-urban migrants revitalizes agricultural production in the village of origin and enables people in the village to draw up their own development plans (Brown

1994, 1997; Adams 1998; Ahlburg and Brown 1998; Regmi and Tisdell 2002; de Haan 2002). In some regions, fund transfer for rural development was carried out systematically by migrant associations in the cities (Kato 1986: 414–415). However, there has been little research on the influence of urban dwellers on resource management and distribution of property. Considering the behavior of the Iban in Sibu, who actively exploited living and migration strategies, including their desire to keep rural property, we can easily examine this important research theme, the influence of urban sojourners on rural development.

In relation to property management, Stark and Lucas (1988) and Hoddinott (1994), for instance, focused on land inheritance rights because they regarded the remitting behavior of rural-to-urban migrants as a long-term contract between parents living in the village and adult children working in the cities. As numerous studies indicate, many urban sojourners intend to return home to the village in the future (Lucas and Stark 1985; Ogura 1988, 1990; Galor and Stark 1990, 1991; Hoddinott 1994; Ellis 1998; Rigg 1998). It is reasonable to assume that these people are anxious to secure rural property and improve their position in their village of origin.[7] For Southeast Asian countries, which have promoted development policies, an important issue is how to manage and exploit 'peripheral' land and natural resources that governments regard as having been left idle. As well as rural residents having a direct interest in government proposals for resource distribution, many urban migrants are highly sensitive to tactful approaches from the macro-society to rural property in their village of origin. Therefore, family relationships around resource problems are often influenced by the socio-political situation at a macro-level.

Thus, in the same way that rural societies have been transformed through interaction with the wider world, the value of the rural village to urban dwellers has changed considerably. Although this situation is largely accepted, previous rural-to-urban migration studies have not taken this perspective into account. This omission is probably related to the division between rural and urban studies.

The Iban in Sibu

How can the discussion in this section be applicable to the Iban case in the research area? In the relatively early stage of their in-migration into Sibu, many Iban had obtained jobs in the formal sector. This may not be a feature of a small-scale local town, because, as Dwyer (1975) pointed out, every intermediate city and small town in Southeast Asia had 'urban problems' such as squatter settlements, unemployment of migrants and enlargement of the informal labor market. The case of Sibu should be considered as a feature of the cities in Malaysia. For instance, it is reported by Fujimaki (1998) that many government employees live in squatter settlements in Kuala Lumpur, which is considerably different from the situation of squatters in other developing countries. The relatively well-off situation of squatters in Sibu and other cities in Malaysia is largely related to Malaysian national policy, especially the so-called *bumiputera* policy. In the case of Iban squatters in Sibu, many of them not only engaged in jobs in the formal and government sector, but also acquired legal lots in a resettlement scheme. These were closely related to their interaction and negotiation with other ethnic groups, regional political leaders and national development politics. However, it is not fair to overemphasize their shrewd and cunning characters, because from the structuralist point of view, the Iban in Sibu have obviously been marginalized. They are often regarded as 'rustic,' excluded from the major stream in Sarawak politics as non-Muslim, and also forced to occupy the lower strata of the urban economic structure. Burdened with this multiple marginality, the Iban in Sibu have endeavored to establish living strategies within a limited range of choices.

The Iban have a another peculiar feature that is different from the urban poor in other countries, that is, the process by which they established their urban community in Sibu. Previous studies on urban-to-rural migrants have emphasized the mutual-aid functions of the community composed of the urban poor. Some researchers even declare that the foundation of the associations organized by the urban in-migrants can be attributed to common backgrounds or kinship, and not just ethnicity (Matsuda 1990). However, the importance of homeland-based or kinship-based organizations is tacitly emphasized on the basis that there is a considerably large population in the original villages of squatter residents. As for the case of the Iban or other non-Muslim *bumiputera* in Sarawak, however, the scale of their village is rather small because their village communities are usually organized in the form of a 'longhouse.' The small population of the home village (longhouse) hardly gives them the opportunity to compose homeland-based associations in urban areas. Instead of forming such a community, the Iban in Sibu established a relatively loose mutual-aid network, which was based on the same ethnicity in Kampung Usaha Jaya squatter settlement (Kg. UJ). Moreover, they were also prepared to take a pragmatic approach and cooperate with Muslims and Chinese when needed, in order to draw benefits from this alliance.

As for their jobs in Sibu, what is interesting is that most of the Iban in Kg. UJ had secured job contracts before migrating out of the village into the town, a practice rarely discussed in the literature. This feature is probably attributed to the close accessibility between Sibu and its hinterland longhouses. As described in Chapter 5, origins of the Iban in Kg. UJ are mostly within the range of 100 kilometers from the town of Sibu. They are able to wait for a job opportunity and until one arises they stay in their longhouse of origin.

This geographical accessibility has significance in that the Iban in Sibu can easily return to their longhouse whenever they need. Since many of the urban dwellers intend to return home after retirement, they have to maintain ties with their parents in the original *bilek* and the longhouse community. Indeed, in principle, the geographical distance is not proportional to the intimacy between the family and village members. However, as the Iban themselves emphasize, it can be safely said that living in the neighboring town Sibu, positively influences their capacity to keep emotional ties with their parents in the village.

The accessibility also enabled urban Ibans to intervene more easily in the economic development and improvement of infrastructure in their villages of origin. They act as catalysts to introduce government-led development projects to the longhouse community and manipulate village people to take part in development politics, to some extent. In particular, the fact that many longhouse heads (*tuai rumah*) live in Sibu symbolically illustrates relations between the development policy and ethnicity in Sarawak.

These phenomena are made clear by observing migrants at the micro level, both from rural and urban perspectives. In this sense, analyzing people moving between and around rural and urban locations in a relatively small vicinity such as Sibu and its hinterland provides us with creative approaches to discuss rural–urban interactions. In other words, observation of migrants in their different settings is an important analytical method. This perspective has not been developed enough in previous studies on rural–urban migration.

Rural and urban studies: the possibility of articulation

Rural-to-urban migration and its impact on social change have drawn considerable scholarly interest. A substantial amount of research has been conducted from both rural and urban perspectives. One point to note, is that although discontinuity between studies on rural households and studies on urban migrants has frequently been noted, very few have attempted to comprehensively examine both the rural and urban setting. This section identifies several points of view that may have value for developing an integrated analysis of migration and rural–urban interactions.

Rural–urban interactions

The conventional wisdom of the urban/rural dichotomy has been increasingly questioned and challenged (Hugo 1992; Afsar 1999). This is partly because major changes in the mobility of people, goods, services, capital and ideas have considerably blurred the distinction between urban and rural populations (Afsar 1999). Although some work mentions reciprocal rural–urban linkages, few succeed in taking an inclusive view of both the urban and rural dwellers. This study tried to provide a comprehensive view in the previous chapters. In order to place this work in the context of the literature on rural–urban interactions, I will undertake a brief examination of some of the key studies.

Potter and Unwin (1995: 65) stated: 'The interactions that take place between rural and urban areas are central to any understanding of the processes of social and economic change in developing countries, but they remain poorly articulated and little understood.' As Watts (1996) and Rigg (1998) have suggested, research on rural–urban interactions, linkages and interdependency is rapidly becoming an important subfield within development geography and rural studies in general.

The word 'interaction' implies an attempt to comprehend the 'dynamism' of the various phenomena that occur between rural and urban spaces. Unwin (1989), a human geographer, pointed out that although geography has a long tradition of rural-to-urban migration studies, the discipline has focused on urban and rural development separately and failed to accumulate wide-ranging research on the linkages and interactions between the two localities. As Lin (2001) also indicated, in recent years a growing number of scholars from various disciplines have become increasingly critical of the adequacy of the arbitrary urban/rural dichotomy (Friedman 1996; Douglass 1998; Tacoli 1998).

According to Unwin (1989: 13–14), since the late 1950s three basic, interrelated ideas have dominated much of this literature: the 'growth pole' concept, the distinction between 'top-down' and 'bottom-up' development, and the conceptualization of cities as being either 'parasitic' or 'generative.'

Rural–urban interactions, however, have become increasingly complicated, and so-called '*desakota*' zones (McGee 1989, 1991; McGee and Greenberg 1992)[8] have emerged around not only primate cities but also intermediate cities and smaller towns in various developing countries. Furthermore, the flow of human resources, goods, money, technology, information and ideologies has become reciprocal between urban and rural areas. As for human migration, the dominant conceptualization of migration and migrant adjustment as a one-way journey is inadequate, as many individuals and groups forge connections and social fields across expanses of space and time (McHugh 2000: 71).

In reconsidering Lipton's (1977, 1982) concept of 'urban bias,' Unwin (1989: 17) was critical that Lipton failed to satisfactorily explain the flow of surplus resources between country and town. Unwin attributed this failure to Lipton's equation of 'people' with 'places.' While it is relatively easy to identify places as being either rural or urban, this is a much more difficult exercise as far as people are concerned. It is suggestive that this kind of criticism is presented by a geographer. As was mentioned in Section 2 of this chapter, people move constantly between rural and urban areas, and it is almost impossible to assign discrete spatial addresses to them (Rigg 1998). Moreover, considering the emergence of '*desakota*' regions in Third World towns and cities of all sizes, allotting people, households, groups, and resources to a single category such as rural or urban is unrealistic.

While it is not always possible to distinguish clearly between urban and rural people, there are nevertheless a number of different types of linkages between the town and country that provide a basis for measuring these interactions. Using these variables, some researchers have tried to produce a balance of flows for particular case studies, which could be used to indicate a net transfer of resources and to assess the degree of exploitation that existed (Lipton 1977; Stöhr and Taylor 1981; Rondinelli 1983). However, Unwin is skeptical of these attempts because he thinks it is extremely difficult to interpret the results of such an approach in the study of rural–urban interaction. As Unwin (1989) and Dixon (1987) pointed out, it is people rather than places that exploit and are exploited, and it is not rural and urban areas, or rural and urban classes, that interact, it is people who interact. The important point here is that we need to look at who is trying to gain access to which resources to derive benefit. In other words, the strategies of the various actors in rural–urban interactions should be the focus of the discussion. In this sense, it is significant to analyze rural–urban interactions by focusing on the Iban who are moving between and around rural and urban areas.

Development policy, rural resources and urban residents

Nowadays, research on a particular region, society, or ethnic group must take into account their relationship to the macro-society, such as to the government, nation-state, international enterprise and world economy. This study regards those who move between the rural and the urban as the 'actors.' However, the notion of actor is not limited to the individual, but is applicable to the urban administration, nation-state, enterprise, ethnic group, rural community and so on, and what is important is to grasp the interactions of actors (Bryant and Bailey 1997). This study tried to describe these interactions from the perspective of rural–urban migrants, because it was thought that diversified relations between these actors have been reflected in the living strategies of migrants. Therefore, focusing on a particular ethnic group or specific community does not necessarily fall into the 'exceptionalism' or the excavation of anecdotes. Investigation into indigenous logics is aimed at clarifying how people recognize different social groups, the nation-state, government, and world economy, and how they reestablish their ways of living and thinking in their interaction with such macro-societies. In Southeast Asian countries, where multi-ethnic societies are the norm, it is inevitable to clarify the logics of different communities respectively even when examining the social structure at a macro-scale.

We should not ignore the fact that the transformation of rural societies, changing living strategies of rural households, and sharpened perceptions of rural-to-urban migrants about their native villages all reflect the socio-cultural background that is peculiar to each ethnic group. If diverse groups have varied interests in a common area, they may take different approaches to it based on their respective ways of thinking, which can result in friction. In the relationships between rural-to-urban migrants and rural society, land management often becomes a point of conflict because, while the land is still recognized as an important basis for living by rural communities, diverse actors such as urban residents, developers, and governments have increasingly been gaining access to the natural resources in the rural regions.

In Southeast Asian countries, which have promoted rural development in the name of 'development policy,' it is obvious that land resources have become an increasingly important issue not only for rural communities but also for various social and political actors. The topic of land has been discussed from a range of perspectives—environmental economics, cultural ecology, environmental sociology, and political ecology—all of which tend to attribute friction and conflict concerning rural resources to the defective introduction of modern institutions intermingled with partial approval from the perspective of traditional customs. In Sarawak, too, land has been a controversial topic that is related to environmental degradation and to the deprivation of people's rights to land resources. This book, however, has focused on how urban dwellers were concerned with land development issues. The Iban in the case study have been making strenuous efforts to maintain their rights to land and draw benefit from resource development within the plurality of land institutions.

It is widely recognized that 'plural institutions' relating to resource distribution is the result of colonial and post-colonial development policies. For example, Mizuno (1991, 1997) described the development of Indonesian land institutions, Ganjanapan (1994) pointed out the discrepancy between customary land tenure systems and national land laws in northern Thailand, and Prill-Brett (1994) commented on indigenous land rights and legal pluralism among the Philippine highlanders.

These studies have profound implications in that they highlight the vulnerability of rural residents to government development policy. However, the situation in individual countries is too complicated to be described within the framework of confrontation between powerful governments and vulnerable peasants. As we observed in the previous chapters, rural-to-urban migrants are deeply involved in both politico-economic bargaining in urban areas and socio-cultural activities in their village of origin. In other words, those who migrate between the two areas often play important roles as intermediaries between macro and micro-societies. As well, they also provide a new basis for analyzing rural–urban interactions.

The living space of the movers

Focusing on the movers

Previous studies of rural–urban relationships can be broadly summarized as follows: first of all, the study of rural–urban interactions from the perspective of population movement has been inadequate. Some scholars do indeed mention 'organic' relationships and the sequence of urban and rural societies with reference to migration (Kato 1983; Kumagai 1990; Fujimaki 1993). However, they do no more than indicate various kinds of flow between the two areas and present the emergence of urban ethnic communities that are based on rural principles.

Secondly, the change in, or expansion of the 'living space' of rural-to-urban migrants has not been considered in previous studies. For example, the rural 'household' now often crosses over spatial village boundaries, which means the household economy no longer fits easily into current models and frameworks. Furthermore, there has been little research on the significance to urban dwellers of village society, household structure, and rural property. These problems can be attributed to a neglect of the migrants' own view of themselves.

The third point is the relationship to the macro-society. While rural communities have greater access to macro-society through the movement of rural-to-urban migrants, urban dwellers are also increasingly involved, as resource redistribution in rural areas becomes a vital interest for diverse political and economic actors. How do they make use of intertwined channels to other groups and strata of society? Investigating this issue may help clarify the living strategies of migrants.

Here, I would like to put forward a suggestion. As we observed in the previous chapters, it is difficult to assign discrete addresses to these people. However, the terms such as migration and migrants force us to imagine a sedentary base or address for the individual. This gap may have disturbed our understanding of those who are in frequent and reciprocal movement. As Skeldon (2005) stated, migration is a complex system of various types of movement and it is better termed 'mobility,' in which non-permanent forms are as important. In the same way, those who frequently move between town and country and try to establish multiple living bases in different places are better called 'movers,' not migrants.

This study has focused on 'human mobility' between rural and urban areas in order to explain how 'movers' establish a holistic living space between and around the two areas. In other words, in an attempt to comprehend the dynamism of changing notions of ruralness and urbanness, we investigated the behavior of the movers, who simultaneously embodied both aspects. It is reasonable to assume that those who move assimilate both rural knowledge and urban ways of thinking, and that their experiences of the two locations are intermingled and integrated into their lives. People indeed choose their attitudes according to situations, but this does not mean a split personality or institutional discontinuity between their rural and urban lives. The opportunistic behavior of individuals simply reflects the holistic personality of those who interact with diverse actors in various situations. Multiple identities—both 'rural' and 'urban'—or 'rural' and 'urban' ways of life are integrated into his or her 'living space' at the individual level (Figure 8.1).

Concluding remarks: the expansion of living space at the individual level

This book has examined key dimensions of rural–urban interaction as reflected by Iban society. After describing the brief history of Rantau Kemiding in Chapter 3, we observed the outflow of the Iban from the longhouses to Sibu, especially the departure of married women in Chapter 4. The chapter also

Figure 8.1 Blurred rural-urban divide

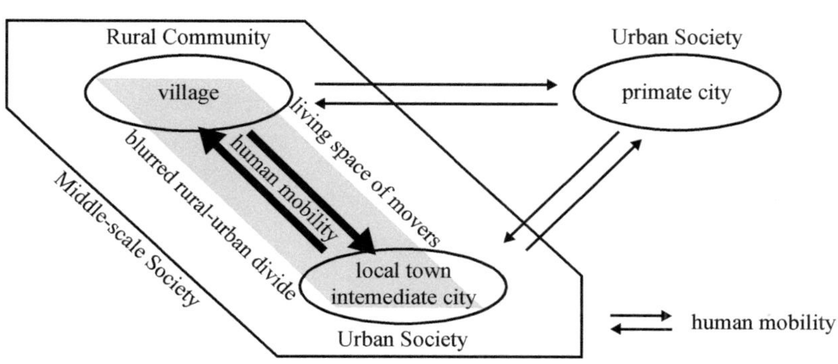

pointed out the changes in agricultural practices and their destabilizing effect on the structure of the longhouse community. Chapters 5 and 6 looked at the living strategies of urban Iban from socio-economic and political perspectives, where various actors played a role in connecting rural and urban societies. Chapter 7 examined family relations and property inheritance in Iban society in light of the discussion in previous chapters, and suggested that the expansion of their living space was an important factor for urban Iban.

As mentioned in Chapter 5, the Iban in the Rajang Basin do not necessarily move only to primate cities. Many of them live for long periods in the town of Sibu, and some apparently stay permanently in that small urban center. Below, we consider the implications of this fact.

One of the most important topics within rural-to-urban migration studies has been the subject of remittances. However, observation of the movement of Iban people between the rural and the urban shows that payment of funds are not necessarily the main factor in maintaining rural–urban connections. It is possible to regard financial aid from urban sojourners to their parents in the village as a long-term contract relating to inheritance and succession, but we saw many urban sojourners give money directly to their parents when they returned to the longhouse or when their parents visited them in town. We should note of course that the relatively short distance between the parents in the village and their adult children in the town probably makes remittances less significant. In other words, greater accessibility enables the urban Iban to maintain relations with their parents and their original village community not only through financial aid but also through other activities. For instance, they frequently travel back and forth between the areas to take part in festivals, ritual ceremonies, village meetings, agricultural activities, and other programs. The voting system in Sarawak also means that they are often more active during an election period. Opinion leaders in the village, such as the longhouse head, often live in town. Changes in relations between parents and children are also the result of a broader interpretation of their customs. These factors are all possible because of the short distance between the town and its hinterland villages, ensuring easy access between the two locations.

The importance attached to these factors by the Iban in the area is related to their long-term life plans and explains why they prefer living in a local town, Sibu, rather than in a larger city or primate city much further away from their original village.

The social sphere in which many of the Iban carry out their activities can be regarded as a 'middle-scale society,' and its spatial range has been established in this book as the local town, Sibu, and its hinterland, Kanowit. Previous studies have neglected small regional centers as having little importance in the national economic sense, and thus the living strategies of those residing in these areas have not been explored. Our focus on a regional center and its hinterland villages as a spatial analytical unit has enabled us to illustrate the linkages between urban and rural settings by observing in detail, and from several aspects, people who continually move between and around the two areas. To gain a clearer understanding of rural–urban interactions it is important to understand the holistic lives of the movers.

Most of the Iban in this area who have experienced urban life in Sibu, even temporarily, still cling to their membership of the longhouse community, as we observed in Chapters 5, 6 and 7. However, we should not view their adherence to their origins as simply emotional and sentimental. The Iban are keenly aware of their marginality in both the national and regional contexts. It is easy to surmise that the self-identification of their marginalized existence would be sharpened by their interaction with other ethnic groups and the macro-society in the cities. The construction and stabilization of the nation-state and the promotion of development politics has imposed structural marginality on indigenous peoples. Under these conditions, the Iban pursue a more stable existence, in both rural and urban localities. Their strategy is to establish living bases in both areas and to integrate the different living spaces into one larger sphere of economic, social, and political activity. This viewpoint is important in understanding the holistic lives of the Iban and the dynamism of rural–urban interactions in Sarawak, Malaysia.

Rural-to-urban migration, which has long attracted academic interest, has been regarded as a strategy used by poor peasants to maintain a subsistence level of income. This study also initially discussed rural-to-urban migration from the perspective of the rural community. However, a detailed examination of the many facets of Iban life compels us to note that what should be stressed here is not migration itself, but the Iban's strategic expansion of their living space between and around rural and urban areas. Paradoxically, careful examination into the lives of the movers may release us from the deadlock of the rural/urban divide, so dominant in migration studies literature. The Iban in the research area have moved continually between the two areas and attempted to create new living spaces to tackle their social, economic, and political difficulties. This has resulted in them recognizing the two locations as a single spatial unit in terms of their lives. In other words, the movers simultaneously integrate and embody rural and urban lives at the individual level.[9] In this sense, attention on the movers themselves can provide a new dimension to the study of rural–urban articulation.

9
Conclusion: The Iban as Agents on the Move

The previous chapter provided a comprehensive analysis of the Iban movers with regard to the literature on migration and rural–urban interactions. In this concluding chapter we propose that focusing on the movers is central to the articulation of rural/urban perspectives. Here, we also review the latest discussion on the topic that criticizes the 'sedentary bias' and emphasizes the substantial mobility of people in the Third World. Finally, by drawing upon the concept of 'agency,' we examine how Iban mobility has significance in the broader context of Sarawak.

Mobility as a premise

As mentioned above, the dominant conceptualization of migration and migrant adjustment as a one-way journey is inadequate (McHugh 2000). Recently, there has been a tendency to explain reciprocal migration patterns in terms of 'migrant institutions' or 'networks.' In addition, the primacy of a purely economic model of migration has been challenged through the exploration of issues of identity and social networks, which are not easily incorporated into such a model (Hampshire 2002).

Migration studies can be roughly classified into two approaches. The first is a neo-classical one based on a 'dual economy' model, which includes the premise of the rational movement of laborers, and the second is a Marxist model that stresses structural factors rather than migrant agency (Mosse et al. 2002). Although the division of these approaches has been cause for pessimism (Goss and Lindquist 1995), studies since the late 1990s seem to find common ground in that they admit substantial mobility of migrants and sometimes rightly criticize the sedentary bias (de Haan 1999; Mosse et al. 2002; Leinbach 2004).

De Haan (1999) asserted that previous models of migration and migrants have often been based on an assumption of 'sedentarism.' Mosse et al. (2002) also stated that migration and rural livelihoods are falsely opposed, and that rural development is invariably taken to imply the reaffirmation of a disrupted sedentary agricultural community (Mosse et al. 2002). Another viewpoint is offered by Elmhirst's (2001) case study of Indonesia's transmigration policy, which noted that 'place-based essentialism' undermines the security of settlers, denies their rights to land and erodes possibilities for fostering civil society.

Thus, recent studies, irrespective of the difference in their approaches and viewpoints, reject the assumption of sedentarism and discuss migration by presupposing high mobility of the rural population. Englund (2002: 139) also asserted that 'the challenge of regarding mobility, rather than immobility, as primary in social life confronts not only development policies but much conventional wisdom in the social sciences.'

When this feature of migration is examined in terms of family composition and household strategies, the diversification of family relations are emphasized. Firman (1994: 83) developed the argument of Caces et al. (1985), stating 'theoretically, all members, irrespective of their physical location, continue to maintain important connections with those still living at home and with those living elsewhere.' He calls such families 'bi- or multi-local families' that largely reflect the deployment of the labor force. Families that straddle different agro-ecological and economic zones have been mentioned by many other scholars (de Haan et al. 2002; Kelly 1998; Agesa 2004) in relation to the allocation of labor within a household. For instance, Agesa (2004) presents the concept of 'one family, two households,' and examined the relations between members within households that are permanently separated and maintain two homes.

These arguments have been mostly developed and based on the well-known concept of 'shadow household' (Caces et al. 1985). The Iban in the research area have many points in common with this kind of household and recently presented patterns of family composition that were mentioned above. However, the Iban case has many other points that can add new perspectives to the discussion. For instance, Agesa (2004) emphasized the split between the husband and wife in examining the household types in relation to migration patterns, but erred in asserting that if a wife followed her husband to the city, the migration of the family unit was complete. The Iban case not only illustrates the realization of the spatial expansion of the household by the husband and wife, but also demonstrates that there are other dimensions of family life that need consideration; namely the relationship between the parents in the village and the adult children in the city. This perspective has not been adequately discussed in previous studies of migration. The Iban in Sibu apparently set up an independent household economically, but in a social and cultural sense, they retain the potential to affiliate with either the *bilek*-family of the husband or wife's parents in the longhouse.

Although we discussed the mobility of rural people by focusing on the household and family composition, this notion has long been criticized for its ambiguity and vagueness. It is true that the household, which has been discussed within both the structuralist and functionalist approaches, is a problematic analytical concept (Folbre 1986; Goss and Lindquist 1995). It has been seen as inadequate because as an analytical category it cannot function as a point of articulation between macro and micro-levels of determination, or between structure and agency (Goss and Lindquist 1995). In addition, Bounthong et al. (2004) remarked that even taking the household as the unit of analysis raises the important methodological question of whether certain actions should be conceptualized as part of a household's 'strategy' or as decisions that are best understood from the standpoint of the individual.

Thus, the ambiguity of the notion of the household has been a critical issue when examining the living strategy of the individual (Tacoli 1996; Booth 2004). However, as discussed in Chapter 7, changing the concept of household itself—the broadened interpretation of the '*bilek*-family' in this study—could be the research theme which provides the key to comprehend the holistic life of the Iban on the move. Indeed, the notion of the household is often criticized as an ambiguous concept, but as we saw in the Iban case, the investigation of the changing notion of the household could lead to a comprehensive understanding of their living strategy.

Another and more critical point for studies concerned with human mobility and the household, is that the split in the household or the diversification of household types has been discussed on the premise that actors or members of the household 'migrate' between rural and urban areas. As indicated above, however, there are difficulties in understanding the movement of the Iban within this framework. In effect, the Iban in Kg. Sentosa, Sibu do not regard their stay in Sibu as the result of migration. The Iban has a word '*pindah*' which, according to the definition of Kedit (1993), means migrating permanently as a family group or longhouse community. The Iban in Sibu, however, seldom use this term to explain their mobility. One of the Kg. Sentosa residents said to me:

> Our stay in Sibu is of course now different from *bejalai*, but nor is it *pindah*. We came to Sibu to be engaged in wage work and improve our lives. We do not have an adequate word to express our lifestyle in Iban language. Our present situation may be a moderate one, between *pindah*, *bejalai*, and *belelang* (to go on extended and distant journeys, sometimes without returning). [1]

This study demonstrated that Iban mobility between rural and urban areas is complex and is reflected in their 'double (or multiple) residence,' existence of longhouse leaders in the town of Sibu, easier accessibility from the longhouse to the neighboring town of Sibu, and their frequent movement between the two areas. We asserted that it is more realistic to regard their lives as the process of expansion of their living space, which may be substantially different from the notion of 'migration,' which has been discussed on the basis that the household members 'shift' or 'change' their places of residence. The Iban in the research area have endeavored to establish multiple residences at the individual level, resulting in the broad interpretation of the *bilek*-family.

Thus, the taken-for-granted notion of 'migration' itself should be reexamined in the Iban case and it may be inappropriate as an explanatory concept for Iban mobility between and around rural and urban areas. The Iban in the research area, are movers and 'expansionists' rather than migrants.

Structure and agency

Many researchers have argued that both individualistic (or behavioral) models such as the Todaro model (Thadani and Todaro 1984; Lucas and Stark 1985; Katz and Stark 1986) and migration analyses in the Marxist (or structuralist) tradition (McGee 1982; Standing 1985; Rubenstein 1992), have taken a one-sided point of view. Economic models tend to isolate the economic decision-making, and do not analyze the political and social contexts. In contrast, Marxist analyses overemphasize the political-economic contexts that influence migration decisions, and isolate the constraining nature of formal institutions on mobility. As a result, they tend to ignore the migrants' agency (de Haan 1999). As Hampshire (2002) remarked, an exploration of the questions relating to migrants' identity and social networks should be incorporated into economic and/or quantitative investigations.[2]

Goss and Lindquist (1995) identified the theoretical impasse that has been created between functional and structural approaches in understanding labor migration. To overcome these polarities, recent theories have emphasized that analyses need to incorporate both individual motives and the structural factors in which migrants operate in the form of Anthony Giddens' structuration theory (de Haan 2002). The attempt by Goss and Lindquist (1995) to develop a concept of 'migrant institutions' that could articulate various levels of analysis, was among the studies based on 'structuration theory.' In this approach, in which the notion of 'agency' was reinstated and developed (Chant and Radcliffe 1992), and the relationship between structure and agency was examined, researchers often discussed the collapse of the binary oppositions of rural and urban, tradition and modernity, or push and pull, and allowed labor migration to be seen as part of local and diverse livelihood strategies.

Emirbayer and Mische define the agency as the temporally constructed engagement by actors of different structural environments—the 'temporal relational contexts of action—which, through the interplay of habit, imagination, and judgment, both reproduces and transforms those structures in interactive response to the problems posed by changing historical situations (1998: 970).' One of the important issues in the context of migration is whether migrants have choices or they are forced to migrate (Halfacree 1995). In the argument on female migration, Smith (2004) pointed out that Halfacree's portrayal of intentional and unintentional agency embedded within migration decision-making begs questions about whether family migration represents the 'choices' and/or 'constraints' of migrants (Smith 2004). This issue needs further examination.

As for the case of the Iban in the study area considered here, we first have to investigate whether their rural-to-urban flows have been caused by any structural factors, and how urban Ibans find 'choices' in negotiating with other ethnic groups, the urban administration and their family in the longhouse. In Part II of this book, we described the Iban's life and mobility with the term 'living strategy,' and now we would like to reexamine this within the framework of a notion of 'agency.'

The Iban as agents

Agency of the movers

The Iban have often been portrayed by the mass media and NGOs as people who were expelled from the primary forest because of logging and other development processes. Some stress the irony that people excluded from the forest are forced to work at logging sites, thus taking part in the degradation of their own living space. However, it has been established that the Iban have been largely dependent on secondary rather than primary forests (Freeman 1955). It is true that the areas where they reside have experienced deforestation, but an over-emphasis on the oppressed situation of the Iban could lead to a misunderstanding of their living strategy in the context of modernization in Sarawak.

The Iban in the research area, for example, began to introduce new technologies and different ways of thinking through their interaction with the white rulers and the Chinese in the late nineteenth century. Innovations in agricultural techniques enabled them to plant the wet paddies and the introduction of rubber trees brought them cash income, reducing their dependence on even secondary forests during the last one hundred years. In other words, since the early twentieth century the Iban in the research area, had begun, to some extent, to earn their living away from the forest.

This process could be regarded as one of marginalization as a result of structural forces, in that the Iban were 'excluded' from the forest. However, 'traditional livelihoods' in the forest cannot be realized without complete 'neglect' or non-intervention by the government. From the wider socio-economic and political perspective, such a hands-off policy, which is almost inconceivable, would also have led to the marginalization of the Iban. In fact, in the 1980s, some ethnic groups including the Iban in the Upper Rajang and Baram Rivers displayed attitudes of open resistance against the government and logging companies, and demanded the conservation of the forest as their living space. Their attitudes, however, resulted in more radical interference in their lives by the government and the companies, which often ended up worsening their situation. This process may, in fact, be the culmination of the marginalization of indigenous peoples.

In contrast to those in the Upper areas, the Iban in the research area chose another way; that is, they decided to go out of their longhouses in the relatively early stages of Sarawak's modernization process. In the 1960s in particular, rapid development in the logging and oil industries generated a large demand for labor and many young Iban males began to work away from home. In the 1980s the diversification of job opportunities in the city accelerated their flow, taking the family unit with them. While positive in some respects, those Iban that moved to the urban area also began to recognize that their change of residence placed them in a marginal position within the local, state and national context. In other words, their choice to move to the city was also part of the process of marginalization.

Migration is often explained through narratives in which the rural inhabitants, mostly men, migrate in response to negative factors such as environmental change, population growth or increasing economic pressure (de Haan et al. 2002). In addition, views about migration and migrants are often based on an assumption of sedentarism; that is, populations that used to be immobile and have been uprooted by economic environmental forces (de Haan 1999). In this sense, the migration of rural populations into urban areas has often been regarded as a consequence of institutional and structural disadvantage. In the case of the Iban, however, they 'chose to move' to Sibu even if their range of choices was limited.

From the perspective of urban administration, the inflow of rural people into the city has been considered undesirable and regarded as a source of various social problems such as 'overpopulation,' increased unemployment, and housing shortages in urban centers. Much of the literature on migration has been silent about the kinds of policies that were introduced to try to alleviate these problems. De Haan and Rogaly (2002) explain that this is because migration tends to be an uncomfortable area for policy-makers, with studies and policies tending to assume immobile populations, revealing their 'sedentary bias' (de Haan 2002).

Koczberski's statement that the uncertain economic future for the majority of rural and urban populations, and rising inequalities in income opportunities and access to resources, have coincided with greater intolerance of migrant groups and attempts by governments at all levels to restrict internal migration, particularly urbanization (Koczberski et al. 2001; Koczberski and Curry 2004) can be applied to many regions of Southeast Asia. Population movement is seen as a disjuncture, and as such is undesirable. It can be said that such a spatial cognition is socially constructed, sometimes restricting people's movements and sometimes guiding their behavior. In this sense, the rural/urban divide is itself structural in nature.[3] In effect, the Sarawak government has regarded population flow from rural to urban areas as problematic and tried to reduce it because the increase in illegal land occupation and urban unemployment might disturb the urban administration. In effect, the government planned to set up 'Rural Growth Centers' to reduce population flow from rural to urban areas and its incidental urban problems. However, this project has not been very effective. The Iban in the research area not only moved from longhouses to the town of Sibu but also undertook reciprocal, frequent and complicated moves between the two locations. This pattern of movement has been difficult for administrative systems to grasp. Government and policy makers have failed to understand the migration patterns of the Iban people because they have tried to understand their movement in the framework of rural-to-urban migration. However, their urban sojourn should be recognized as a temporary one in a process of continuous flow, rather than the accumulation of rural poverty in the city.

Agents in Sibu

The Iban who moved to Sibu have become more acutely aware of their marginality through their interaction with other ethnic groups and with the macro-society. In Sibu they experience the urban economy that is reflected in Chinese society and have become conscious that Malaysia is a Muslim country. In other words, the town of Sibu is an institution different from that of the longhouse community, and in this sense it is a *'negeri'* for the Iban who come from the hinterland area.

While the difference in society and culture between Sibu and rural areas often disadvantage the Iban, who come from rural longhouses, they have not chosen to adopt an attitude of open resistance. Instead, they devise ways to cooperate and associate with other ethnic groups such as the Malay, Melanau and Chinese groups in the squatter settlement in Sibu, obtaining a more stable living base in Kampung Sentosa resettlement area. As for job opportunities, while the Iban complain about inequality between the Muslim and non-Muslim, they chose to get a tiny share of the profits provided by the *bumiputera* policy. In addition, their pro-government demonstrations during election periods were an elaborated strategy to bring government-led development projects to the longhouse with an eye to their future return in their long-term life plan.

In observing these strategies, one may regard that the Iban tamely enjoy a lower but relatively steadier life in a 'second class *bumiputera* status.' However, they have not necessarily been domesticated or structurally embedded in the urban economy and national policy. Their voting tactics, for example, have the potential to reduce the meaning of conventional rural development policy in Sarawak, in that many people endeavor to bring development projects to rural areas, and at the same time, transfer the profit from the longhouse back to the city, in both regular and irregular ways. Their strategy to improve living conditions, in both rural and urban areas, shows that it is impossible to grasp their lives from a viewpoint based on the conventional rural/urban dichotomy. In this process, the government has become forced to negotiate with both rural and urban dwellers even in the promotion of rural development policy.

Another case concerning the election in Kanowit apparently showed an attitude of resistance against the government in that the longhouse community in Rantau Kemiding supported a powerful independent candidate. However, it was not a straightforward and unsophisticated resistance, but rather many supporters took part in the political campaign in the prospect of their future inroads into the power structure of Sarawak's politics. Their attempts had unfortunately proved abortive, but there was a potential to transform the current political structure. People in Rantau Kemiding and the Kanowit District still clearly remember the split in the then Dayak-based political party, SNAP, and the formation of the new party, PBDS. Although many of them narrate the political event as if in self-mockery, they partly evaluate that the event forced the government to be more conscious of rural development especially in the Iban area. It can be said that behind the political activities of the Iban in Rantau Kemiding there was a faint expectation for change in politics in Sarawak. With this expectation, the Iban in the research area sometimes display naïve and unsophisticated attitudes, and at other times enact complicated and rather shrewd strategies.

The *bilek*-family and longhouse community as institutions

We have to discuss the agency of the Iban in the research area in relation to the *bilek*-family and longhouse community, because these can be considered to have institutionalized elements. De Haan et al. (2002: 55), for instance, state 'household and kinship networks structure the movement of individuals, by providing them with some independence while at the same time retaining them within these networks.' Migration and human mobility out of the village does not directly result in the disunity of the rural household. However, movers and migrants sometimes act against the interest of the household for example, they may cheat family members for their own convenience and prepare for a breakaway from the original household (de Haan et al. 2002). Thus human mobility may destabilize the institutions within the household.

This study could not conduct a detailed investigation into labor allocation within the *bilek*-family, but we could make clear that out-migration of females resulted in the older family members engaging in subsistence agriculture in the village and that the extended stay of married children in the city made it difficult for the parents in the longhouse to decide a successor of the *bilek*.

Kedit (1993) emphasized the prescriptive effect of the *bejalai* custom in terms of Iban mobility in the modern context. In other words, their outflow to work away from home had been performed as a kind of traditional cultural institution. As discussed in the previous chapters, however, this cultural institution has been gradually transformed by the outflow of the family unit and the subsequent expansion of their living spaces. Although adult children in Sibu have a great influence in providing financial assistance for the parents in the longhouse, these children in Sibu have established an independent household from the parents at least in terms of their livelihood. As the conventional customs of the Iban was not necessarily comfortable for the town dweller, they tried to interpret the tradition more broadly to deal with the increased uncertainty of *bilek* succession and land inheritance with careful attention to the rural development processes in Sarawak. This performance of urban sojourners affected the changes in family relations among the Iban population in the research area. On the other hand, the parents living in the longhouse are to a greater or lesser degree dependent on the economic support from their adult children in the city, and also anxious about who will be a successor and take care of them when they are aged. This is why the parents in the longhouse tend to acknowledge their children in the city as retaining membership of their *bilek*-family in the longhouse, and also allowing for the broad interpretation of traditional customs. Moreover, the increase in the number of those who were born in the city as the 'second generation' of movers and their new styles of *bejelai* activities, may affect the reproduction system of the *bilek*-family in the longhouse.

Spatially extensive connections between longhouse residents and urban sojourners not only affect family relations within each *bilek*-family, but also have the potential to transform the structure of the longhouse community itself. General opinions and consensus—especially those concerning rural development—among the longhouse residents are often formed under the influence of urban sojourners. In addition, longhouse communities that attach importance on the ability to access and negotiate with macro-societies tend to choose their leaders from the urban sojourners. The growing presence of urban sojourners among the longhouse residents is closely related to the structural changes occurring in the Iban community.

Agents on the move

As shown above, while the Iban in the research area are embedded in various levels of structural social relations and often act as if they are guided by these social constructs, they reiterate negotiations at each level, sometimes successfully and sometimes not. Their various activities—regardless of whether they are intentionally or unintentionally performed—have the potential to transform current structures and can be seen as their 'agency.' These activities encompass the living strategy of the Iban.

When we consider Sarawak politics from a macro-perspective, or consider the 'federal factor' at the national level, the power structure seems to be absolute. A pessimist might think that there is no room for the Iban to transform this structure. However, close observation at a more micro-level shows that the Iban sometimes passively adapt to existing power relations and sometimes counteract the influence of the structures at various levels by adopting both regular and irregular approaches. From the perspective of Iban movers, family and village structures are related to the political trends of the state. Land development in rural areas and the improvement of both rural and urban lives can be achieved through the coordination of family and village members and also through their negotiations with macro-societies. The increased contact between rural residents and macro-society may accelerate change in a social structure that was previously regarded as spatially divided into the rural and the urban. Thus, the social actions of Iban movers in Sibu and its hinterland have articulated different levels of society and at the same time, showed the possibilities of boring a 'wind hole' in the structures at various levels.

This study observed the social actions of the Iban movers with an emphasis on the spatial expansion of their living base. If space is considered to be a social relation that is involved in the production and reproduction of social structures, social action and power and resistance relations (Gotham 2003), then the Iban are social actors who have constructed a new living space straddling Sibu and its hinterland villages, blurring the rural/urban distinction and articulating micro and macro-societies. In the process of changing their mobility patterns, they have tended to break down rather than evoke the urban/rural binary, which makes it difficult for policy makers and social scientists to maintain a structural understanding of this dichotomy. In this sense, the Iban in the research area are agents on the move.

Notes

Chapter 2

1 In 1893 the Kanowit Catholic Church first registered its 161.25 acres of land, most of which was used as a demonstration farm for experimental agriculture.

2 Although Kanowit is linked to Sibu by road, the towns and villages in the upper areas are still only accessible by river.

3 In 1998 a small-scale 'supermarket' was opened, which sold goods only for cash. This also contributed to the weakening of patron-client relations between the Chinese and the Iban.

4 The Foochow is now the second largest Chinese dialect group in Sarawak.

5 According to the *Yearbook of Statistics 2005* (Department of Statistics Sarawak 2005), the estimated number of urban population in the Sibu District was slightly less than in the Miri District. Therefore, Sibu is now the third largest urban center in Sarawak, following Kuching and Miri.

6 Most of the express boats that go along the Rajang River commence at Sibu.

7 As Dwyer (1975) pointed out, very poor quality settlements, such as squatter areas and slums, most of which were constructed by rural-to-urban migrants, can be observed not only in the primate cities but in every city and town in Southeast Asia. Thus, rural-to-urban migrants and low-quality settlements are also important elements of urbanness in Southeast Asia.

8 In this study I define a 'local city/town' as a regional center to differentiate it from primate cities and their satellite cities, which have larger socio-economic importance in the national context. Similar terms such as 'secondary city' and 'intermediate city' are often used in an academic context, but these adjectives are not appropriate to use before the word 'town.' Thus, local city/town can be used in a broader sense.

9 From a case study in Ujun Pandang, however, Yamashita (1986) concluded that it is difficult to define 'urbanness' in a sociological sense because Ujun Pandang is composed of separate and disconnected communities such as the Traja, Bugis and Makassar. The emphasis on the separation of each ethnic group differs little from the concept of 'enclaves in a peasant society.' In this sense, his attempt has proved abortive.

10 However, Rondinelli's suggestion is not realistic in that he expects local leaders to act altruistically to lead development and improvement of the home place (for example, substantial investment in the regional economy and promotion of social reform in cooperation with local residents). For local economic leaders or entrepreneurs, the most important strategy, both in investment and distribution, is access to powerful politicians. Meanwhile, local political leaders are able to lay a foundation for their activities by forming a back-scratching alliance with local entrepreneurs. Moreover, their activities are often under the control of the central government. In this sense, even if such leaders perform locally oriented actions, it is questionable whether they contribute towards raising the standard of living of local residents. As for power mechanisms in local cities, Kawanaka's (2000) case study in the Philippines is relevant.

Chapter 3

1 Because Iban language and its pronunciation have regional differences, the rules of spelling are still inconsistent even among scholars. This book follows the orthography of Kedit (1993).

2 The Iban vocabulary has no word equivalent to 'family.' Therefore, strictly speaking, to adopt the word '*bilek*-family' is questionable. However, those who live together in a *bilek* are recognized as a managing unit of swidden agriculture and this unit is referred to as a *se-bilek,* with the prefix '*se*' meaning 'one.' In this sense, *se-bilek* virtually corresponds to a stem family. This book, following previous studies, calls such a unit the *bilek*-family. The notion of *bilek*-family will be discussed in detail in Chapter 7.

3 Since the 1990s, the Sarawak Government does not approve of the construction of a new longhouse that contains less than 10 *bileks.*

4 This road was partly paved in 2003.

5 A few vans, irregularly but frequently, come and go between the village and the town and the fee for traveling one way in the van is one *Ringgit* Malaysia. One *Ringgit* Malaysia was equivalent to 0.40 $ in 1996, but it was fixed to 0.26 in September 1998 to alleviate the influence of the economic recession brought about in late 1997.

6 This school is managed by the Kanowit Catholic Church.

7 According to Tan Sri Datuk Gerunsin Lembat (1994), the longhouse territory is called '*pemakai menoa*,' which means a certain area occupied by a longhouse or a village community and the area includes agricultural lands, vegetable farms, orchards, graveyards, water sources, forests and so

on. The Iban in Kanowit seldom use the term '*pemakai menoa*,' but instead they usually call such an area '*lumpong*' with almost the same meaning. Old people in Rantau Kemiding remembered that most of the longhouses in the area were established after the 1930s and that a project, which confirmed the village boundaries had been undertaken. At that time, the Land Order of 1931 and the Land Settlement Order of 1933 provided for the registration of village boundaries (Hong 1987: 44–45). This probably encouraged the project to define the village boundaries in the Kanowit area. In the end, however, this project was not completed because it was extremely difficult to demarcate village or community boundaries in strict conformity with the actual situation (Land and Survey Department of Sarawak, Annual Report 1966). Therefore, the research area has no official record on the village boundaries. The boundary shown in Figure 3.1 is simply a rough sketch. According to the villagers, the boundary definition project was promoted on the advice of the Kanowit Catholic Church. There was a loose consensus of neighboring longhouses that the customary land usufruct of each longhouse community should be, in principle, limited to that within the territory. Since there was abundant land suitable for planting dry paddies and also, at that time, rubber gardens were still small in number and size, no conflict or confusion occurred as a result of defining rough village boundaries.

8 As a *tuai rumah* is given a small monthly allowance by the government as the head of the smallest unit of an administrative organization, government employees cannot be a *tuai rumah*. The *tuai rumah* of Longhouse B is not formally approved as the head of the longhouse, because he works for a government office in the Kanowit Town. In this sense, Longhouse B is an informal organization.

9 Although most of the old documents were lost during the period of Japanese occupation, some baptism records are left in fragments in the Kanowit Catholic Church. In the records written in the late 1920s, for example, we can find that Empam baptized several local Ibans during the year.

10 They usually cultivate various kinds of vegetables and fruits on dry paddy fields such as pumpkin, cucumber, corn, gourd, watermelon, bean and cassava. As the harvesting seasons of these crops are different, they are used as supplementary foods before harvesting the paddy in February, and are thought to be a kind of risk dispersion.

11 In those days the Iban used to shift even the wet paddy field almost every year.

12 According to the Sarawak Gazette (March 31, 1970, p.51), the Kanowit Catholic Church planted new crops such as coffee and pepper on the church's demonstration farm and tried to educate the local Iban to adopt these crops.

However, the church did not produce good results until 1910 when Father Adrian Klerk introduced rubber trees.

13 Hong (1987) pointed out that one of the factors that encouraged the Iban to settle down was the government's frequent revision of land laws for the purpose of prohibiting the opening of virgin forests and restricting the migration of indigenous peoples. In addition, Soda (1999) assumes that the concept of exclusive land ownership among the Iban evolved from planting rubber on fallowed land and that the increase in land value contributed to the restriction of the longhouse community's migration.

14 Umpau was appointed as a member of the Kanowit Mixed Local Authority (KMLA) in 1955. This authority was established as a result of the reorganization of Kanowit Sea Dayak Local Authority (KSDLA) for the purpose of training local Ibans to become administrative officers and only allowed membership of local Ibans. KSDLA was dissolved and later reorganized into KMLA, allowing membership by other ethnic groups in Kanowit. The members, at the beginning, included seventeen *penghulus* (Ibans), four Chinese, two Malays, one Rajang (Kanowit) and three Iban women. After serving for KMLA as an administrative officer, Umpau entered Sarawak's political arena to become a state assemblyman in 1963 and in 1965 obtained the post as the Minister of the Department of Land and Mineral Resources.

15 These irrigation systems were intended to afford opportunities to the local Iban to plant wet paddies efficiently. The village people, under the guidance of the Agricultural Department, constructed the systems. As both of the irrigation systems had been buried underground, it is unknown how large the systems were.

16 The Annual Report of District Officer Kanowit appeared in the Sarawak Gazette and described the educational facilities in the district as follows:

The most important educational establishments in the District are the Roman Catholic Mission School at Kanowit, which caters for about 240 Chinese and 95 Dayak children up to Standard 6, and the Rural Development School which teaches improved methods of rural technology to some 30 selected married couples, most Dayaks, across river from Kanowit...In general it may be said that there is still a large undeveloped agricultural potential in the District. There are a number of extensive swamp areas capable of development on a comprehensive scale for the cultivation of irrigated paddy. The example of the Rural Improvement School could be followed on a greatly increased scale. At present the swamp lands support relatively few Dayaks...(Annual Report of District Officer Kanowit, Sarawak Gazette, May 31, 1952, p.103).

17 An article on the lecture about agricultural poison was published in the Sarawak Gazette. It noted that:

Headmen from the District of each *Penghulu* could, on pre-arranged dates, be called down to some convenient place where they could be lectured on the use of the poison and then take it away (Annual Report of District Officer Kanowit, Sarawak Gazette, August 30, 1952, p.189).

18 The Sarawak Government has seen the shifting cultivation practices of indigenous peoples as primitive and exploitative agricultural methods that lead to degradation of tropical forests (Hong 1987). The government introduced wet paddy with the intention of protecting primary forests against agricultural use and utilizing tropical trees for export. It was in 1964 that timber became the primary export of Sarawak, surpassing the export of rubber.

19 Immediately after the death of Duit, his daughter, Eda was considered to be first in line to succeed the *tuai rumah*. However, Eda refused the initial proposal and her husband, Klukok was asked to become the leader (see Figure 3.3).

20 The term 'Dayak' was bestowed on collective ethnic groups who lived in the interior in Borneo during the colonial period. By the middle of the twentieth century, the Iban were often called 'Sea Dayak' and the 'Bidayuh' came to be known as 'Land Dayak.'

21 For details of this political incident, see Chapter 6.

22 According to an interview with an officer of the Kanowit District, many longhouse communities divided and regrouped in the 1980s as a result of Iban-related political affairs.

23 There are various reasons for this, for instance, land shortage, discord among the village members, dealing with the increase in population, keeping losses to a minimum in case of fire, and so on.

Chapter 4

1 I was given advice and assistance by the District Officer of the Kanowit District in deciding on the study area.

2 The Iban vocabulary for job or occupation is closely tied to words concerning migration. Kedit (1993) explained these words as follows in relation to the Iban's migration: *bejalai* is to go on journeys with the view of acquiring wealth, material goods and social prestige, and *bekuli* is to undertake wage-laboring or to take on labor migration, while *kerja* is to work as a non-manual wage-earner.

3 For example, Freeman (1970: 224–225) reported that in an Iban community

of the Balleh region all of the unmarried males between 16 and 30 years old (15 persons) and 75 percent of the married males under 40 years old (16 persons) engaged in *bejalai* for three to six months during his research period in 1949 and 1950. He also calculated, using the data obtained in the surrounding longhouse communities that about 20 percent of adult males were absent from the longhouse throughout the year.

4 This word is thought to derive from the Malay word '*kerja*.'

5 One *Ringgit* Malaysia was equivalent to 0.40 $ in 1996. As for the dollar exchange, see endnote 5 in Chapter 3.

6 In this chapter, I consider the heads of each *bilek*-family and their children to be of Rantau Kemiding origin regardless of their current place of residence. Whether the stay-outs should be regarded as village members or not will be discussed in Chapter 7. For the occupation data, I counted those persons 15 years old and above. Because it was difficult to interview the stay-outs, the data on occupation was obtained mainly through interviews with those who stayed in the village, but I tried to confirm this information as much as possible. Some stay-outs were visited at their current residences in town and some were interviewed when they returned temporarily to the longhouse.

7 In this chapter, those females who engaged in '*ngibun rumah*' (to take care of domestic affairs) are classified as a 'housewife.' It is presumed that among these 'housewives' some are temporarily engaged in informal jobs such as selling homemade cookies, contract work in a factory, or as a babysitter. But if the head of a *bilek*-family does not recognize their daughters' work, I categorized them as 'housewife.'

8 There is a preconception that the Malay and Melanau are in power, the Chinese control the economy, and the Iban supply the manual labor.

9 There is no clear criterion to judge whether an urban dweller is still considered a longhouse member or not. Those who move out to another longhouse to marry are regarded as nonmembers of their original community, though in some cases they return to the original *bilek* with their spouse. As will be mentioned, there are several vacant *bileks* in Rantau Kemiding, which are not necessarily abandoned. In principle, when a *bilek*-family leaves the longhouse to join another community, the family forfeits their various rights in the original longhouse. However, regarding the vacant *bileks* in Rantau Kemiding, the *bilek* owners who currently reside in urban areas are expected to return to the longhouse in the near future. They also retain their rights as community members. The membership of a *bilek*-family will be discussed in Chapter 7.

10 This number cannot be thought uncommon in urban areas. For example, according to the *State Population Report Sarawak 1991*, the urban population of the Iban is 42 982 males and 42 680 females, and among them, those who

are employed (between 15 to 64 years old) number 22 385 males (52 percent) and 8344 females (20 percent) (Department of Statistics Malaysia 1995b). This illustrates the relatively low rate of female employment.

11 In the earlier stage of Sarawak's development, most urban centers were export centers for a specific product. Sibu was an export port for timber products, Miri was the base for a developing oil field, and Bintulu was a center, which produced natural gas. Recently, these towns have also begun to compete with the raw material processing industries and tourist industries by capitalizing on cultural experiences and the natural environment.

12 Many Iban mention the educational disparities between the urban and rural areas. They are also acutely aware of the effects of educational background on job opportunity and wage level. For example, Chinese schools, which are rarely found in rural areas, attract considerable attention from the Iban because of their higher educational level. Thus, some parents of Rantau Kemiding origin send their children to Chinese schools for better future opportunities.

13 Numerous authors pointed out that investment in the education of children and other family members has also become a very important part of rural household asset diversification (Ellis 2000; Booth 2004; Leinbach 2004).

14 Though there are regional and annual differences, the agricultural cycle of planting dry paddies can be roughly summarized as follows: felling trees and mowing underbrush in June and July, burning in August, seeding in September and early in October, and harvesting in February and March. On the other hand, the cycle of wet paddy planting is a little different: mowing and weeding in July, burning in August, making a rice nursery late in August and early in September, transplanting in October, and harvesting in February and March. In both cases, the Iban weed a few times by December and sometimes spray insecticide. (See Figure 3.4 in Chapter 3.)

15 The Iban tend to plant many kinds of paddy on a small piece of land. Even in wet paddy fields, they try to plant dry paddies on a small convex ground. In Table 4.8, such insignificant amounts of planted paddy are indicated as '*mit*' (*mimit*: a little), which, for the sake of convenience, is excluded from the total sum.

16 Out of 39 kinds of paddy, 12 were adaptable to both wet and dry fields.

17 Each *bilek*-family is supposed to have a few kinds of supplementary sacred rice, called *padi sangking,* other than the *padi pun.* This supplementary sacred rice also has a symbolic meaning in the succession of the *bilek*. Freeman (1970: 50–51) assumed that it is possible to trace the family line by retracing the *padi pun* and *padi sangking.*

18 One person asserted that, for those who had converted to Christianity, the sacred rice did not retain its significance any longer.

19 *Bilek* and *ruai* are regarded as having contrasting functions, which is

related to the dichotomous pattern generally found in Iban society. See Uchibori (1991) for further information about these relations, categories and symbols.

20 Because the Malaysian Government has an age-limit system for the retirement of government employees (55 years old as of 1996), in this book those who are 55 years old and above are regarded as old people.

21 Refer to Figure 3.6 in Chapter 3.

Chapter 5

1 Dwyer (1975) pointed out that the definition of 'illegal settlement' might depend on arbitrary judgment where the government's legal system is incomplete or where the customary laws of several ethnic groups are interwoven with each other. Therefore, he advocated the use of the term 'spontaneous settlement' in substitution for the term 'squatter settlement' which lays stress on its 'illegality.'

2 Even within the field of geographical study we can find extensive literature on Southeast Asian cities (McGee 1967, 1971, 1975; Dwyer 1975; Hugo 1981, 1983; Drakakis-Smith 1987; McGee and Robinson 1995).

3 Latin American countries paved the way for studies on the emergence of the urban poor.

4 The marginality theory of the urban poor emerged from the study of Latin American cities, which subsequently led to lively discussions. The details of these discussions are well explained in Yonemura (1991b).

5 In the field of social anthropology, since the work of Radcliffe-Brown and Evans-Pritchard, an individual was recognized as being structurally involved in a society and controlled by it. In the same way, the urban poor and their social networks established in urban areas were regarded as the extension of the social relations that had been traditionally constructed in their home villages. It was not until the 1970s that, apart from such classical structuralism, a new viewpoint was proposed that urban in-migrants were enclosed within another structure such as a state or the modern world system. These views were flourishing particularly in the field of urban anthropology in Africa (Matsuda 1990).

6 The conceptualization of the existence of the urban poor, such as 'peasants in cities' or 'marginal man' is a good example (Mangin 1970; McGee 1973; Roberts 1978; Fujimaki 1993).

7 For instance, see Kato (1986), Stark and Lucas (1988), Zenno (1994), Firman (1994), Erman (1998), Hataya (1998), and Matsuda (1998).

8 In the 1960s the Malaysian government, began to create so-called 'New

Towns,' which were intended to ease the over-concentration of population into the Kuala Lumpur metropolitan area and to create new labor opportunities in rural areas, but the government did not propose any policy on existing local cities and towns (Lee 1987). In Sarawak, on the other hand, in 1991, the state government designated several local towns as 'Rural Growth Centers' and agreed to redevelop the existing local towns to ease migration to urban centers. However, there was no perceptible effect on the development of rural areas or a reduction of out-migration of the rural indigenous population.

9 On the matter of the peripheral situation of Sarawak in the national context of Malaysia, see King (1988, 1990).

10 '*Bumiputera* policy' is officially called the 'New Economic Policy,' See Chapter 2.

11 An article reported that an Iban man in Peninsular Malaysia was not approved as a *bumiputera*; this was closely related to his background of Sarawak origin and his Christian religious beliefs (Far Eastern Economic Review, June 12, 1997: 27).

12 Strictly speaking, non-*bumiputera* includes Indian, Indonesian, and other small groups besides the Chinese, and non-Muslim *bumiputera* includes Bidayuh, Kayan, Kenyah, Christian Melanau, and so on. In the administrative reports in Sibu, however, details of ethnic groups are not specified, but the terms Chinese, Malay/Melanau, and Iban are used synonymously with non-*bumiputera*, Muslim *bumiputera*, and non-Muslim *bumiputera*. To avoid this difficulty and for the sake of convenience, this book follows the terminology of the administrative reports.

13 The research in Sibu was mainly conducted from June to September 1999 and January 2000. Additional fieldwork was carried out in 2002. This chapter uses survey data as of September 1999 unless otherwise stated.

14 This is according to the interview with a staff member of the Enforcement Section, the Land and Survey Department (Sibu Branch).

15 In 1996 there still existed a number of squatters who had not yet built a new house in the Kg. Sentosa resettlement area. In the early 1990s there were squatter huts on the vacant land on this side, although they had already moved to Kg. Sentosa.

16 Even bicycles and motorbikes went on this narrow path.

17 According to the report prepared by the Land and Survey Department in 1983, 57 percent of *bumiputera* were employed in the government sector even though the report did not distinguish between the Iban and the Malay (Land and Survey Department, Sibu Branch 1984).

18 This means that local towns in Sarawak have been moving various development programs into the fringes of urban areas. Concerning Kg.

UJ settlement, squatter clearance was set in motion for the purpose of the construction of an exclusive residential district with Chinese-based capital.

19 However, any clear criterion to approve an application was not specified.

20 As of 1991, one *Ringgit* Malaysia was approximately equal to 0.37 US dollars.

21 According to the Land Law of Sarawak, the entire land of Sarawak belongs to the state. Therefore, so-called land title means the rights to lease state land. The period of the lease is limited to within 60 years, which can be renewed so as to extend the period. As for the land administration in Sarawak, see Hong (1987) and Soda (1999).

22 This is according to the interview with the Chairman of JKKK of the Iban area in Phase 1 and a staff member of the Enforcement Section, Land and Survey Department (Sibu Branch).

23 For example, the average number of households (*bilek*-family) in a longhouse is 18.1 (Sibu District Office, *Senarai ketua-ketua masyarakat dan ketua-ketua kaum di daerah Sibu*, 1999). Similarly, the average number of households in a longhouse in the Kanowit District is 17.9 (Kanowit District Office, *Senarai ketua kaum di bawah bidangkuasa ketua masyarakat daerah Kanowit*, 1996). As longhouses began to take on the character of permanent residence and the population of the longhouse community increased naturally, fairly large communities have emerged and now it is not unusual for a village community to have multiple longhouses. However, it is still rare to find a village, which contains more than 200 households.

24 A man who was born in 1953 and served in the military between 1973 and 1995 confessed that since 1973 he lived in quarters within the military camp with his wife and two children, but that in 1982 he constructed a house in Kg. UJ. This was because he believed the rumor that if he built a house in Kg. UJ he would be given a lot by the government. Some of his friends tried to discourage him from moving to the squatter area, but he ignored his friend's advice because he knew that many government employees and even policemen had already established their living base in Kg. UJ.

25 The reason why the construction of their houses is seriously delayed is that most of the residents cannot afford to employ professional carpenters, but they themselves are engaged in the construction and they can only scrape up the cost of constructing their houses little by little. Some people live in rented rooms in urban centers until their houses in Kg. Sentosa are built. This is why even the Land and Survey Department does not grasp how many people really live in Kg. Sentosa at the present time.

26 In this book, 'conjugal family' means a family consisting of a conjugal couple and their unmarried children, and 'stem family' refers to the

conjugal couple of a child of the household head. A 'joint family' contains more than two conjugal couples within the same generation.

27 Of those who were in secondary school in Sibu, most of them returned to their original longhouse after graduation. Incidentally, there were four registered household heads that were born in town and have never lived in the longhouse community.

28 Those over 15 years old, except for school attendants, were counted.

29 In Kg. Sentosa every ethnic group in Phase 1 and Phase 2 has its own JKKK organization individually and each JKKK has a chairperson (chief). It was not until the end of 1999 that JKKK of the Iban area in Phase 1 was first registered belatedly because there had been repeated inefficient handling in the process of formal registration.

30 Most of the land that is said to be held in the village is so-called 'Native Customary Land,' which has no registered land title. See Soda (1999) for the perception of land holding in Iban society.

31 This was one of the periodical markets recognized by the municipality. On Sundays, Chinese and Iban people of neighboring villages came to market to sell their perishable foods. Many of the Kg. Sentosa residents went to this market every Sunday to buy fresh food at a reasonable price. This place was very important for both sellers and customers to exchange information. However in 2003, this market was abolished because of sanitary problems.

32 In Sarawak state, the first to the third of June are public holidays for the *Gawai* festival. Many urban dwellers take leave for at least a week to go to their home village during the *Gawai* season.

33 Many people, including urban dwellers, came together at a longhouse in the lower Rajang Basin to celebrate the installation of a small-scale drainage system for the paddy field.

34 While some of Kg. Sentosa residents return home to the village during the New Year holidays, many of them celebrate their new year in Sibu. During Christmas and New Year, many longhouse residents come to Sibu to visit their relatives in town.

35 This point will be re-examined in Chapter 7.

Chapter 6

1 Useful examples in Asia are provided by the following studies: Nagata (1981), Kato (1993), Harrell (1994), Segawa (1995), Winzeler (1997), and papers in the special publication of *Southeast Asian Journal of Social*

Science (10) 1 (1982). For case studies on Sarawak, see Pringle (1970), King (1982), Uchibori (1987), and Ishikawa (1997).

2 See also Lumb (1993), and articles in *Law and Society Review* (28) 3 (1994). Recently, there have been lively discussions in the field of 'political ecology.' Details regarding the emergence of political ecology and its subsequent development can be found in Shimada (1998).

3 For example, see Ayabe (1994) and Russel (1989).

4 There is also the policy of population adjustment, such as encouraging migration from overpopulated areas to agricultural frontiers, for example the construction of FELDA in Malaysia, the transmigration program in Indonesia, and SALCRA in Sarawak. See Bahrin (1988), Jayum (1994), and Elmhirst (1999).

5 On the other hand, it is also relatively easy to 'become an Iban,' and even among those who are categorized as Iban, there exist various ethnic identities such as Memaloh and Bekatan. See Uchibori (1994) and Okuno (2000).

6 These terms are often used with political overtones. The category of *bumiputera* was instrumental in defining the privileged status of indigenous peoples apart from Chinese and Indian, while Dayak, as mentioned later, was raised to inspire unity among non-Muslim indigenous peoples.

7 For the different attitudes of each ethnic group toward the acceptance of the label 'Dayak,' refer to Mason (1995).

8 If we consider the Dayak groups who have converted to Islam (*masuk Melayu*) or a number of non-Muslim *Melanau* subgroups, it is apparent that the concept 'Dayak' does not strictly coincide with that of 'non-Muslim *bumiputera*.' In this study, the convoluted issue of ethnicity will not be addressed.

9 On this point refer to Mason (1995).

10 The PBDS seceded from the Sarawak State coalition, although it still remained in the federal coalition (*Barisan Nasional*), which seemed to the electorate to be a glaring contradiction. Furthermore, the PBDS challenge to the state coalition was undertaken without putting forward a candidate for the Chief Minister of Sarawak in the event of its victory in the election. The failure of the PBDS to show a more aggressive attitude in scrambling for political power disappointed its supporters.

11 According to the 1991 Census, the Iban accounted for 67 percent of the total Dayak population. Iban leadership of the Dayak community is obvious, but the lack of consideration toward other Dayak groups dampened interest in the unity of the community.

12 According to research conducted in 1991 by the Land and Survey Department, Sibu, the Iban occupied some 605 squatter houses. Considering

that the Dudong constituency, which included the squatters' area, had only 18 619 voters (in the 1991 election for State Assemblymen), it is thought that the squatters had some influence on the elections.

13 Aside from the above cases, there have been instances of double and even triple voting registrations in different constituencies, or other instances of bargaining for votes or selling votes. These are illegal activities. A man explained that those who are traveling on official business during the polling period could use a postal vote. He also professed: 'I know the way to register multiple votes both in ordinary registration and postal voting registration. As the registration of voters in Sarawak has not been computerized yet, such illegal registrations are seldom discovered.'

14 Of the remaining five seats, three seats (all from urban constituencies) were occupied by the Chinese-based opposition party.

15 In addition to these two candidates, there was another independent candidate who drew very little public support.

16 Regarding the concept of Native Customary Land and its related problems, see Hong (1987) and Soda (1999).

17 A candidate and his supporters are walking to the Kanowit District Office to file his candidacy for the State Assembly.

18 The supporters of the independent candidate asserted that they should secure their land rights so that their descendants could inherit them. Actually, the supporters of the incumbent candidate also felt unease about the security of their land rights, but their narrative is very different from the assertion of the independent candidate. One of them told me that: 'It may be possible that our land rights will be taken away, but 60 years later, we, our children and even grandchildren will have died already. Rather than being anxious about such a distant future, we should think of how to improve the present stagnant situation of the Iban. Our land is left idle. The plantation may be a chance to accumulate our funds to develop Iban society.'

19 During festivals and election periods many urban dwellers temporarily return to their home village. The road in front of the longhouse is crowded with cars and motorbikes.

20 For example, see the *Sarawak Tribune*, 19 August 1996; the *Sarawak Tribune*, 20 August 1996; and the *Borneo Post*, 3 September 1996.

21 However, due to the torturous and drawn-out process of resolving differences of opinion among the longhouse communities, the application to open the plantation was eventually withdrawn.

22 Another independent candidate gained only 121 votes.

23 The villagers form a line to vote in the election for the State Assembly in

1996. A polling station was set up in a classroom of the government primary school next to Longhouse A.

24 Most of them seemed prepared to approve the plantation scheme on the condition that they could secure a small parcel of land for planting paddies and title deeds to the land intended to be developed for the plantation.

25 From the viewpoint of the traditional cycle of shifting cultivation, 'underutilized' land is important as fallow land. But in this case, the word 'underutilized' (*nadai guna*) indicates the remote possibility of using the land for swidden agriculture in the near future, or it refers to the condition of land covered by rubber trees that are left untapped. Therefore, these types of un-tended land are now rarely recognized as 'fallow land,' but tend to be regarded as idle.

26 Therefore, important longhouse meetings tend to be held on the weekend for the convenience of the urban dwellers. The most popular means of notification is by word of mouth brought by those who frequently move back and forth between urban and rural areas. Communications through message-exchanging programs provided by local radio stations are also important for the rural residents. There are still very few longhouses with telephones installed, but recently some longhouse dwellers have started using mobile phones.

27 The officials who openly participated in these campaigns were transferred to distant places immediately before the voting date through the oppressive intervention of the Sarawak government. Therefore, most government officers try to stay clear of political activities.

28 Concerning the work experiences of these *tuai rumahs*, at the time of my research, one was a taxi driver, one formerly served in the Department of Welfare, one worked for a state hospital as a professional driver, and two were contract workers. The remaining one had no work experience in Sibu.

29 Since primary schools are found even in the remotest parts of the country, one cannot overlook the political influence of schoolteachers in rural communities. As for the roles of schoolteachers in politics in Peninsular Malaysia, see Shamsul (1986).

30 Immediately after the 1987 state election in which the PBDS challenged the state coalition government, many government employees who supported PBDS were forced to resign, and councilors and *penghulu*s on the PBDS side were replaced (Mason 1995). Even in the mass media, politicians often reaffirm that the government has the power to replace such local representatives as *penghulus* and councilors. In practice, the power to

appoint those local leaders is under the jurisdiction of local branches of the Government parties.

31 These seven bureaus are in charge of revitalization activities concerning 'Youth and Culture (*Belia and Kebudayaan*),' 'Women and Livelihood (*Wanita and Urus Rumah Tangga*),' 'Economic Development (*Penbangunan/ Economi*),' 'Welfare (*Kebajikan*),' 'Security and Hygiene (*Keselamatan and Kesihatan*),' 'Education (*Pendidikan*),' and 'Religion (*Keagamaan*).'

32 When rural people apply for development projects, the application will be viewed in a favorable light if it bears the signatures of persons who have strong connections with the government. In short, what is important is how to develop and maintain close ties with *penghulus*, councilors, high administrative officials, and so on.

Chapter 7

1 For example, the Rantau Kemiding Village is not an officially registered name, but the village is administratively named following the name of the longhouse head. Therefore, the village name changes according to the replacement or take-over of the head.

2 In most cases the head of the longhouse community also holds the post of the head of the village JKKK.

3 The concept of Native Customary Land will be described in the following section.

4 Land in Sarawak can be classified into five categories, that is, Mixed Zone Land, Native Customary Land, Native Area Land, Interior Area Land and Reserved Land. The land mentioned in this paper mostly belongs to Native Customary Land. As for the details of the land tenure system and land administration in Sarawak, see, for example, Zaidi (1985).

5 For instance, see Wilk (1989), Takada (1991), and Koppel and Hawkins (1994).

Chapter 8

1 On this point, Reardon et al. (2001) also outlined a suggestive case of income diversification of the 'educated landless' in Central and South America.

2 In this context, Hoddinott (1994) uses the word 'contract' on the assumption that the most important card for parents in the village is inheritable land. By analyzing the parent-child relationship in terms of land inheritance and remittance, he tried to generalize the so-called Todaro (1969) model.

3 Koppel (1986, 1991) and Koppel and Hawkins (1994) assert that, taking economic development in Asia into account, it is unreasonable to consider the terms 'rural' and 'agrarian,' or 'urban' and 'industry and services' as replaceable. They pointed out that the concepts of 'rural' and 'urban' is no longer representative of socio-economically different patterns of development.

4 According to Koppel and Hawkins (1994), previous studies looking at nonagricultural activities considered the 'nonagricultural labor market' in the urban sector as the counterpart of the 'agricultural labor market' in the rural sector. This led to the recognition that 'rural' was equal to 'agricultural.'

5 'Over-urbanization' and 'pseudo urbanization' are used to describe conditions in cities where increases in population have obviously surpassed improvements in the industrial structure and urban infrastructure. The term, 'subsistence urbanization,' describes the state of cities where a large proportion of the urban population has difficulty in maintaining even a minimum standard of living (Niitsu 1973; Fujimaki 1993).

6 For expansion of this argument, see Wazaki (1987) and Matsuda (1990).

7 The converse has also been noted. Schrieder and Knerr (2000) reported that young urban migrants from rural regions in Cameroon have been observed to neglect their traditional obligations to support their elderly parents, especially if they do not intend to return to their native village, do not expect any sizable inheritance, and have no reciprocal insurance commitment with their parents.

8 *Desakota* means a spatial form of intensive rural–urban interaction that is emerging adjacent to and between major urban centers (Lin 2001). This notion was formulated by McGee (1989, 1991) to illustrate an urbanization process that is peculiar to Asian countries. He also compared the form to the '*konjuuka*' zone in Japan, where a mixture of rural–urban population and land use is seen. '*Desa*' is an Indonesian word meaning village or settlement, and '*kota*' means town or urban area.

9 We would like to take an instance that presents the embodied space of the rural and the urban. I undertook an interview with an unmarried young Iban man who was born in Sibu but had *bejalai* experiences to distant places such as the Peninsular Malaysia and Papua New Guinea. In replying to my question he said: 'Although I have a stable job in Sibu now, I used to go for *bejalai* to many places to look for better wage-earning jobs. But, even when I was in distant places, I always returned to Sibu during the *Gawai* festival period and also followed my parents to the longhouse downstream from Sibu. Still now I go back to the longhouse when rituals and events are held, because my home place is Sibu and the longhouse.' In his statement

we can find the simultaneous and overlapping presence of rural and urban spaces in his life. Even those who were born in Sibu often go for *bejalai* a long way, but during the festival season 'return' to the longhouse of their parents' origin. They usually recognize that not only Sibu but also the parent longhouse is simultaneously their home place.

Chapter 9

1 Kedit (1993) explained that the meaning of *belelang* in the modern sense refers to working overseas or in urban centers that prevent or discourage returning home until retirement. This may be adequate for explaining the situation of the Iban in Sibu. However, Kedit also stated that *belelang* may result in losing contact with their traditional background and breaking away from home. This is a very different situation that was indicated in the findings of my research in Sibu.

2 Smith (2004) also pointed out that previous quantitative-based studies have over-privileged economic-related outcomes, and masked the underlying social and cultural decision-making processes of family migrants. In emphasizing the perceived merits of qualitative frameworks to tease out the 'non-economic' dimensions of family migration, Smith asserted that a more sophisticated analysis is required for the study of migration.

3 As for the relation between space and structure, Gotham (2003) conceptualized space as a social construction that shapes social action and guides behavior.

References

Adams, R. H. Jr. (1998), 'Remittances, investment, and rural asset accumulation in Pakistan', *Economic Development and Cultural Change*, 47 (1), pp. 155–173.

Adams, R. H. Jr. (2002), 'Non-farm income, inequality, and land in rural Egypt', *Economic Development and Cultural Change*, 50 (2), pp. 339–363.

Aeria, A. (1997), 'The politics of development and the 1996 Sarawak state elections', *Kajian Malaysia*, 15, pp. 57–83.

Afsar, R. (1999), 'Rural–urban dichotomy and convergence: emerging realities in Bangladesh', *Environment and Urbanization*, 11 (1), pp. 235–246.

Agesa, R. and S. Kim (2001) 'Rural to urban migration as a household decision: evidence from Kenya', *Review of Development Economics*, 5, pp. 60–75.

Agesa, R. U. (2004), 'One family, two households: rural to urban migration in Kenya', *Review of Economics of the Household*, 2, pp. 161–178.

Ahlburg, D. A. and R. P. C. Brown (1998), 'Migrants' intentions to return home and capital transfers: a case study of Tongans and Samoans in Australia', *The Journal of Development Studies*, 35 (2), pp. 125–151.

Ahmad, M. A. and F. Y. Noran (1991) 'Development and change in Batang Ai, Sarawak: perception of a resettled Iban community', *Sarawak Museum Journal*, 63, pp. 267–282.

Alderman, H. P., A Chiappori, L. Haddad, J. Hoddinott, and R. Kanbur (1995), 'Unitary versus collective models of the household: is it time to shift the burden of proof?', *World Bank Research Observer*, 10, pp. 1–19.

Appell, G. N. (1997) 'The history of research on traditional land tenure and tree ownership in Borneo', *Borneo Research Bulletin*, 28, pp. 82–97.

Armstrong, W. and T. G. McGee (1985), *Theatres of Accumulation: Studies in Asian and Latin American Urbanization,* London: Methuen.

Ayabe, M. (1994), 'Tai hokubu sanchishakai to heichiseitai: 'Kokkyou' no seijuku e koo shita *chau-khau* no keisei (Upland society and lowland political system in northern Thai: the formation of *Chaau-Khau* in response to the establishment of national boundaries)', *Shakai Jinruigaku Nenpou* (Annual Bulletin of Social Anthropology), 19, pp. 65–90.

Bahrin, T. S. (1988) 'Land settlement in Malaysia: a case study of the Federal Land Development Authority projects', in A.S Oberai (ed.), *Land*

Settlement Policy and Population Redistribution in Developing Countries, New York: Preager, pp. 89–128.

Bajracharya, B. N. (1995) 'Promoting small towns for rural development: a view from Nepal', *Asia-Pacific Population Journal*, 10 (2), pp. 27–50.

Booth, A. (2004), 'The changing importance of off-farm income for agricultural household in Indonesia', in T. R. Leibach (ed.), *The Indonesian Rural Economy: Mobility, Work and Enterprise,* Singapore: ISEAS, pp. 15–37.

Bounthong Bouahom, Douangsavanh Linkham and J. Rigg (2004) 'Building sustainable livelihoods in Laos: untangling farm from non-farm, progress from distress', *Geoforum*, 35, pp. 607–619.

Brown, R. P. C. (1994), 'Migrants' remittances, savings and investment in the South Pacific', *International Labour Review*, 133 (3), pp. 347–368.

Brown, R. P. C. (1997), 'Estimating remittance functions for Pacific Island migrants', *World Development*, 25, pp. 613–626.

Bryant, R. L. and S. Bailey (1997), *Third World Political Ecology,* New York: Routledge.

Bryceson, D. F. (1996) 'Deagrarianization and rural employment in sub-Saharan Africa: a sectoral perspective', *World Development*, 24 (1), pp. 97–111.

Bryceson, D. F. (1997), 'Deagrarianization in sub-Saharan Africa: acknowledging the inevitable', in D. F. Bryceson and V. Jamal (eds), *Farewell to Farms: Deagrarianization and Employment in Africa*, Aldershot: Ashgate (African Studies Center research series 1997/10), pp. 237–256.

Bryceson, D. F. (2000), 'Peasant theories and smallholder policies: past and present', in D. Bryceson, C. Kay and J. Mooij (eds), *Disappearing Peasantries?: Rural Labour in Africa, Asia and Latin America*, London: ITDG Publishing, pp. 1–36.

Bryceson, D. F. (2002), 'The scramble in Africa: reorienting rural livelihoods', *World Development*, 30 (5), pp. 725–739.

Burawoy, M. (1976), 'The functions and reproduction of migrant labour: comparative material from southern Africa and the United States', *American Journal of Sociology*, 81 (5), pp. 1050–1080.

Butterworth, D. R. (1970), 'A study of the urbanization process among Mixtec migrants from Tilantongo in Mexico City', in M. Mangin (ed.), *Peasants in Cities: Readings in the Anthropology of Urbanization*, Boston: Houghton Mifflin, pp. 98–113.

Caces, F. F. A., J. Fawcett and R. Gardner (1985), 'Shadow households and competing auspices: migration behaviour in the Philipines', *Journal of Development Economics*, 17 (1/2), pp. 5–25.

Cederroth, S. and I. Gerdin (1986), 'Cultivating poverty: the case of the green revolution in Lombok', in I. Norlund, S. Cederroth and I. Gerdin (eds), *Rice Societies: Asian Problems and Prospects,* London: Scandinavian Institute of Asian Studies and Curzon Press, pp. 124–150.

Chambers, R. (1983), *Rural Development: Putting the Last First*, Essex: Longman.

Champion, T. and G. Hugo (2001), 'Introduction: moving beyond the urban-rural dichotomy', in T. Champion and G. Hugo (eds), *New Forms of Urbanization: Beyond the Urban-Rural Dichotomy*, Burlington: Ashgate, pp. 3–42.

Chant, S. and S.A. Radcliffe (1992), 'Migration and development: the importance of gender', in S. Chant (ed.), *Gender and Migration in Developing Countries*, London: Belhaven Press, pp. 1–29.

Chin, J. (1996), 'PBDS and ethnicity in Sarawak politics', *Journal of Contemporary Asia*, 26 (4), pp. 512–526.

Choguill, C. L. (1989), 'Small town and development: a tale from two countries', *Urban Studies*, 26, pp. 267–274.

Cleary, M. and P. Eaton (1995), *Borneo: Change and Development,* Kuala Lumpur: Oxford University Press.

Cohen, A. (1969), *Custom and Politics in Urban Africa: a Study of Hausa Migration in Yoruba Towns*, London: Routledge & Kegan Paul.

Cramb, R. A. (1986), *The Evolution of Iban Land Tenure*, Monash University: Centre for Southeast Asian Studies, Working Paper no.39.

Cramb, R. A. (1989), 'Explaining variations in Bornean land tenure: the Iban case', *Ethnology*, 28, pp. 277–300.

Cramb, R. A. (1992), 'Problems of state-sponsored land schemes for small farmers: the case of Sarawak, Malaysia', *Pacific Viewpoint*, 33, pp. 58–78.

Cramb, R. A. and I.R. Wills (1990), 'The role of traditional institutions in rural development: community-based land tenure and government land policy in Sarawak, Malaysia', *World Development*, 18 (3), pp. 347–360.

Curry, G. and G. Koczberski (1998), 'Migration and circulation as a way of life for the Wosera Abelam of Papua New Guinea', *Asia Pacific Viewpoint*, 39 (1), pp. 29–52.

Curtain, R. L. (1981), 'Migration in Papua New Guinea: the role of the peasant household in a strategy of survival', in G.W. Jones and H.V. Ritcher (eds), *Population Mobility and Development: Southeast Asia and the Pacific*, Sydney: Development Studies Center, Australian National University (Development Studies Center Monograph No. 27), pp. 187–204.

Danaraj, N. (1995), 'Challenges, options and prospects for higher value-added industrialisation for Sarawak: beyond primary processing', in H. Solhee, B.J. Bujang and S.A. Hua (eds), *Sarawak the Next Step,* Kuching: Heng Sing Brothers Press, pp. 27–56.

De Haan, A. (1999), 'Livelihoods and poverty: the role of migration a critical review of the migration literature', *The Journal of Development Studies*, 36 (2), pp. 1–47.

De Haan, A. (2002), 'Migration and livelihoods in historical perspective: a case study of Bihar, India', *The Journal of Development Studies*, 38 (5), pp. 115–142.

De Haan, A., K. Brock and N. Coulibaly (2002), 'Migration, livelihoods and institutions: contrasting patterns of migration in Mali', *The Journal of Development Studies*, 38 (5), pp. 37–58.

De Haan, A. and B. Rogaly (2002), 'Introduction: migrant workers and their role in rural change', *The Journal of Development Studies*, 38 (5), pp. 1–14.

Department of Statistics Malaysia (1995a), *Population Report for Local Authority Areas 1991 (Population and housing census of Malaysia 1991)*, Kuala Lumpur: Department of Statistics Malaysia.

Department of Statistics Malaysia (1995b), *State Population Report Sarawak 1991 (Population and housing census of Malaysia 1991)*, Kuala Lumpur: Department of Statistics Malaysia.

Department of Statistics Sarawak (1998), *Yearbook of Statistics Sarawak 1998*, Kuching: Department of Statistics Sarawak.

Department of Statistics Malaysia (2001), *Population Distribution and Basic Demographic Characteristics 2000 (Population and housing census of Malaysia 2000)*, Kuala Lumpur: Department of Statistics Malaysia.

Department of Statistics Sarawak (2002), *Yearbook of Statistics Sarawak 2002*, Kuching: Department of Statistics Sarawak.

Department of Statistics Sarawak (2005), *Yearbook of Statistics Sarawak 2005*, Kuching: Department of Statistics Sarawak.

Dixon, D. (ed.) (1987), *Rural–urban Interaction in the Third World,* London: Developing Area Research Group, Institute of British Geographers.

Douglass, M. (1998), 'A regional network strategy for reciprocal rural–urban linkages', *Third World Planning Review*, 20 (1), pp. 1–33.

Drakakis-Smith, D. (1987), *The Third World City*, London: Methuen.

Dwyer, D. J. (1975), *People and Housing in Third World Cities*, London: Longman.

Edward, L. and P. W. Stevens (1971), *Short Histories of the Lawas and Kanowit Districts*, Kuching: Borneo Literature Bureau.

Ellis, F. (1998), 'Household strategies and rural livelihood diversification', *The Journal of Development Studies*, 35 (1), pp. 1–38.

Ellis, F. (2000), 'The determinants of rural livelihood diversification in developing countries', *Journal of Agricultural Economics*, 51 (2), pp. 289–302.

Elmhirst, R. (1999), 'Space, identity politics and resource control in Indonesia's transmigration programme', *Political Geography*, 18, pp. 813–835.

Elmhirst, R. (2001), 'Resource struggles and the politics of place in North Lampung, Indonesia', *Singapore Journal of Tropical Geography*, 22 (3), pp. 284–306

Elmhirst, R. (2002), 'Daughters and displacement: migration dynamics in an Indonesian transmigration area', *The Journal of Development Studies*, 38 (5), pp. 143–166.

Elson, R. E. (1997), *The End of the Peasantry in Southeast Asia: A Social and Economic History of Peasant Livelihood, 1800-1990s*, The Australian National University: Canberra.

Emirbayer, M. and A. Mische (1998), 'What is agency?', *American Journal of Sociology*, 103 (4), pp. 962–1023.

Endo, G. (1996), 'Tai ni okeru chihou jitsugyouka no jigyou tenkai: chenmai wo jirei toshite (The development of provincial businessmen in Thailand: a case study of Chiangmai)', *Ajia Keizai* (Monthly Journal of Institute of Developing Economies), 37 (9), pp. 54–82.

Englund, H. (2002), 'The village in the city, the city in the village: migrants in Lilongwe', *Journal of Southern African Studies*, 28 (1), pp. 137–154.

Epstein, A. L. (1981), *Urbanization and Kinship: The Domestic Domain on the Copperbelt of Zambia 1950–1956*, London: Academic Press.

Erie, S. (1988), *Rainbow's End: Irish-Americans and the Dilemmas of Urban Machine Politics, 1840-1985*, Berkeley: University of California Press.

Erman, T. (1998), 'Becoming "urban" or remaining "rural": the views of Turkish rural-to-urban migrants on the integration question', *International Journal Middle East Studies*, 30, pp. 541–561.

Fawcett, J. T., S. E. Khoo and P.C. Smith (eds) (1984), *Women in the Cities of Asia: Migration and Urban Adaptation*, Boulder: Westview Press.

Fidler, R. C. (1973), *Kanowit: An Overseas Chinese Community in Borneo*, Unpublished Ph.D. thesis, The University of Pennsylvania.

Fidler, R. C. (1978), 'Chinese-Iban economic symbiosis', *Southeast Asian Journal of Social Science*, 6 (1/2), pp. 56–77.

Fielding, T. (1992), 'Migration and culture', in T. Champion and T. Fielding (eds), *Migration Processes and Patterns, Volume I: Research Progress and Prospects*, London: Belhaven Press, pp. 201–212.

Firman, T. (1994), 'Labour allocation, mobility, and remittances in rural households: a case from Central Java, Indonesia', *Sojourn*, 9, pp. 81–101.

Folbre, N. (1986), 'Cleaning house: new perspectives on households and development', *Journal of Development Economics*, 22, pp. 5–40.

Frank, A. G. (1967), *Capitalism and Underdevelopment in Latin America*, New York: Monthly Review Press.

Freeman, J. D. (1955), *Iban Agriculture*, London: Her Majesty's Stationery Office.

Freeman, J. D. (1970), *Report on the Iban*, London: The Anthlone Press.

Freeman, J. D. (1981), *Some Reflections on the Nature of Iban Society*, An Occasional Paper of the Department of Anthropology, Research School of Pacific Studies, The Australian National University.

Friedman, J. (1996), 'Modular cities: beyond the rural–urban divide', *Environment and Urbanization*, 8, pp. 129–131.

Fujimaki, M. (1993), 'Toshi no murabito' ron saikou: kaihatsu tojoukoku sekai toshika kenkyuu no kaiko to tenbou (A review on studies of 'urban villagers' in the developing countries)', *Tenri Daigaku Gakuhou* (The Tenri University Journal*)*, 174, pp. 31–49.

Fujimaki, M. (1998), 'Kuara rumpuru no ikirareta sukuottaa kanpon: 1980 nendai mareishia toshi kasou syakai no fuukei (Squatter kampungs in Kuala Lumpur as lived space: landscape of lower strata society in Malaysia in the 1980s)', in N. Eguchi (ed.),*"Hinkon no bunka" saikou* (Rethinking "The culture of poverty"*)*, Tokyo: Yuuhikaku, pp. 113–176.

Galie, L. G. (1988), 'Choosing locations for small town development to enable market and employment expansion: the case of Kenya', *Economic Geography*, 64 (3), pp. 242–254.

Galie, L. G. (1992), 'Improving rural–urban linkages through small town market-based development', *Third World Planning Review*, 14 (2), pp. 131–148.

Galor, O. and O. Stark (1990), 'Migrants' savings, the probability of return migration and migrants' performance', *International Economic Review*, 31 (2), pp. 463–467.

Galor, O. and O. Stark (1991), 'The probability of return migration, migrants' work effort, and migrants' performance', *Journal of Development Economics*, 35, pp. 399–405.

Ganjanapan, A. (1994), 'The northern Thai land tenure system: local customs versus national laws', *Law & Society Review*, 28, pp. 609–622.

Gans, H. J. (1962), *The Urban Villagers: Group and Class in the Life of Italian-Americans*, New York: The Free Press.

Glick, J. (1973), 'Urban anthropology', in J. Honigmman (ed.), *Handbook of Social and Cultural Anthropology*, Chicago: Rand McNally, pp. 979–1029.

Goss, J. and B. Lindquist (1995), 'Conceptualizing international labor migration: a structuration perspective', *International Migration Review*, 29 (2), pp. 317–351.

Gotham, K. F. (2003), 'Toward an understanding of the spatiality of urban poverty: the urban poor as spatial actors', *International Journal of Urban and Regional Research*, 27 (3), pp. 723–737.

Haddad, L., J. Hoddinott and H. Alderman (1997), 'Introduction: the scope of intrahousehold resource allocation issues', in L. Haddad, J. Hoddinott and H. Alderman (eds), *Intrahousehold Resource Allocation in Developing Countries: Models, Methods, and Policy,* Baltimore and London: John Hopkins University Press, pp. 1–16.

Halfacree, K. H. (1995), 'Household migration and the structuration of patriarchy: evidence from the USA', *Progress in Human Geography*, 19, pp. 159–182.

Halfacree, K. and P. Boyle (1993), 'The challenge facing migration research: the case for a biographical approach', *Progress in Human Geography*, 17, pp. 333–348.

Halfacree, K. and P. Boyle (1995), 'A little learning is a dangerous thing': a reply to Ron Skeldon', *Progress in Human Geography*, 19, pp. 97–99.

Hampshire, K. (2002), 'Fulani on the Move: Seasonal Economic Migration in the Sahel as a Social Process', *Journal of Development Studies*, 38 (5), pp. 15–36.

Harbison, S. F. (1981), 'Family structure and family strategy in migration decision making', in G. F. de Jong and R. W. Gardner (eds), *Migration Decision Making*, New York: Pergamon Press, pp. 225–251.

Harrell, S. (1994), 'The history of the history of the Yi', in S. Harrell (ed.), *Cultural Encounters on China's Ethnic Frontiers*, Seattle: University of Washington Press, pp. 63–91.

Hart, K. (1973), 'Informal income opportunities and urban employment in Ghana', *Journal of Modern African Studies*, 11, pp. 61–89.

Hart, G. (1992), 'Household reproduction reconsidered: gender, labor conflict, and technological change in Malaysia's Muda region', *World Development*, 20, pp. 809–823.

Hart, G. (1995), 'Gender and household dynamics: recent theories and their implications', in M.G. Quibria (ed.), *Critical Issues in Asian Development*, Hong Kong: Oxford University Press, pp. 39–74.

Hataya, N. (ed.) (1998), *Hatten tojoukoku no toshi juumin soshiki: sono shakai kaihatsu ni okeru yakuwari* (Urban people's organization in developing countries: its role for social development*)*, Tokyo: Institute of Developing Economies.

Hinderick, J. and M. J. Titus (1988), 'Paradigms of regional development and the role of small centres', *Development and Change*, 19 (3), pp. 401–423.

Hoddinott, J. (1994), 'A model of migration and remittances applied to western Kenya', *Oxford Economic Papers*, 46, pp. 459–476.

Hong, E. (1987), *Natives of Sarawak: Survival in Borneo's Vanishing Forest*, Penang: Institut Masyarakat.

Hugo, G. J. (1981), 'Village-community ties, village norms and ethnic networks: a review of evidence from the Third World', in G. F. de Jong and R. W. Gardener (eds), *Migration Decision Making: Multidisciplinary Approaches to Micro-level Studies in Developed and Developing Countries*, New York: Pergamon Press, pp. 186–224.

Hugo, G. J. (1983), *Population Mobility and Wealth Transfers in Indonesia and Other Third World societies*, Honolulu: East-west Population Institute.

Hugo, G. J. (1992), 'Migration and rural–urban linkages in the ESCAP region', in Economic and Social Commission for Asia and the Pacific (ed.), *Migration and Urbanization in Asia and the Pacific*, New York: United Nations, pp. 91–117.

Inglot, T. and J. P. Pelissero (1993), 'Ethnic political power in a machine city: Chicago7s poles at Rainbow's End', *Urban Affairs Quarterly*, 28 (4), pp. 526–543.

Inoue, M. (2002), 'Ekkyou suru fiirudo kenkyuu nokanousei (The potentiality of field research beyond the frontier)', in H. Ishii (ed.), *Knkyo Gaku no Gihou* (Social methods of environmental studies*)*, Tokyo: The University of Tokyo Press, pp. 215–257.

Ishikawa, N. (1997), 'Minzoku no katarikata: sarawaku marei towa dareka (Who are the Malay of Sarawak?)', in M. Uchibori (ed.), *Minzoku no seisei to ronri* (Formation and logic of ethnicity), Tokyo: Iwanami Shoten, pp. 135–148.

Ishikawa, N. (1998), 'A benevolent protector or a failed exploiter?: an examination of local response to agro-economic policies under the second Rajah, Charles Brooke (1868-1917) of Sarawak', in A.B. Shamsul and T. Uesugi (eds), *Japanese Anthropologists and Malaysian Society: Contributions to Malaysian Ethnography (Senri Ethnological Studies no.48)*, Osaka: National Museum of Ethnology, pp. 71–98.

Jackson, J. C. (1968), *Sarawak: A Geographical Survey of a Developing State*, London: University of London Press.

Jagannathan, N. V. (1987), *Informal Markets in Developing Countries,* New York: Oxford University Press.

Jayum, A. J. (1991), *The Ethnic Factor in Modern Politics: The Case of Sarawak, East Malaysia,* Hull: Center for South-East Asian Studies, The University of Hull.

Jayum, A. J. (1993), 'The Sarawak State General Election of 1991,' *Kajian Malaysia*, 11 (1), pp. 1–21.

Jayum, A. J. (1994), *Iban Politics and Economic Development: Their Patterns and Change*, Selangor: Penerbit UKM.

Jayum, A. J. and V. T. King (1997), 'The Ibans of Sarawak: the nature of their peripherality and its political and economic consequences', *Contributions to Southeast Asian Ethnography*, 11, pp. 33–59.

Kaboy, T. (1965), 'The murder of Steele and Fox: two versions', *Sarawak Museum Journal*, 25/26, pp. 207–214.

Kato, T. (1983), 'Toshi to ijuumin: jakaruta zaijuu minankabau no jirei (Cities and migrants in Southeast Asia: a case of Minangkabau migrants in Jakarta)', *Tonan Ajia Kenkyuu* (Southeast Asian Studies*)*, 21 (1), pp. 47–61.

Kato, T. (1986), 'Indoneshia no toshi ni miru shuzoku ketsugou: nettowaaku to doukyoukai (Urban ethnicity in Indonesia: networks and locality-based associations)', *Tonan Ajia Kenkyu* (Southeast Asian Studies*)*, 23 (4), pp. 391–418.

Kato, T. (1993), 'Shiiku sareru esunishiti (Ethnicity domesticated)', in T. Yano (ed.), *Chiiki kenkyuu no furontia* (Frontier of area studies*)*, Tokyo: Koubundou, pp. 153–189.

Katz, E. and O. Stark (1986), 'Labor migration and risk aversion in less developed countries', *Journal of Labor Economics*, 4, pp. 131–149.

Kawanaka, T. (2000), 'Firipin chihou toshi ni okeru kenryoku mekanizumu: naga shi no jirei (The mechanism of power in a Philippine city: a case of Naga city)', *Ajia Keizai (Monthly Journal of Institute of Developing Economies)*, 41 (1), pp. 2–33.

Kedit, P. M. (1980), *Modernization Among the Iban of Sarawak*, Kuala Lumpur: Dewan Bahasa dan Pustaka.

Kedit, P. M. (1989), 'Ethnicity in a multi-cultural society: Dayak ethnicity in the context of Malaysian multi-cultural society', *Sarawak Museum Journal*, 61, pp. 1–8.

Kedit, P. M. (1993), *Iban Bejalai*, Kuala Lumpur: Ampang Press.

Kelly, P. F. (1998), 'The politics of urban-rural relations: land use conversion in the Philippines', *Environment and Urbanization*, 10 (1), pp. 35–54.

King, V. T. (1976), 'Some aspects of Iban-Maloh contact in West Kalimantan', *Indonesia*, 21, pp. 85–114.

King, V. T. (1979), *Ethnic Classification and Ethnic Relations: A Borneo Case Study*, University of Hull: Center for South-east Asian Studies, Occasional Paper No.2.

King, V. T. (1982), 'Ethnicity in Borneo: an anthropological problem', *Southeast Asian Journal of Social Science*, 10 (1), pp. 23–43.

King, V. T. (1988), Models and realities: Malaysian national planning and East Malaysian development problems, *Modern Asian Studies*, 22 (2), pp. 263–298.

King, V. T. (1990), 'Why is Sarawak peripheral?' in V.T. King (ed.), *Margins and Minorities: The Peripheral Areas and Peoples of Malaysia*, Hull: Hull University Press, pp. 110–129.

King, V. T. and A. J. Jayum (1996), 'The Ibans of Sarawak, Malaysia: ethnicity, marginalization and development', In D. Dwyer and D. Drakakis-Smith (eds), *Ethnicity and Development: Geographical Perspectives*, Chichester: Wiley, pp. 195–214.

King, V. T. and W. Wilder (eds) (1982), *Ethnicity in Southeast Asia (Southeast Asian Journal of Social Science* 10 (1)), Singapore: Joint Publication of the Institute of Southeast Asian Studies and the Department of Sociology of the National University of Singapore.

Kiu, M. K. (1997), *The Diffusion of Foochow Settlement: in Sibu-Binatang Area, Central Sarawak 1901-1970*, Sibu: Sarawak Chinese Cultural Association.

Koczberski, G., G.N. Curry and J. Connell (2001), 'Full circle or spiralling out of control?: state violence and the control of urbanisation in Papua New Guinea', *Urban Studies*, 38 (11), pp. 2017–2036.

Koczberski, G. and G. N. Curry (2004), 'Divided communities and contested landscapes: mobility, development and shifting identities in migrant destination sites in Papua New Guinea', *Asia Pacific Viewpoint*, 45 (3), pp. 357–371.

Koppel, B. (1986), 'Janus in metropolis: an essay on the political economy of urban resources', *The Developing Economies*, 24, pp. 3–25.

Koppel, B. (1991), 'The rural–urban dichotomy re-examined: beyond the Ersatz debate?', in N. Ginsburg, B. Koppel and T.G. McGee (eds), *The Extended Metropolis: Settlement Transition in Asia*, Honolulu: University of Hawaii Press, pp. 47–70.

Koppel, B. and J. Hawkins (1994), 'Rural transformation and the future of work in rural Asia', in B. Koppel, J. Hawkins and W. James (eds), *Development or Deterioration?: Work in Rural Asia*, Boulder: Lynne Rienner Publishers, pp. 1–46.

Krokfors, C. (1995), 'Poverty, environmental stress and culture as factors in African migrations', in J. Baker and T. Akin aina (eds), *The Migration Experience in Africa*, Uppsala: Nordiska Afrikaninstitutet, pp. 54–64.

Kumagai, K. (1990), ' Jakaruta no 'nijuu kuozou' to sono henyou: infoomaru sekutaa to kanpon wo megutte ('Dual structure' and its transformation in Jakarta: concerning the informal sector and kampung)', in Ajia Chiri Kenkyuukai (ed.), *Henbous suru ajia: NIEs, ASEAN no kaihatsu to chiiki henyou* (Changing Asia: development and regional transformation*)*, Tokyo: Kokon Shoin, pp. 155–179.

Land and Survey Department of Sarawak, (1966), *Annual Report 1966*, Kuching: Land and Survey Department.

Land and Survey Department, Sibu Branch, (1984), *Annual Report 1984*, Sibu: Land and Survey Department, Sibu Branch.

Lanjouw, J. O. and P. Lanjouw (2001), 'The rural non-farm sector: issues and evidence from developing countries', *Agricultural Economics*, 26, pp. 1–23.

Lee, B. T. (1987), 'New towns in Malaysia: development and planning policies', in D.R. Phillips and A. G. O. Yeh (eds), *New Towns in East and South-east Asia*, Hong Kong: Oxford University Press, pp. 153–169.

Leigh, M. B. (1974), *The Rising Moon: Political Change in Sarawak,* Sydney: Sydney University Press.

Leinbach, T. R. (1992), 'Small towns, rural linkages, and employment', *International Regional Sciences Review*, 14 (3), pp. 317–323.

Leinbach, T. R. (2004), 'The Indonesian rural economy', in T.R. Leibach (ed.), *The Indonesian Rural Economy: Mobility, Work and Enterprise*, Singapore: ISEAS, pp. 3–14.

Leones, J. P. and S. Feldman (1998), 'Nonfarm activity and rural household income: evidence from Philippine microdata', *Economic Development and Cultural Change*, 46 (4), pp. 789–806.

Lin, G. C. S. (2001), 'Evolving spatial form of urban-rural interaction in the Pearl River Delta, China', *Professional Geographer*, 53 (1), pp. 56–70.

Lipton, M. (1977), *Why Poor People Stay Poor: Urban Bias in World Development,* Massachusetts: Harvard University Press.

Lipton, M. (1982), 'Why poor people stay poor', in J. Harris (ed.), *Rural Development: Theories of Peasant Economy and Agrarian Change*, London: Hutchinson, pp. 66–81.

Loeb, E. M. and J. O. M. Broek (1947), 'Social organization and the longhouse in Southeast Asia', *American Anthropologist*, 49, pp. 414–425.

Lucas, R. E. B. and O. Stark (1985), 'Motivations to remit: evidence from Botswana', *Journal of Political Economy*, 93 (5), pp. 901–918.

Lumb, R. D. (1993), 'Native title to land in Australia: recent high court decisions', *International and Comparative Law Quarterly*, 42, pp. 84–100.

Maggs, P. and J. Hoddinott (1999), 'The impact of changes in common property resource management on intrahousehold allocation', *Journal of Public Economics*, 72, pp. 317–324.

Mangin, W. (ed.) (1970), *Peasants in Cities: Readings in The Anthropology of Urbanization*, Boston: Houghton Mifflin Company.

Masing, J. (1988), 'The role of resettlement in rural development', in R.A. Cramb and R. H. W. Reece (eds), *Development in Sarawak: Historical and Contemporary Perspectives*, Victoria: Center for Southeast Asian Studies, Monash University, pp. 57–84.

Mason, R. (1995), 'Parti Bansa Dayak Sarawak and the Sarawak state elections of 1987 and 1991', *Kajian Malaysia*, 13 (1), pp. 26–58.

Matsuda, M. (1990), 'Kousoku to souzou: afurika toshi dekasegimin no dainamizumu: kenia, maragorijin no baai (Restriction and creation: urban emigration in Kenya, a case study)', *Rekishigaku Kenkyuu* (Journal of Historical Studies), 612, pp. 31–43.

Matsuda, M. (1996), *Toshi wo kainarasu: afurika no toshi jinruigaku* (Domesticate Africa), Tokyo: Kawade Shobou.

Matsuda, M. (1998), *Urbanization From Below: Creativity and Soft Resistance in the Everyday Life of Maragoli Migrants in Nairobi*, Kyoto: Kyoto University Press.

McGee, T. G. (1967), *The Southeast Asian City: A Social Geography of the Primate Cities of Southeast Asia,* London: G. Bell and Sons.

McGee, T. G. (1971). *The Urbanization Process in the Third World: Exploration in Search of a Theory*, London: Bell.

McGee, T. G. (1973), 'Peasants in the cities: a paradox, a paradox, a most ingenious paradox', *Human Organization*, 32 (2), pp. 135–142.

McGee, T. G. (1975), 'Malay migration to Kuala Lumpur city: individual adaptation to the city', in B.M. Dutoit and H.I. Safa (eds), *Migration and Urbanization: Models and Adaptive Strategies*, Hague: Mouton Publishers, pp. 143–178.

McGee, T. G. (1982), 'Labour mobility in fragmented labour markets: the role of circulatory migration in rural–urban relations in Asia', in H.I. Safa (ed.), *Towards a Political Economy of Urbanization in Third World Countries*, Delhi: Oxford University Press, pp. 47–66.

McGee, T. G. (1989), 'Urbanisasi or kotadesasi?: evolving patterns of urbanization in Asia', in F.J. Costa, A.K. Dutt, L. J. C. Ma and A. G. Noble (eds), *Urbanization in Asia: Spatial Dimensions and Policy Issues*, Honolulu: University of Hawaii Press, pp. 93–108.

McGee, T. G. (1991), 'The emergence of desakota regions in Asia: expanding a hypothesis', in N. Ginsburg, B. Koppel and T.G. McGee (eds), *The Extended Metropolis: Settlement Transition in Asia*, Honolulu: University of Hawaii Press, pp. 3–26.

McGee, T. G. and C. Greenberg (1992), 'The emergence of extended metropolitan regions in ASEAN: towards the year 2000', *ASEAN Economic Bulletin* 9 (1), pp. 22–44.

McGee, T. G. and I.M. Robinson (1995), *The Mega-Urban Regions of Southeast Asia*, Vancouver: UBC Press.

McHugh, K. E. (2000), 'Inside, outside, upside down, backward, forward, round and round: a case for ethnographic studies in migration', *Progress in Human Geography*, 24 (1), pp. 71–89.

Mizuno, K. (1991), Nishi jawa ni okeru tochi shoyuuken no kakunin shorui hoyuu joukyou (Right of land ownership and documents to certify its right in rural West Java)', in H. Umehara (ed.), *Tounan ajia no tochi seido to nougyou henka* (Land tenure and agricultural change in Southeast Asia), Tokyo: Institute of Developing Economies, pp. 251–308.

Mizuno, K. (1997), 'Indoneshia ni okeru tochiken tenkan mondai: shokuminchiki no kindaihou tochiken no tenkan mondai wo chuushin ni (Conversion of land titles in Indonesia: with special reference to land titles registered modernly in colonial era)', in K. Mizuno and S. Shigetomi (eds), *Tounan ajia no keizai kaihatsu to tochi seido* (Economic development and land system in South-East Asia), Tokyo: Institute of Developing Economies, pp. 115–154.

Morrison, P. (1993), 'Transition in rural Sarawak', *Pacific Viewpoint*, 34 (1), pp. 45–68.

Mosse, D., S. Gupta, M. Mehta, V. Shah, J. Rees and the KRIBP Project Team (2002), 'Brokered livelihoods: debt, labour migration and development in tribal Western India', *The Journal of Development Studies*, 38 (5), pp. 59–88.

Mountjoy, A. B. (1976), 'Urbanization, the squatter and development in the Third World', *Tijdschrift voor Economische en Sociale Geografie*, 67 (3), pp. 130–137.

Murai, Y. (1978), 'Indoneshia no minsyuu seigyou (Pedlers and vendors in Indonesian cities)', *Ajia kenkyuu (Asian Studies)*, 24 (4), pp. 57–82.

Nagata, J. (1981), 'In defense of ethnic boundaries: the changing myths and charters of Malay Identity', in C.F. Keyes (ed.), *Ethnic Change*, London: University of Washington Press, pp. 87–116.

Nakanishi, T. (1988a), 'Firipin ni okeru toshi hikoushiki bumon (I): manira shutoken no suramu sumikomi chousa kara (The urban informal sector in the Philippines (I))', *Ajia Keizai* (Monthly Journal of Institute of Developing Economies), 29 (1), pp. 17–33.

Nakanishi, T. (1988b), 'Firipin ni okeru toshi hikoushiki bumon (II): manira shutoken no suramu sumikomi chousa kara (The urban informal sector in the Philippines (I))', *Ajia Keizai* (Monthly Journal of Institute of Developing Economies), 29 (2), pp. 48–62.

Ngidang, D, (1995), 'The politics of development in longhouse communities in Sarawak, East Malaysia', *Development in Practice*, 5 (4), pp. 305–312.

Niitsu, K. (1973), 'Minami ajia ni okeru kouto idousha no toshi taiou youshiki (The adapting style of city migrants in South Asia)', *Shakaigaku Hyouron* (Japanese Sociological Review), 24 (2), pp. 34–49.

Niitsu, K. (1989), 'Joshou: gendai ajia ni okeru suramu mondai no shozai (Introduction: slum problems in modern Asia)', in K. Niitsu (ed.), *Gendai ajia no suramu: hatten tojoukoku toshi no kenkyuu* (Slum in modern Asia: studies on cities in developing countries), Tokyo: Akashi Shoten, pp. 13–91.

Ogura, M. (1988), 'Zanbia ni okeru nouson-toshi kan roudou idou: idousha ni yoru nouson tono chuutai (The rural–urban migration in Zambia: migrants' ties with their home villages)', *Ajia Keizai* (Monthly Journal of Institute of Developing Economies), 29 (7/8), pp. 77–89.

Ogura, M. (1990), 'Keizai suitai ka no zanbia toshi juumin to nouson no chuutai: rusaka chousa ni yoru bunseki (Zambian urban dwellers and their ties with home villages in the period of economic decay: a report on Lusaka survey)', *Ajia Keizai* (Monthly Journal of Institute of Developing Economies), 31 (8), pp. 46–59.

Okuno, K. (2000), '19 seiki ikou no Sarawak ni okeru Memaloh no ginzaiku zukuri no tabi (The Memaloh's traveling into Sarawak with silver-smithing)', *Tabi no Bunka Kenkyusyo Kenkyu Hokoku* (Bulletin of Institute for the Culture of Travel), 9, pp. 65–78.

Padoch, C. (1982a), *Migration and its Alternatives Among the Iban of Sarawak*, Hague: The Hague-Martinus Nijhoff.

Padoch, C. (1982b), 'Land use in new and old areas of Iban settlement', *Borneo Research Bulletin*, 14 (1), pp. 3–14.

Papanek, G. F. (1975), 'The poor of Jakarta', *Economic Development and Cultural Change*, 24 (1), pp. 1–27.

Perlman, J. E. (1976), *The Myth of Marginality; Urban Poverty and Politics in Rio de Janeiro*, Berkeley: University of California Press.

Potter, R. B. and T. Unwin (eds) (1989), *The Geography of Urban-Rural Interaction in Developing Countries: Essays for Alan B. Mountjoy*, London: Routledge.

Potter, R. B. and T. Unwin (1995), 'Urban-rural interaction: physical form and political process in the Third World', *Cities*, 12 (1), pp. 67–73.

Prill-Brett, J. (1994), 'Indigenous land rights and legal pluralism among Philippine highlanders', *Law & Society Review*, 28 (3), pp. 687–697.

Pringle, R. (1970), *Rajahs and Rebels: the Iban of Sarawak Under Brooke rule, 1841-1941*, London: Macmillan.

Prothero, R. M. and M. Chapman (1985), *Circulation in Third World Countries*, London: Routledge & Kegan Paul.

Ranis, G. and F. Stewart (1993), 'Rural nonagricultural activities in development: theory and application', *Journal of Development Economics*, 40, pp. 75–101.

Reardon, T., J. Berdegue and G. Escobar (2001), 'Rural non-farm employment and incomes in Latin America; overview and policy implications', *World Development*, 29 (3), pp. 395–409.

Regmi, G. and C. Tisdell (2002), 'Remitting behaviour of Nepalese rural-to-urban migrants: implications for theory and policy', *Journal of Development Studies*, 38 (3), pp. 76–94.

Richards, A. J. N. (1949), 'The migration of the Ibans and their poetry', *Sarawak Museum Journal*, 1, pp. 77–87.

Rigg, J. (1998), 'Rural–urban interactions, agriculture and wealth: a southeast Asian perspective', *Progress in Human Geography*, 22 (4), pp. 497–522.

Rigg, J. (2001), *More than the Soil: Rural Change in Southeast Asia*, Harlow: Prentice Hall.

Rigg, J. and S. Nattapoolwat (2001), 'Embracing the global in Thailand: activism and pragmatism in an era of deagrarianization', *World Development*, 29 (6), pp. 945–960.

Roberts, B. (1978), *Cities of Peasants: The Political Economy of Urbanization in the Third World*, London: Edward Arnold.

Rondinelli, D. A. (1983), *Secondary Cities in Developing Countries: Policies for Diffusing Urbanization*, Beverly Hills: Sage Publication.

Rondinelli, D. A. (1985), *Applied Methods of Regional Analysis: The Spatial Dimensions of Development Policy*, Boulder: Westview.

Rooney, J. (1981), *Khabar Gembira: A History of the Catholic Church in East Malaysia and Brunei, 1880-1976,* London: Tien Wah Press.

Root, B. D. and G. F. de Jong, (1991), 'Family migration in a developing country', *Population Studies*, 45, pp. 221–233.

Rubenstein, H. (1992), 'Migration, development and remittances in rural Mexico', *International Migration*, 30 (2), pp. 127–157.

Russel, S. D. (ed.) (1989), *Ritual, Power, and Economy: Upland-Lowland Contrasts in Mainland Southeast Asia*, DeKalb: Northern Illinois University Center for Southeast Asian Studies.

Sandin, B. (1956), 'The westward migration of the Sea Dayaks', *Sarawak Museum Journal*, 7, pp. 54–81.

Sandin, B. (1967), *The Sea Dayaks of Borneo Before White Rajah Rule*, London: Macmillan.

State Government of Sarawak (1997), *Internal Migration Study, Sarawak*, Kuching: State Government of Sarawak.

Sather, C. (1990), 'Trees and tree tenure in Paku Iban society: the management of secondary forest resources in long-established Iban community', *Borneo Review*, 1, pp. 16–40.

Sather, C. (1994), 'Introduction: sources of Iban traditional history', *Sarawak Museum Journal*, 67 (Special Monograph No. 7), pp. 1–78.

Schrieder, G. and B. Knerr (2000), 'Labour migration as a social security mechanism for smallholder households in Sub-Saharan Africa: the case of Cameroon', *Oxford Development Studies*, 28 (2), pp. 223–236.

Scott, J. (1985), *Weapons of the Weak: Everyday Forms of Peasant Resistance*, New Heaven: Yale University Press.

Searle, P. (1983), *Politics in Sarawak 1970-1976: The Iban Perspective*, Singapore: Oxford University Press.

Segawa, S. (1995), 'Kokumin kokka wo miseru: 'Utsukushii indoneshia mini kouen' ni okeru zuan, cchi, yomi no senyuu (The nation-state visualized: beautiful Indonesia in miniature park and the monopoly of design, location and reading)', *Jinbun Chiri* (Human Geography), 47 (3), pp. 215–236.

Sekine, K. (1979), 'Ronguhausu wo meguru kuukan kouzou: iban no baai (Spatial structure in and around longhouse: a case of the Iban)', *Kikan Jinruigaku* (Quarterly Journal of Anthropology), 10 (2), pp. 54–107.

Shamsul, A. B. (1986), *From British to Bumiputera Rule: Local Politics and Rural Development in Peninsular Malaysia*, Singapore: Institute of Southeast Asian Studies, Singapore.

Shamsul, A. B. (1996), 'Promise versus performance: formal organizations in rural Malaysia', in M. Hoadley and C. Gunnarsson (eds), *The Village Concept in the Transformation of Rural Southeast Asia*, Richmond: Curzon Press, pp. 140–161.

Shand, R. T. (ed.) (1986), *Off-Farm Employment in the Development of Rural Asia*, Canberra: Australian National University.

Shimada, S. (1998), 'Naijeria nougyou kenkyuu no atarashii chihei: poriticaru ekorojii ron no kanousei wo megutte (New perspectives of studies of African Agriculture: feasibility of political ecology)', in J. Ikeno (ed.), Afurika *nouson henyou to sono akutaa* (Rural transformation in Africa and actors), Tokyo: Institute of Developing Economies, pp. 1–29.

Shiraishi, T. (1994), ''Kaihatsu' kokka no seiji bunka (Political culture of 'developmentalism' state)', in K. Tsuchiya (ed.), *Nashonarizumu to kokumin kokka* (Nationalism and nation state), Tokyo: The University of Tokyo Press, pp. 229–248.

Siddiqi, A. (1993), 'Small town growth and development policy in Pakistan', *GeoJournal*, 30 (4), pp. 421–434.

Skeldon, R. (1990), *Population Mobility in Developing Countries: A Reinterpretation*, New York: Belhaven Press.

Skeldon, R. (2005), 'Jinkou idou to jinkou idou kenkyuu: jinkou ryuudoushi hensan ni muketeno joron (Migrations and thinking about migrations: introductory remarks towards a historiography of population movement)', in Y. Ishikawa (ed.), *Ajia taiheiyou chiiki no jinkou idou* (Migration in the Asia-Pacific region), Tokyo: Akashi Syoten, pp. 29–54.

Smith, D. P. (2004), 'An 'united' research agenda for family migration: loosening the 'shackles' of the past', *Journal of Ethnic and Migration Studies*, 30 (2), pp. 263–282.

Smith, P. C., S. E. Khoo and S. P. Go (1984), 'The migration of women to cities: a comparative perspective' in J. T. Fawcett, S. E. Khoo and P.C. Smith (eds), *Women in the Cities of Asia*, Boulder: Westview Press, pp. 15–35.

Soda, R. (1999), 'Sarawaku iban jin syakai ni okeru shiteki tochi syoyuu kannen no keisei (The evolving concept of land ownership among the Iban of Sarawak, Malaysia)', *Human Geography*, 51 (4), pp. 329–351.

Soda, R. (2000), 'Living strategies of the urban poor in a local town in Sarawak, Malaysia: population mobility of the Iban between urban and rural areas,' *Geographical Review of Japan (Series B)* 73 (2), pp. 139–164.

Soda, R. (2001), 'Rural–urban migration of the Iban of Sarawak and changes in long-house communities,' *Geographical Review of Japan (Series B)* 74 (1), pp. 92–112.

Soda, R. (2003), 'Development policy and human mobility in a developing country: voting strategy of the Iban in Sarawak, Malaysia,' *Southeast Asian Studies* 40 (4), pp. 459–483.

Soda, R. (2006), 'Agents on the move,' *The Annual Report on Cultural Science (Hokkaido University)* 119, pp. 79–101.

Solhee, H. (1994) 'The district development plan: towards enhancing the role of the resident and district officer in development planning and implementation', *Jurnal AZAM*, 10 (1), pp. 10–17.

Standing, G. (1985) 'Circulation and labour process', in G. Standing (ed.), *Labour circulation and labour process*, London: Croom Helm, pp. 1–45.

Stark, O. and R. E. B. Lucas, (1988) 'Migration, remittances, and the family', *Economic Development and Cultural Change*, 36 (3), pp. 465–481.

Stöhr, W. B. and D. B. F. Taylor (eds) (1981), *Development from above or below?: the dynamics of regional planning in developing countries*, Chichester: Wiley.

Sugimoto, N. (1971), 'Tounan ajia no juukyo (Houses in Southeast Asia)', *Kikan Jinruigaku* (Quarterly Journal of Anthropology), 2 (3), pp. 147–191.

Sutlive, V. H. (1972), *From Longhouse to Pasar*, Ph.D. Dissertation, The University of Pittsburgh.

Sutlive, V. H. (1985), 'Urban migration into Sibu, Sarawak', *Borneo Research Bulletin*, 17 (2), pp. 85–94.

Sutlive, V. H. (1986), 'Urban migration into Sibu, Sarawak: II', *Borneo Research Bulletin*, 18 (1), pp. 27–45.

Sutlive, V. H. (1991), 'Keling and Kumang in town', in V.H. Sutlive (ed.), *Female and Male in Borneo*, Williamsburg: Borneo Research Council, Inc., pp. 489–515.

Sutlive, V. H. (1992), *The Iban of Sarawak: Chronicle of a Vanishing World*, Kuala Lumpur: S. Abdul Majeed & Co.

Sutlive, V. H. and G. N. Appell (1991), 'Introduction', in V.H. Sutlive (ed.), *Female and Male in Borneo*, Williamsburg: Borneo Research Council, Inc., pp. xi–xlvi.

Tacoli, C. (1996), 'Migrating 'for the sake of family?': gender, life course and intra-household relations among Filipino migrants in Rome', *Philippine Sociological Review*, 44, pp. 12–32.

Tacoli, C. (1998), 'Rural–urban interactions: a guide to the literature', *Environment and Urbanization*, 10 (1), pp. 147–166.

Takada, M. (1991) ''Noumin shakai,' 'noumin,' nougyougai roudou: bangur-adeshu no shokugyo kouzou no jirei kara ('Peasant society,' 'peasants,' non-farm work: a case study of a village in Bangladesh)', *Minzokugaku Kenkyuu* (The Japanese Journal of Ethnology), 56 (1), pp. 20–44.

Tan Sri Datuk Gerunsin Lembat (1994), 'Native customary land and adapt', Proceeding paper presented in a seminar on *Pembangunan Tanah Pusaka Bumiputera* held in Santubong, Sarawak, Malaysia on 29th September – 3rd October, 1994.

Thadani, V. N. and M. P. Torado (1984), 'Female Migration: a conceptual framework', in J.T. Fawcett, S.E. Khoo and P.C. Smith (eds), *Women in the Cities of Asia*, Boulder: Westview Press, pp. 36–59.

Todaro, M. (1969), 'A model of labour migration and urban unemployment in LDCs', *American Economic Review*, 59, pp. 138–148.

Tokman, V. E. (1978), 'An exploration into the nature of informal-formal sector relationships', *World Development*, 6 (9/10), pp. 1065–1075.

Uchibori, M. (1978), *The Leaving of this Transient World: A Study of Iban Eschatology and Mortuary Practices*, Australian National University, Unpublished Ph.D. Dissertation.

Uchibori, M. (1984), 'Transformations of Iban social consciousness', *Senri Ethnological Studies*, 13, pp. 211–234.

Uchibori, M. (1987), 'Kokumin kokka to buzoku shakai: sarawaku iban no keiken (Nation state and tribal society)', in A. Itou (ed.), *Modern Social Anthropology 3*, Tokyo: The University of Tokyo Press, pp. 57–82.

Uchibori, M. (1991), 'Sakashima no sekai (The world upside-down)', in S. Maeda (ed.), *Tounan ajia no bunka* (Cultures in Southeast Asia), Tokyo: Koubundou, pp. 170–191.

Uchibori, M. (1994), 'Minzoku no shoumetsu ni tsuite: sarawaku bukitan no joukyou o megutte (On the extinction of an ethnic group: the case of Bukitan of Sarawak)', in E. Kuroda (ed.), *Minzoku no deau katachi* (Interaction between different ethnic groups), Tokyo: Asahi Shinbunsha, pp. 133–152.

Uchibori, M. (1996), *How to Eat Forest*, Tokyo: The University of Tokyo Press.

Uchibori, M. and S. Yamashita (1986), *Shi no jinruigaku* (Anthropology of death), Tokyo: Kobundo Publishing Company.

Unwin, T. (1989), 'Urban-rural interaction in developing countries: a theoretical perspective' in R. B. Pttoer and T. Unwin (eds), *The Geography of Urban-Rural Interaction in Developing Countries*, London: Routledge, pp. 11–32.

Wadley R. L. (1997), *Circular Labor Migration and Subsistence Agriculture: A Case of the Iban in West Kalimantan*, Indonesia, Unpublished Ph.D. dissertation, Arizona State University.

Waterson, R. (1990), *The Living House*, Singapore: Oxford University Press.

Watts, M. (1996), 'Development III: the global agrofood system and late twentieth century development (or Kautsky redux)' *Progress in Human Geography*, 20, pp. 230–245.

Wazaki, H. (1987), 'Gendai toshi jinruigaku no tenkai: chiiki jinruigaku to esunishiti no shikaku (Modern city and development of urban anthropology: perspective of regional anthropology)', in H. Fujita and N. Yoshihara (eds), *Toshi: shakaigaku to jinruigaku kara no sekkin* (City: approaches from sociology and anthropology), Kyoto: Minerva Shoten, pp. 46–79.

Wazaki, H. (1988), 'Toshi jinruigaku kara mita 'toshi no honshitsu': toshi seikatsusha no 'ikinuki' senryaku to esunikku baundarii ron (The essence of the city from the urban anthropology view point)', *Toshi Mondai Kenkyuu* (Journal of Municipal Problems), 40 (2), pp. 79–95.

Wilk, R. R. (ed.) (1989), *The Household Economy: Reconsidering the Domestic Mode of Production*, Boulder: Westview Press.

Williams, L. B. (1989), 'Postnuptial migration and the status of women in Indonesia', *Journal of Marriage and the Family*, 51, pp. 895–905.

Willis, K. and B. Yeoh (2000), *Gender and Migration*, Cheltenham: Edward Elgar Publishing.

Winzeler, R. (ed.) (1997), *Indigenous Peoples and the State: Politics, Land,*

and Ethnicity in the Malayan Peninsula and Borneo, New Haven: Yale University Southeast Asia Studies (Monograph series 46).

Wolf, D. L. (1992), *Factory Daughters: Gender, Household Dynamics, and Rural Industrialization in Java*, Berkeley: University of California Press.

Wright, L., H. Morrison and K. F. Wong (1972), *Vanishing World: the Ibans of Borneo*, New York: Weatherhill/Serasia.

Yamashita, S. (1986), 'Ujun pandan no toraja shakai: indoneshia chihou toshi kenkyuu (The Toraja community in Ujung Pandang: a study on a local city in Indonesia)', *Tonan Ajia Kenkyu* (Southeast Asian Studies), 23 (4), pp. 419–438.

Yamazaki, H. (1977), 'Kokkateki tougou to noumin (National integration and the peasantry)', *Keizaigaku Zasshi (Journal of Economics)*, 76 (4), pp. 1–24.

Yamazaki, H. (1978), 'Toshi bakuhatsu to noumin rison (Urban explosion and out-migration of rural peasants)', in K. Yoshioka and H. Yamazaki (eds), *Gendai daitoshi no kouzou* (Structure of modern metropolis), Tokyo: The University of Tokyo Press, pp. 269–301.

Yonemura, A. (1991a), 'Raten America ni okeru tosi kasou kenkyuu no rironteki tenkai (I): kindaikaron teki paradaimu kara juuzoku riron teki paradaim (Process and backgrounds of paradigm change in Latin American urban poor studies: from modernization theory to dependency theory (I))', *Ajia Keizai (Monthly Journal of Institute of Developing Economies)*, 32 (4), pp. 2–13.

Yonemura, A. (1991b), 'Raten America ni okeru tosi kasou kenkyuu no rironteki tenkai (II): kindaikaron teki paradaimu kara juuzoku riron teki paradaim (Process and backgrounds of paradigm change in Latinamerican urban poor studies: from modernization theory to dependency theory (II))', *Ajia Keizai* (Monthly Journal of Institute of Developing Economies), 32 (5), pp. 28–47.

Yoneyama, T. (1987), 'Daisan sekai ni miru toshi no hougateki keitai: zaiiru kyouwakoku buranbika no baai (Early stage of urban growth in the Third World: a case study in Zaire)', *Shunjuu Seikatsugaku* (Synjuu Life Studies), 1, pp. 202–210.

Zaidi Khaldin Zainie (1985), 'Land tenure system in Sarawak', *Sarawak Gazette*, 1985 July: 14–17.

Zenno, M. (1994), 'Sonraku zaijuusha to toshi ijuusha no shakai soshiki no sougo kankei: mekishiko, oahaka shuu, myunteka kouchi no ichi sonraku no jirei kara (The inter-relationship of the social organizations of rural villagers and urban migrants: a case study of a aillage in Mixteca Alta in Oaxaca, Mexico)', *Minzokugaku Kenkyuu* (The Japanese Journal of Ethnology), 59 (3), pp. 193–220.

Index